THE STRATEGY OF DESIRE

The Strategy of Desire

by ERNEST DICHTER

1960 DOUBLEDAY & COMPANY, INC.

GARDEN CITY, NEW YORK

Library of Congress Catalog Card Number 60–11380

Printed in the United States of America
First Edition

Design: Charles Kaplan

Excerpts from the following appear in this book.

Professor Anne Roe Address before the American Psychological Association, August 1958.
Introduction to Logic and Scientific Method, by Morris R. Cohen and Ernest Nagel, Harcourt Brace, Inc.
Sharing a Business by Franklin J. Lunding, The Updegraff Press, Ltd. "The Psychology of Imagination" by Frank Barron, *Scientific American*, September 1958.

To my son, who might receive guidance from this book, and to my wife and daughter, who stuck it out with me.

ACKNOWLEDGMENTS

First, a vote of thanks goes to the many hundreds of clients who, over the last two decades, have shown a pioneering spirit and the readiness to accept new ideas and concepts. To a large extent it has been their support and interest which has made our work and consequently this book possible.

During these years, many people have worked with me, especially the following who have made particular contributions: Dr. Tibor Koeves, Irving Gilman, Alex Gachfeld, Dr. John Vogel, and Cecil Lubell. The study directors who have worked on many of the studies mentioned in this book deserve special thanks.

Some of the paragraphs in the book have previously appeared in trade publications—"The Analysis of Westerns" in *Broadcasting Magazine,* September 1957, and "Dichter on Dracula" in *Sponsor,* November 1957. Some paragraphs in the chapter on "Goals" appeared in the *Harvard Business Review* under the title "Psychology of Prosperity." Some paragraphs appeared in *Motivations,* the publication of the Institute for Motivational Research.

I want to thank particularly Elliott Schryver for his help in editing this book, and Peggy Munson for painstakingly typing a difficult manuscript and Fan Friedman for supervisory work.

CONTENTS

INTRODUCTION 11

ONE: PERSUASION STARTED WITH EVE

1: THE MASK OF BEHAVIOR 25

2: THE DISCOVERY OF MOTIVATIONS 33

3: COMMAND OR PERSUASION 48

4: MEASURING HUMAN EMOTIONS 60

5: THE SOUL OF THINGS 85

6: WE THINK AS WE PLEASE 111

7: THE WHOLISTIC APPROACH 144

TWO: STRATEGY IN A CONFLICT ERA

INTRODUCTION 165

8: THE PSYCHO-ECONOMIC AGE 167

9: THE VISIONS BEFORE US 187

10: THE FEAR OF CHANGE 205

11: THE SEARCH FOR IDENTITY 226

12: MISERY OF CHOICE 242

13: THE "BURDEN" OF THE GOOD LIFE 253

14: SEARCH FOR A GOAL 265

APPENDIX I 283

APPENDIX II 289

INTRODUCTION

Some time ago, after a lecture I delivered in Western Germany, a lady rose to her feet during the discussion period and asked me in an aggrieved tone: "Isn't it true that activities like yours help in realizing the terrible predictions George Orwell made in his book *1984*?"

Back in the middle forties, Edward R. Murrow told me that he was afraid of the power social scientists might eventually wield by using their knowledge of how to influence people.

Vance Packard's book, *The Hidden Persuaders*, has expressed similar fears and has joined in warning the world at large against shaping the mind of contemporary man by what to him are occult influences. "The motivational analyst and symbol manipulator," Mr. Packard warns, "pooling their talents and with millions of dollars at their disposal, make a fascinating and at times disturbing team. These depth manipulators are, in their operations beneath the surface of American life, starting to acquire a power of persuasion that is becoming a matter of justifiable public scrutiny and concern."

The Americans or the Russians or both are almost certain to put a man into space during the sixties. We see ourselves surrounded by a world of push-buttons, boundless leisure, and electronic marvels. But what about the man of 1970? Will he be improved, will he have learned the art of living? Even without the threat of war, even with eternal peace guaranteed, will we have discovered the mystery of the goal of life? In all the hundreds of predictions about the next decade, little has been said about the inner man: his ability to control his desires, his hopes, and his fears. In all the changes in the world around us, is he to remain the same as he was at the beginning of civilization; or are we learning to solve, bit by bit, the problems anchored in human nature?

It is the human factor in the equation of progress and evolution which is decisive. There is a long list of assignments which await solution or at least improvement: juvenile delinquency, racial understanding, desire for independence; overcoming the fear of change; gaining insight into the motives and desires of others, whether friends, marital partners, children, or employees. The list is long, and it provides enough for us to do, no matter how much additional time automation will make available.

Ever since we built the first fire or devised the first clothing, we have attempted to improve upon the world. Each faster plane or better fertilizer or electronic computer represents another step forward in this evolution. We have made some progress in understanding human nature, but we have been painfully slow in learning how to bring about behavioral change. We have no qualms about tampering with nature in many of its manifestations. We use artificial insemination in cattle breeding and discuss seriously the fact that plowing, although practiced for thousands of years, may be a poor agricultural technique.

For a long time we simply did not have the tools to bring about behavioral change. As the social sciences have progressed we are evolving these tools very slowly. The mass media developed over the last few decades have given us the means of reaching millions of people with the verbal and non-verbal cues which could bring about changes and the utilization of the human factor. Applying these techniques, however, to the commercial and social problems on the list of assignments has aroused fears of hidden persuasion, manipulation.

In a letter which I recently received, I was accused of having stumbled onto a powerful weapon. "You know how to use it, but you lack a set of humanistic values and a sense of responsibility, and consequently you are making some glorious blunders. You are like a child which has suddenly found a machine gun and on learning how to operate it sets out to show people that he knows how by shooting at them. I think you psychologists should be learning how to motivate man so that he will desire more education and knowledge rather than creating needs for economic commodities."

In these discussions various issues are raised. Some people consider any kind of interference with human nature wrong and immoral; others object to the goals for which these persuasion techniques are used. It is interesting that there is so much emotional anxiety connected with this subject of persuasion. Why are we so afraid of being influenced, of being persuaded? Maybe what we are really afraid of is the growth and evolution of the individual and of the human race. The story of Adam and Eve repeats itself in our individual lives and in the evolution of human groups. It symbolizes the eternal conflict between the desire to stay in the paradise of ignorance and static tranquility, and the desire to live in the world of knowledge, striving, challenge, and growth. Who did the first persuading? Was it Eve, was it the apple, or was it the serpent? And why did Adam *take* the apple?

We still are attempting to escape back into the Nirvana of womb-like warmth and dreamy ignorance. We are afraid of persuasion techniques because they are the flaming sword sharpened on the grindstone of science that prevents our return to what we possibly erroneously call paradise. Human desire is the raw material we are working with. The strategy of human desire is the tool of shaping the human factor, the most important aspect of our worldly arsenal. Human progress is a conquest of the animal within us. No conquest is possible without strategy.

This whole controversy, if it is one, about the "art of influencing" gains much in clarity if we realize that the words "persuasion" or "education" cannot stand by themselves. Just as you cannot use the word "brother" without accepting the existence of a second individual, so no one is an educator or a persuader by himself. He needs a pupil, a "persuadee." Moreover, he also needs a goal, a purpose. He has to educate for something. We are then dealing with a trinity: the persuader, the subject of his persuasion, and the goal of his persuasion.

Since we are seeking the solution of a moral problem, it is best to approach it with some measure of scientific detachment. We must examine first not how people *should* behave but how they *do* behave.

And we must keep in mind that ethical standards operate within an existing cultural, economic, and philosophical framework.

Cannibalism, bigamy, and human sacrifice have at one time or another been approved aspects of human behavior. In our own society, under certain circumstances, wars, executions, deprivation of freedom, and economic coercion are also accepted standards of behavior.

Ideally, we may wish that people should never be influenced. The truth is they are continuously being influenced, and not only by people (parents, teachers, clergymen, friends) but also by the poverty or wealth of their society, and even by their physical environment, the landscape and the climate.

I hear many objections to "emotional" influences. This is to be expected since man (the persuadee) has been brought up for thousands of years under the banner of rationality and intellect. Emotions and irrationality have been described as forces to be controlled and to be despised. Ever since Plato, emotions have been compared to wild horses which must be tamed by *homo sapiens*, the thinking, rational man.

But this dichotomy represents a distortion of the psychological reality. We are not dealing with an either-or proposition. Emotions are part of the same continuum which governs the rational factors in human motivation. To complain about the existence of emotions or their inclusion in the human equation is unscientific. It does no good to wish people were made in a certain way; science must proceed from what people *are*. Wherever decisions are involved, whether in the choice of a mate or the choice of a car, emotions are present. To wish them away will make it impossible to understand the why of human behavior. Whatever your attitude toward modern psychology or psychoanalysis, it has been proved beyond any doubt that many of our daily decisions are governed by motivations over which we have no control and of which we are often quite unaware.

Thus, in view of these circumstances surrounding the subject of persuasion, the only really debatable factor is the *goal* of education or the *purpose* of the persuasion. While these goals vary in different historical periods and in different cultures, this relativity can be translated into absolute values when the clinical and psychological well-being of the individual is being taken into consideration.

For example, we face a major alternative when we educate our children. We can either make them content and satisfied with things the way they are, or we can make them discontent. If we assume that it is part of the basic nature of life, man, and man's place in this world to change continuously and constructively, then creative discontent is a healthy goal of persuasion and education. If, on the other hand, we believe that we now live in the best of all possible worlds, then contentment should be the goal.

Only the philosophical outlook of "Big Brother" fosters the concept that we have reached the best of all possible worlds. "Big Brother" cannot afford malcontents. They are dangerous, they ask too many questions. So they are given happiness pills. They are being persuaded in hidden and in overt ways that everything is fine.

I believe that a real danger in our contemporary life is a kind of superficial sophistication which prevents many people from admitting that they are influenced by advertising and propaganda, in the broadest meaning of this poor word. In many studies we have conducted we find that weak and defensively rational individuals cannot bring themselves to admit that they too have emotions—that they too have been swayed by the irrational two-tone design of a new streamlined car, even though they realize their old car would have lasted another five years.

Is it moral to help convince people of the beauty of a new car, to make them spend the $3,000 or $4,000 which they could have used for something else? And if it is immoral, where shall we draw the line? Do you really need the fireplace in your house when you have automatic oil heat? Was it right to buy the garbage-disposal unit which flushes into the sewer valuable food residues which might have been put into the compost pile for the organic garden?

Men's ties, women's Easter hats, and gaudy admirals' uniforms are all irrational. Why should we take it for granted that the silly plot of a boring Broadway musical is more desirable, simply because it is theater, than an exquisitely performed TV program which reaches millions of people?

Yes, there are standards. And they have been continuously discussed since the dawn of civilization. Persuasion, like education and atomic power, can be used for good and for evil. Even the all-out attacks on psychological persuasion, such as Vance Packard's book, are desirable ones. They draw attention to an important aspect of a form of modern communication—the use of emotional appeals in addition to rational ones in order to sway people. Most uninhibited people with wisdom and maturity are aware of this aspect of human interrelations. Those who have denied its existence may now be forced to acknowledge that many things in life are play-acted and exaggerated to enlist our sympathy, our anger, or our love. But just as we have stopped shooting the good actor who portrays the villain in the theater or on the screen, we might consider the possibility of letting the persuader persuade us.

Most of us will claim that we resent high-pressure salesmen. Yet when the salesman stops selling and tells us to choose rationally, we feel let down and downright insulted by his indifference.

Demosthenes, two thousand years ago, took lessons in hidden persuasion by putting pebbles in his mouth. President Eisenhower took them from Robert Montgomery. Neither did anything unethical or dangerous. Persuasion is good if there is a correct goal. In the context of commercial persuasion, modern psychology helps define at least one major goal: we may call it frivolous buying or we may call it an invitation to new experiences, to a more creative and more fulfilled life.

Strictly speaking, a new car, a color TV set, cigarettes, beer, or French wines are not necessities. But they all represent aspects of a full life. Modern psychology considers a man well adjusted when he can strike a proper balance between the cycles of tension and satisfaction, when he can continuously grow and expand his power for enjoyment and creative exploration to the utmost of his capacities. Such an expansive life can be considered ethical not only from the point of view of the individual but also from that of the society. The combined creative fulfillments of all the citizens in a society add up to the total capacity of the group or culture within which the individual and the family live.

The products or services that are being consumed and used as vehicles and tools of such fulfillment are incidental. If the desire for freedom and discovery can be expressed through the glamor of a new convertible, I willingly accept responsibility for combining two strong human desires for the benefit of the car advertiser—and ultimately for the benefit of both the national economy and the creative happiness of the individual. It is only when the goal of persuasion is to instill static and stale contentment that it results in eventual maladjustment and unhappiness and thus becomes clinically incorrect and morally undesirable. If everything in this world is in flux, then we must persuade more, rather than less; we must persuade mankind to push the big ball actively up the hill of human history. Each step in our growth is part of a maturing process; each step is represented by a conflict. The aimless playing of a pre-school child is eventually replaced by rigid schedules. More and more discipline, more and more responsibility are being placed on our reluctant shoulders. It is a continuous fight between remaining a beachcomber of life and becoming an active modern citizen. Persuasion, education, communication must be used continuously in order to make us take the next step.

We have learned to perfect the techniques of persuasion and communication. Often the assignment given our organization for conducting motivational research was a very sober and concrete one. How could we convince people that they should buy more of a brand of soap, chewing gum, or beer? Often the aim is far loftier. How could we get people to give more blood, to vote, to participate in elections? How could army officers be taught to make decisions? How could we get people to give to charity or to keep the city clean? How could we stop the new wave of anti-Semitism? How could we get more people to join the Air Force? In some instances the problem we investigated was concerned with broad philosophical goals. How could we get Americans to stop being afraid of bigness? How could we create better understanding between the races? How could the image of America abroad be improved and how could American goals and strategy be determined? What is the psychology and what are the motivations of young nations? What should be the relationship between recently liberated countries and their former protectors? In each one of these cases, techniques of persuasion and communication were employed.

This book will deal with these techniques. I shall attempt to report on the knowledge we have acquired on what makes people act the way they do and on how we can motivate them.

The major lesson we learned in serving as a sort of strategy council for many institutions, organizations and companies was the need for a different kind of thinking—motivational thinking. This kind of thinking implies freeing oneself from the shackles of many misconceptions, some of them comfortable and time-honored. Our world is changing. Yet we insist on approaching this changing world with the same concepts and stereotypes which supposedly worked fifty years ago. We are in the midst of a silent war—on the outside with Russia and on the inside with our old concepts of thinking.

Our daily problems have changed. We are being asked to defend our goals and our philosophy of life when we listen to a discussion between a socialist or Communist and someone living in a free country. If a cocktail party progresses beyond idle chatter, it rapidly becomes involved in a discussion of the quality of the American educational system, the desirability of having the "right" amount of chrome on your car, or the degree of conformism or non-conformism in the average American as compared with other nationalities.

When we discuss how differently modern youth behaves toward grownups compared to the youth of thirty years ago, when we question the desirability of making lots of money against working for happiness, we find that each one of these areas requires a new set of psychological outlooks.

This is a book about human strategy. If we want to get people to behave the way we think they should, we must stop making theological demands on them. Instead of embellishing the Ten Commandments, we must start worrying about why we have been unable to fulfill these demands. We are all against sin, but the problem has always been and still is one of finding the best method of making people less sinful.

The strategy of human conduct has two approaches: the theologian's and the social scientist's. Neither one has been too effective up to now, and no balance sheet needs to be drawn up to prove this point.

In her 1958 presidential address to the American Psychology Association, Anne Roe of Harvard University had this to say:

> There is no need to belabor the point that only man is a danger to man. Surely, then, it is incumbent upon us as students of man, as well as upon other social scientists, to reassess our roles, and if need be to redirect our activities. I do not decry our past preoccupations, but I confess to a great weariness with the present concentration upon technical minutiae, with better and better research design for matters of less and less importance. Indeed, it often seems that the correlation between goodness of design and importance of project is remarkably high, and negative.
>
> Since as individuals or as a species we cannot evade our responsibilities and remain men, let us cast up our assets and liabilities, let us make some decisions, let us at least not lose the world by default.

The social scientists have been so preoccupied with finding out the *truth* about human nature and with putting it down in decimal points that they have not had enough time to concern themselves with the sober daily problems encountered by the businessman and the civic leader.

The client who approaches the applied social scientist wants to know in clear terms what he can do next week to influence citizens to vote in favor of the new school or influence his consumers to buy his product. The tragedy is that when the scientist barricades himself behind the escape of "true" science, when he says that he does not know the complete answer or that it would take him three years to find it, then the practical businessman often makes his decision without even the most rudimentary information the social scientist could have given him. There are literally hundreds of daily problems which belong in the domain of social science, yet few answers are offered.

Social scientists have tried to jump the phase of concept-formulation, have tried to start measuring before being quite clear about what was being measured. The Aristotelian belief in empiricism and deduction from observation, from objective data, is highly questionable in the light of modern epistemology and semantics. Effective scientific research, I believe, must start with a hypothesis.

It is further questionable whether the customary sharp division between diagnosis and therapy is a correct approach in a field which is called upon for concrete and practical recommendations. Problem-solving research asks different questions, sets up different forms of investigation from those of research where the primary demand is to know the facts. Too often, in my experience, I have discovered that a helpless client, small or large, after having supposedly assembled all the facts and having been given the diagnosis of his ills, still asks, "What do I do now?"

Our research, our motivational thinking, concentrates more on the techniques of human strategy which are necessary to bring about the desired goal. The question we ask ourselves, before undertaking and analyzing a motivational problem, is "What will I have to know in order to be able to advise the client on the proper advertising, sales program, propagandistic or educational approach?" This pragmatic viewpoint has led me to recognize that the individual problems confronting a particular institution are not very different from the enormously larger problems on the national and international scene. They are not so confusing and impossible to attack as they may at first seem to be. Here, as in the business world, there are a number of typical errors in communication which are being made again and again. With proper understanding and recognition of these errors we can help bring about an improved form of persuasion communication.

For example, we are still guided by illusions as to the efficacy of verbal, logical, direct approaches. We have been brought up for so long in a physical world that even two thousand years after Christ, and five thousand years after Moses, we still do not truly believe in the power of the mind and the soul. Only now are we gradually becoming aware that we have entered an age of psychology. We are fighting a sham battle with rockets and hydrogen bombs while underneath the real struggle, the silent war, is for the possession of men's minds. We are witnessing a series of mental and psychological conflicts. An understanding of these conflicts, a decision to use more efficient techniques of communication in order to help us recognize the right alternative, seems to be one of the most important tasks in almost every phase of life.

This book may have undertaken too ambitious a task; but I feel that unless we attempt to arrive at some global, all-encompassing configuration of human goals and strategy, we cannot see and we cannot solve individual tasks in the proper fashion. What we need is a new freedom—the freedom to think in new channels. Motivational research thus represents the application of social science techniques to the problems of human motivations.

We are faced today with a misery of choice between holding on to old ideas or abandoning them and reappraising our attitudes toward the new world which has arisen all around us. Wars have become impossible, a four-day work week seems possible, new nations are springing up every year. From the psychological point of view, the basic conflict we face is one between wanting to hold on to the *status quo*, wanting to return to the womb, to hide, to be fatalistic, or to face the world by accepting change as a challenge. We need to crack the whip of constructive discontent by using all methods of modern communication and persuasion. This is one of the answers—if not the most important answer—to the present conflict between our present level of economic prosperity and the future goals of Western living.

ONE ■ PERSUASION STARTED WITH EVE

1 ■ THE MASK OF BEHAVIOR

Every morning paper tells us that Americans ought to be more interested in education, ought to go to church more often. We are urged to do something about racial prejudice, about juvenile delinquency. We are told that artificial absolescence of products is dangerous for our economy, that inflation is caused by human demands, and that humans should co-operate in order to prevent inflation.

This is primitive, prescientific communication. We state a goal with an exclamation point after it and we think that *presto!* the job has been accomplished. By tearing off the mask of human behavior, by seeing humans the way they really are, by starting from the premise of their prejudices, inhibitions, and emotions, a better job can be done of lifting them up, educating them, bringing them to a higher level.

The techniques of selling, advertising, public relations, and motivational research are directly applicable, not only to commercial problems but also to those of a wider and more socially oriented purpose.

Over the last few thousand years of human existence we have concerned ourselves so much with the glorification of goals for human society that we have paid little attention to how we might achieve them. There are a number of reasons for this retarded orientation.

PHYSICAL VS. PSYCHOLOGICAL THINKING

Throughout most of human history a paradox has existed. As social animals, human beings must learn to exist with each other. Looking outside themselves they found a physical world with physical tools. This dominance of the physical world resulted logically in a search for physical means of strategy and communication. In order to protect themselves, people built walls and barricaded themselves, or used existing caves. In order to provoke fear in other people, they reached for clubs, slings, and stones. To arouse respect and admiration they adorned themselves with feathers, paint, and precious metals. Many of these physical strategy weapons persist today.

At the same time, however, men also discovered the possibility of psychological stratagems such as smiles and the first forms of symbolism and persuasion.

Today, as you look back over human history, the success and failure of states and empires have reflected both the physical and the psychological forces. To a large extent, however, it was the psychological strategy people and nations exerted upon each other which resulted in final success. We still have not written the history of ideological and psychological warfare which has taken place over thousands of years. If we did, we might discover that the ideological weapons are, in most instances, even more powerful than the purely military ones.

We are now again faced with such a dilemma in the missile race and in the competition to conquer outer space. It seems as if all the lessons of thousands of years have been forgotten again. We seem to be much more concerned with shooting our rocket a hundred or two hundred miles high than with producing the kind of ideology and the kind of psychological strategy which will result in greater happiness for mankind. We make believe that the culture which will win out is the one that has the better engineers and the more powerful missiles, rather than the one which has the more powerful ideas. That these mistakes are still being made after thousands of years is a challenging problem for the modern social scientist. It is he who at least claims to be concerned with the strategy of communication and human relationships.

Over twenty new nations have come into being during the last ten years. Each of them was motivated by a desire to be independent. In Marrakech an Arab cab driver told me (in perfect French) that it was true they had more unemployed now than while they were under French protection. "But," he said, "they are our own unemployed." At the same time, in a study conducted for a French dairy company, in Casablanca we found that Moroccans preferred to have the labels on milk bottles printed in French rather than in Arabic. "What is good enough for the French is good enough for us," they said.

Each one of these new nations is confronted with many problems, problems to a large extent of a psychological nature: how to play their new roles, how to teach their citizens to accept their own authority rather than that of a foreign nation. And not only young nations but also older ones must learn to adjust themselves to new roles. The United States has failed to define its goals clearly either for itself or for the outside world. Without such definition the goals of the individual also remain unclear. We want and need answers to the questions of where we are going and why we are going there.

I believe the social sciences can help to provide those answers. But to do so, we must first see man and society as they exist, not as we would wish them to be. And we must also rid ourselves of false assumptions.

FALSE ASSUMPTIONS

Dr. Victor Victoroff, in an article called "The Assumptions We Live By" (*General Semantics Magazine*, Autumn 1958), describes one of the main jobs of a psychiatrist as the examination of assumptions.

> The insufferable circumstance for most humans is to be confronted with a problem, particularly involving something new, unknown and to find no answer to it. The resulting discomfort provides the mind with stimulus to start thinking. To counteract this threat of the unknown, an answer must be found and characteristically it is found. Unhappily it is not necessary to furnish the right answer. The first answer which promises to work will meet the requirements and alleviate anxiety. The mind, defensive as usual, justifies its slipshod work with rationalizations and excuses, afraid that the truth beyond the guess will raise new and worse issues if discovered. Because we sometimes dread or cannot handle the truth, our honest perceptions about a mystery may have to be squelched or denied and more acceptable stereotyped hypotheses substituted.
>
> It is difficult to view the inner man. We elaborately protect ourselves from knowing our motivations for doing things. The 20,000 people a year who kill themselves, had been unwilling or are hopelessly unable to use

reasoning and they elect to blast out their brains rather than amend their false assumptions.

An example of false assumptions occurred in a study we did for a baby-food company. The problem was how best to advertise the various types of baby foods. The obvious assumption was that the best method was to promise the mother that this baby food would contribute to the health of her child. Since the approach of motivational research is unbiased and realistic in its attitude to problems of human motivations, we did not accept this assumption. Through 350 interviews which permitted mothers to talk realistically about babies, motherhood, and feeding problems, we discovered that while this mother love was partially operative, a much more tangible and effective motivation at work was the mother's interest in making her feeding chore more convenient and pleasant. Promising her, therefore, that this particular brand of baby food would be enjoyed by her child, would be less likely to result in rejection, and would cut down feeding time considerably proved to be a more effective appeal. In the prescientific approach of daily life and economics we often assume that mother love, patriotism, morality, etc., are such basic human motivations that we fail to even consider the possibility of much more realistic and truly human motivations.

Mother-love and concern with the baby's growth and health sound much nicer than the practical motivation of convenience. The moralist, of course, becomes shocked by such a discovery. He turns against the advertising man and against the motivational researcher and blames them for having made an appeal to the baser instincts. The dilemma we're dealing with here is one of the most vital ones in the whole science of man.

Suppose a physician were to tell us that he knows certain pains in the body are caused by a disturbance in the digestive tract but that he is not going to concern himself with the examination of the digestive tract because it might force him to touch unpleasant, baser aspects of the human body. It is obvious that we could reject such a value system as unscientific. We certainly would not permit the doctor to move his attention to the more elegant-sounding heart functions. Why then do we condone this attitude when we are dealing with psychological factors in human motivations? It is certainly not the invention of the social scientist that a mother is more interested in herself than she is in her baby. It is a phenomenon which can easily be observed once the nicer-sounding but unrealistic assumptions of mother love have been carefully and objectively examined.

What we're trying to do with motivational research and motivational thinking is to go back to the reality of human behavior. The Cancer Society was interested in getting our advice on how people could be persuaded to see a physician regularly in order to permit early detection of possible cancer. Everybody ought logically to be interested in regular checkups, but the fact that the Cancer Society did ask us for advice shows that this motivation, while a very logical and reasonable one, apparently was not enough. What we found was a less rational but a more human explanation. There were at least as many people who did not go for a checkup because they thought nothing was wrong with them as there were those who did not want to go because they were afraid something would be found. People in our interviews would say, "I wasted my money. After all the thorough examinations, I felt like a fool when the doctor told me that my fears were unwarranted and that there was nothing wrong with me."

In other studies in the medical field we found again and again that certain types of people go from one physician to another until they are finally told the things they want to hear, giving them an excuse to slow down, to take a vacation, to feel pity for themselves, or arouse sympathy.

The Safety Council is very much concerned with preventing death from auto accidents. This is certainly a desirable and logical goal. Yet statistics of the holiday seasons every year show very little change in the death toll. The reason is, again, a wrong approach to the problem of safe driving. Accidents are not the result of a logical decision to speed, to pass someone, to be careless. They are the result of a series of emotional motivations. They therefore cannot be cured by logical appeals. Accident prevention must be approached emotionally. Careless driving is often caused by frustration which results in aggressive tendencies. The car becomes the instrument of destructive tendencies and often, at the same time, self-destructive tendencies.

There is little doubt that the modern car is a power symbol. It is an extension of one's personality and an enormous multiplication of the limited power of the physical frame of the individual. Our recommendation to the people concerned with safety was to provide other outlets for these aggressive feelings and at the same time, through posters and signs, to tap people psychologically on the shoulder and say "Better not!" In a non-authoritative fashion they could be reminded to think it over at the very moment when they were about to make a wrong decision, such as passing someone on the highway.

You may have had a conference this morning trying to decide how to organize your office operation more efficiently, or you may have discussed with your wife the necessity of changing your job. In both cases, scientific knowledge of decision-making would have helped you. No ten minutes pass by in daily life without the need to make some kind of decision.

When I am asked as a psychologist why people buy, why they act as they do, I am usually expected to give my questioner a clear-cut, enumerated list of motivations and reasons. In the course of my work, an impatient advertiser has challenged me and said that all he wants to know is why his soap is not selling while his competitor's soap is successful, although both brands are almost alike in appearance and general quality. He is saying to me: "We do not want a complicated explanation. All we want to discover is why people do not buy our product and which is the most important psychological factor which we have to consider."

What is in the mind of an advertiser when he asks such questions? He has the feeling that the psychologist, who, after all, claims to be an expert on human nature, has a ready-made check list available which he needs only to hand over to the practical businessman so the latter can find out which of the important factors he has considered and which ones he has overlooked.

Unfortunately, the problems are not quite so readily solved. Why is it not possible to set up check lists for human motivations? To say that satisfactions of sex, hunger, need for shelter, etc. represent the basic human motivations, while not untrue, is a superficial and inaccurate attempt to explain human nature. Even if this list is more sophisticated and longer, it is misleading. The fact that you are not wearing your red tie today cannot be explained by a very simple one-two-three list of motivations. If you are a normal human being, an almost incredible number of factors exerted their influence on you, not only today but in all the preceding days, sometimes going back as far as your childhood. We must consider many conscious and unconscious factors such as the mood created by weather and the kind of people with whom you associate, the state of your health, family relations, etc. All of these things often operate and work together in such a simple choice as that between a red or green tie.

You would be amazed to find how often we mislead ourselves, regardless of how smart we think we are, when we attempt to explain why we are behaving the way we do. Our first difficulty stems from the fact that we have a great desire to behave as rational human beings, and therefore we seek rational explanations for our behavior. The truth of the matter is that we behave irrationally more often than not, and since we do not want to be reminded of our irrationality, we become blocked. We do not wish to admit the real reason for our behavior. Any person whose job is to mold public opinion, to affect the attitudes and desires of people, will fail in his task if he forgets this fundamental law of human nature. A rational explanation is always a more suspicious type of answer than one which goes back to a less pleasant but more realistic analysis of our attitudes.

A second factor which makes it difficult to get to the bottom of people's behavior is that much too frequently we tend to judge by appearances. What would seem safer than to explain a girl's interest in her boy friend on the basis of human desire for romance and sex? Surely here we are dealing with a basic motive. Yet many of our psychological studies have shown that even in our sexual relations we are less interested in the partner than we are in ourselves. Even in the physiological moment we are often more concerned with, and prouder of, our own prowess and ability to experience pleasure than we are with the love partner.

It is easier, however—and a more accepted pattern of human

thinking—to explain events on the basis of outward appearances, to place an accepted label on an observed attitude and feel that in this fashion a real explanation has been given. Again and again I encounter this difficulty with manufacturers and advertisers when they tell me that, of course, they know why their product is bought or rejected; it is simply a problem of habit and inertia. It is often a long-drawn-out job to prove to them that such an explanation is utterly meaningless—a pseudo-explanation. It is only after such a statement is made that the real psychological research job begins. Then we must find out what kind of people the buyers are, why they were influenced by a habit, and what is the meaning of this habit which makes people stick to one particular brand, or influences them to switch to a different one.

A third difficulty in analyzing human behavior results from the fact that the majority of propagandists or practical businessmen are very proud of their product or their message. It is inconceivable to them that observation of human behavior has shown that most purchases or actions are made less because of the quality of the product than because of the satisfaction promised to the consumer's ego. We never buy anything or take action unless there is some kind of deep psychological need for it. Often this need has very little to do with the outward appearances. Therefore, one of the most important jobs to be undertaken by the human strategist, the public official, the advertiser, the businessman, or anyone who wishes to understand why people buy or act is to become thoroughly aware of these hidden needs and aspirations.

In the chapters which follow I would, therefore, like to explore some of these psychological needs, to illuminate them through the findings of motivational research, and to indicate some of the things we know about motivating people.

2 ■ THE DISCOVERY OF MOTIVATIONS

It is interesting in itself that the term "motivational research" and all it stands for have become so controversial. More than twenty years have passed since I began to practice what has acquired the trade label of M.R. About a dozen books and many articles have been written about motivational research. Often the very same book or article would state that motivational research is useless, unscientific, and villainous and at the same time would passionately discuss who really originated it. I think the time has come for a little factual and unemotional clarification.

The first study I conducted is now in the library of the Institute for Motivational Research. It concerned itself with the problems of Ivory Soap. It was, I think, one of the first commercial applications of motivational thinking. The new idea involved was that effective copy appeals and some answers to the problems posed by the advertising agency might be arrived at by letting people talk at great length about their use of this soap. I decided to talk to people about such things as daily baths and showers, rather than to ask people various questions about why they used or did not use Ivory Soap. I personally conducted a hundred non-directive interviews where people were permitted to talk at great length about their most recent experiences with toilet soap. The consequent analysis of these hundred interviews revealed that taking a bath before a date, before a special or festive occasion, seemed to have a greater significance than the daily routine bath. I also found that people bathed more carefully, stayed longer in the tub or shower, in their preparations for such an occasion. I also found that people did not judge soaps so much by their price, appearance, lather, or color, but by a combination of all these various factors plus an additional intangible element which I called the personality of a soap. Ivory Soap, I found, had at that time more of a somber, utilitarian, thoroughly cleansing character than the more glamorous personalities of other soaps such as Cashmere Bouquet, for example. This study was conducted in 1939, and it was here that I developed the concept of the "personality" or "image" of a product.

The second research study I conducted which could be termed motivational was carried out for the Chrysler Corporation and dealt with the problems of the Plymouth car in 1939–40. The problem presented was "Why do about 70 per cent of motorists keep on buying the same make of car?"—Ford buyer repeating a Ford, Chevrolet buyer repeating a Chevrolet. This was of particular concern to the Plymouth people because Plymouth had entered the market only a few years before. They were confronted, therefore, with a perpetuation of purchase in the two major competitive brands.

The conventional market research approach to this problem was to go out and ask three thousand people why they had bought the same make of car. The expected answer to this sort of question was "Because I was satisfied with the one I had before." This, however, was a typical example of tautology, or circular evidence, in which one term is substituted for another without really providing an explanation of human behavior. In order to get at the real reason, I proposed to the Chrysler Corporation that we use the modern techniques of social science and the interviewing techniques developed in clinical psychology and psychiatry. This was done. The study revealed among other things that of the two hundred or so motorists interviewed, the majority had a fear of the unknown as far as the then relatively new Plymouth car was concerned. They felt more comfortable buying a car in which the basic elements and engineering features were familiar to them.

Even more important was the personality, the image of the car, as it had developed in their minds. Up to that point (1939) Plymouth had held up the image of difference. "This car is different from any other one you have ever tried," was the basic appeal being used in Plymouth ads. This aggravated the average motorist's fear of change. Seventy per cent of the people kept on buying the same make of car they drove before. We suggested that this fear of change be counteracted by new advertising appeals which emphasized that it would take only a few minutes to feel familiar with the new Plymouth car.

In this study we also discovered some of the basic motivations at work in the driving of cars. We found, for example, that his very first car has more emotional meaning to a man than most of the other cars he may later own. People we interviewed spent three to four times as much time talking about the first car they owned than about more recent and more expensive cars. Our hypothesis about the emotional significance of the first car was further confirmed by another test in which we attempted to ascertain what trips were taken with the first car. We found that a preponderance of these trips led away from home and were often of several days' duration. The significance of these trips as expressed consciously by one person was, "I wanted to find out how free I really was." The car thus served as a vehicle for testing his wings. It is well known that the first car is often the place where first erotic experiences occur.

In this study we also found that while relatively few people bought convertibles, the majority of them dreamt of owning one. Seventy per cent of the two hundred people interviewed in this second motivational study admitted that they had either seriously considered buying a convertible or had at least dreamt of owning one.

These interview results were further confirmed by a number of experiments in which convertibles were put into showroom windows for a period of two weeks and comparisons were made between the number of people who stopped and entered these showrooms as against others where only sedans were displayed. Interviews with salesmen also confirmed this dream of the convertible. We felt, therefore, that the evidence justified our recommending to the Chrysler Corporation that they consider in their advertising appeals the great desire for convertibles despite the low sales figure of 2 per cent which convertibles then represented. We felt it was correct to tell them that considerably more than 2 per cent of their advertising budget should be allocated to convertibles. We also found in this study that the influence of women in car buying was considerably greater than had been normally assumed. This again was uncovered through careful analysis of the interviews and observation of actual sales situations in hundreds of cases. (See Appendix for details of Plymouth study.)

The convertible, we found, often could be compared to the "mistress," the sedan to the wife. The open car was the symbol of youth, freedom, and human dreams. The sedan was sedate, conservative, and practical. This finding was blown up and exaggerated in Vance Packard's book and in other publicity stories. In itself it is a rather sober and common-sense observation.

These two brief examples from early studies illustrate the motivational approach to problems. Let us now dig a little deeper into the meaning of motivational thinking.

To begin with, there are two phases in motivational research. One is to find out why people behave the way they do. The second is to prescribe a remedy and to determine how people might be motivated. It is the second phase which critics refer to when discussing the ethics of persuasion.

Attempting to find out why people behave the way they do leads us directly into the whole field of the psychology of personality and human behavior. Some authors have stated that there is no such thing as unconscious motivation. Such a position is hardly worth debating when we consider the tremendous developments in psychosomatic medicine and the recognition that possibly more than half of all human diseases are psychogenic. More and more evidence is being accumulated to indicate that worry, maladjustment, and other emotional disturbances can be responsible for almost anything from heart attack to cancer.

Our lives are full of motivational "whys." How could Joe ever have married such a wife? Why do these people keep on living in a house that is much too large for them? Why has one of two brothers become a success and the other a failure? Why do many men smoke cigars but more men smoke cigarettes? Why do women use perfume or nail polish? What is the motivation for eating potato chips? Why do we spend or waste time in front of a television set?

Let us discuss some of these motivations. A basic human motivation for almost all our activities and needs is the desire for security in one form or another. We married the girl we did because in the last analysis we felt more comfortable with her. Our biological role as lover, our psychological role as provider, as the man striving for success, seemed to be more assured with one type of woman than with another. No matter how attractive, no matter how rich or desirable, very few men will marry a woman who makes them feel insecure. We drive the car we do because it gives us more prestige, buys us respect with others, gives us a feeling of success. Of course, we may also buy it because it is more economical and better engineered. But even there the final motivation is that we want to be successful as buyers. We don't want to have the feeling that we have been made fools of, that we did not shop or buy wisely.

Recently I visited some of the ruins of the ancient Inca Empire near Cuzco in Peru, and admired the tremendous buildings constructed out of huge stone blocks, so perfectly fitted without cement or any other binding material that not even a razor blade could be inserted between them. The mountain retreat of Machu Picchu, which was only discovered in 1911, is hidden on a mountain slope facing deep valleys in the Andes. While many of the foundations of the buildings have withstood erosion, earthquakes, and the ravages of time, and escaped discovery by the Spanish conquerors, they still are no more than ruins. They are a dramatic example of the human desire for security and at the same time of the failure to achieve security by physical means.

The cultural anthropologist asks continuously why. He is concerned with motivations, either those of the Incas or of the American tribe. But what is a motivation? A motivation is a composite of factors which result in a specific action intended to change an existing situation into a future one. I am hungry, I search for food, I eat. I am not hungry any longer. A need has been satisfied. The term "need," however, is itself a complex one. It may mean simply a basic physiological need. But even when we talk about eating, why do I eat a particularly rich-looking dish rather than an equally nourishing but plainer one? When buying a car, do I buy it because I really need it? The automobile industry would go bankrupt overnight if cars were bought only by those people who actually need them. Even the Indians living near Iquitos near the upper Amazon River whom I visited adorn themselves with feathers of toucan birds and paint their faces with ochre. Neither of these activities is strictly utilitarian. Modern cosmetics, mink coats, and men's ties are equally useless. We must then turn to the concept of *psychological* needs to explain human motivations, but here too many problems arise. We may need solitude, we may need prestige. Some people get it by keeping up with the Joneses, others by doing exactly the opposite. Some people need to express their individualism; they are non-conformists. This need for non-conformity may in turn foster another form of conformism.

In our work at the Institute for Motivational Research, we have developed a more relevant definition for motivation. We believe that most human actions are the result of tensions. Whenever tension differentials become strong enough, they lead to action. For example, I may have been wanting a car for a long time. I am unhappy with my car for a number of reasons. My children have complained about the fact that it looks shabby and all their friends have much better-looking and newer cars. Furthermore, I read in the papers about the new car models. I see advertisements extolling the improvements of the new cars. Finally, something minor happens to my car, which could be easily repaired, but it provides the final stimulus to visit a showroom and to shop for a new car. What happened as far as my motivations were concerned? Why indeed did I buy this new car?

We are dealing with a series of events, some coming from the inside, some from the outside, some from technical factors, others from psychological factors, all building up to a tension which results in action. The tension differential, borrowing this term from the physical sciences, has become so great that the action is finally triggered off. In order to understand the origin of such an action, such a decision, a number of factors must be considered. Let us look at them briefly.

We have been using three major principles:

1. The Functional Principle.
2. The Dynamic Principle.
3. The Principle of Fundamental Insights.

1. THE FUNCTIONAL PRINCIPLE: CULTURAL ANTHROPOLOGY

This implies that we cannot answer the question of why people continue to buy the same make of car, for instance, unless we know first why they buy cars at all. Car buying, at the same time, must be connected with life style, personality, and other general factors if it is to be thoroughly understood. When we investigate cigarette smoking, for instance, we must put this activity in its proper context and frame of reference. We must analyze smoking in a way that will not disturb its natural ties with all its related activities and phenomena such a working habits, leisure time, occupation, health, etc.

Only when we understand the function of television or radio as centers of the home around which the family gathers, can we arrive at a proper understanding of why one commercial is more effective than another, why one program draws more viewers or listeners than another.

The application of this functional principle makes it clear that much of the work called motivational research is really applied cultural anthropology. Margaret Mead, the well-known anthropologist, states:

> Anthropological science gains its importance from the fact that it attempts to see each individual which shares a common culture in its natural context.

In her book, *Cooperation and Competition among Primitive Peoples*, she says:

> The mere recording of the fact that a group of men were accustomed to building a canoe together would have no comparative significance unless one knew the sociological constitution of the group who build these canoes, the way in which this canoe-building group fitted into the total social structure, the ends for which each individual in that group was working, sanctions which lay behind their working together, the extent to which this group activity, whether it was defined as cooperative or merely as collective, was representative of the usual behavior of members of the society. One would, furthermore, have to know the nature of the material environment within which the group got its livelihood and the existing state of technology.

Motivations seldom consist of lists of reasons arranged in a linear manner to be added up arithmetically. Motivations are complicated structures that are best compared to machines with many moving parts, where every part has a very particular influence on the next and where the interaction takes place in a definite timely order. A practical problem of policy decision, whether in the political, commercial, or international field, therefore, cannot really be undertaken unless this functional principle has been understood and considered.

For example, we found in one of our surveys, after a thorough investigation, that soap preference is not necessarily based on outward appearance, odor, and similar factors. In order to really understand why people select one brand of soap rather than another, many factors must be considered. The personality of the soap must be considered. There are young and old soaps, there are flirtatious, "conservative" soaps, and there are more basic factors. Soap is one of those products which comes into very intimate contact with our bodies. It is also held in the palm of the hand. We investigated this relationship between soap and the palm in a number of our studies. We found that we had to go back to the basic biological functions of our hands in order to understand the role played by the shape of a cake of soap.

The human animal distinguishes himself from other animals by his ability to oppose the thumb, to grip things. Even the embryo is positioned in such a way that the thumb presses against the palm of the hand, thus creating a zone of sensitivity. This sensitivity is never lost. Often we prefer one tool to another because of the more pleasant feeling the tool leaves in the palm of the hand. Therefore we prefer soaps that offer a good grip. One of the modern soaps which has created a shape that fits perfectly into the palm of the hand, no matter which way it is being held, is Dove by Lever Brothers. Our study of Dove showed that this shape represented one of the product's important appeals.

Only after I have developed this insight into the biopsychological meaning of the shape of things, the shape of soap, the palm-fitting quality of these products, when I have applied the functional principle, can I go out and make a quantitative investigation of how many people actually prefer a soap that fits the palm of the hand and how many don't. Had I not applied this functional principle, had I not had this insight I may very well have been investigating a very superficial and meaningless characteristic of the product.

This motivational insight into the functional principle of the palm of the hand has many applications. It applies to locks and door handles, as we found in a study for the Qwik-Set Company. It applies to levers on many machines.

The necessity of understanding human motivations in terms of their frame of reference exists not only in the solution of commercial problems but in almost every field. We are often captives of our own reference systems without realizing it. When you think of a Chinese, for example, which mental image is more likely to come to your mind? A coolie or an ambassador? When you think of a Negro, what picture do you see? A laborer or a physician? How many times have you thought of a Russian soldier as a loving father? Racial and color concepts still often get in our way. This is probably one reason why the habits of the American tribe, the motivations of our everyday modern life, have not yet been made the subject of sufficient scientific investigation. To the professional anthropologist it seems more dignified to concern himself with the primitive Trobriand Islanders or far-off Samoans than with the fact that a large group of American teen-agers, when they get their first car, rip out part of the front end and denude the car of almost all its chromium adornments. As our study showed, this is an attempt to superimpose the individuality of the owner of this first car, usually a second-hand one, over the personality of the make of the car. In my mind this is as fascinating an observation and a subject for investigation as the tribal customs and initiation rites of a primitive people.

Almost every day we go out and buy something. We do hundreds of things in our daily lives which have meaning only because we are members of a special tribe, because we live in a special kind of society and culture. For example, we are still guided by principles of value standards which made a great deal of sense during the pioneer days but which have lost their significance today. Many people still buy merchandise on the basis of its weight. Have you ever observed a man select a lighter, a mechanical tool, a shaver, or some similar object? He will handle it, weigh it in one hand and then the other, judge how it feels in the palm of his hand and also how heavy it is.

We were once asked to investigate why engineers would not believe that huge vats made out of Duraluminum were as sturdy as steel vats. The reason was that the irrational evaluation of weight stood in the way of the scientific fact that Duraluminum was technically as strong as steel. It simply did not weigh as much. Being light meant being weak. In most instances, a heavier tool is not really the better one. The heavier shaver is not necessarily the better one. Stone, in the building of homes, still gives us a feeling of security and reliability, yet it does not have as much insulating power as, for instance, aluminum foil. We still have not shed our cave-man beliefs in areas where overwhelming evidence exists to prove us wrong in our irrational attitudes.

2. THE DYNAMIC PRINCIPLE: THE ASPIRATION SCALE

Not only do human motivations have to be understood within a series of frames of reference, but they change and develop ontogenetically and phylogenetically, within the lifetime of one individual and with the historical development of a cultural group or the whole human race. The human race, as a whole, keeps on changing and each individual keeps on repeating, to a large extent, the over-all change brought about over thousands of years in his own life and every so often pushing humanity one or two steps ahead in the phylogenetic racial development. However, the genetic principle implies two things. On one hand, it implies dependence to some extent on our racial and cultural inheritance and on our childhood experiences. On the other hand, it implies the freedom to develop beyond our environment and beyond our background.

This second aspect of the genetic principle is a dynamic one. Freeing ourselves from the concept that our present civilization and culture is more advanced than others may be an important result of the application of this dynamic principle. Julius Lips, in his book *The Savage Hits Back,* tells the following story:

The chief of Kikuyu had seen the first white men enter his territory, and his father and the medicine men went to meet them, taking to the strangers whom they regarded as gods a sacred offering of goats. After this child of Africa had studied white civilization he became convinced that it spelled ruin to his people. "Look," he said, "if I marry in my own country and want to build a house, everybody will help me and my mother will simply cook the dinner we'll all share. But among the white men no one will help me. Every man has his own interests, there is no unity."

Applying this dynamic principle to commercial problems, we find, for instance, that we can better understand why a man bought a particular make of car if we know what car he previously owned. We will know even more if we try to establish a complete biographical line on all the cars he has owned and what they have meant in his life. In cigarette smoking we can learn a lot by getting a person to talk about his first cigarette. In understanding the motivations of a family it is more important to know whether or not their earning power has changed than it is to know the actual amount of money they now make.

Many sociological and market-research studies overlook this fact of dynamics in human motivations. Whether or not a person belongs to a particular social group may be less important than whether or not he is happy in this group, whether he feels he is in this group only temporarily, whether he has just reached this group or whether he feels he is on his way out, up, or down.

This aspect of human motivations has been investigated in many of our studies through a testing technique we call the "Aspiration Scale." (One such test is included in the Appendix.) This consideration of the dynamic principle can often help to explain why we are doing certain things that are otherwise puzzling. At the same time, it can show us our present position on the road of our lives and help us determine where we want to go from here. Living can be compared to driving a car along many, often winding, roads. The unscientific man is very much like the new driver who still has his eyes fixed on the front of his car and does not look far enough ahead. His driving will be awkward, wavering, and insecure. The scientific thinker, on the other hand, takes a steady course by focusing on goals ahead.

This dynamic viewpoint can often have a wholesome effect in

helping us make decisions and also in interpreting the values of many of our personal actions and the actions of nations and people as a whole. An anecdote told among anthropologists makes this point clear. A scientist had a conversation with a cannibal and tried to explain how superior his society was because it had no cannibalism. The cannibal, on the other hand, who had heard a lot about the white man's wars, accepted the fact that cannibalism was bad but wanted to know, "What does the white man do with so much human meat that is being made available in each war?" When the scientist tried to explain to him that they killed people without eating them afterwards, the cannibal was confounded by the absurdity and stupidity of such behavior.

3. FUNDAMENTAL INSIGHTS: THE FETISH OF RATIONALITY

Tons of books have been and will continue to be written about human behavior, but unless the description of human behavior leads to understanding and insight, it has only limited value. For instance, I might collect very accurate data on the behavior of people in a public library. I could state, based on observations carried on with proper regard for scientific accuracy, that when human beings enter a library they generally walk to the walls of the room, pick out an oblong object, walk to a table, place it before them, open it up, and at regular intervals turn the white sheets with which this object is filled. They do this while sitting down. After several hours they close this object and put it back where they found it. I could tell the color of the objects, the temperature of the room, the number of shelves, and so on. I would still be millions of psychological light years away from describing or understanding what reading means, the importance of the tiny black hieroglyphs on the pages and the enormous complexity of the process of reading and thinking.

Many of our motivations are, of course, clear. This does not mean, however, that all our motivations have to be conscious. Why did you really buy the house you live in? Why did you really become a lawyer, a psychologist, a businessman? In most instances we do not have to know. When the social scientist approaches us, however, he cannot be satisfied with easy, ready-made explanations which we may have fabricated to explain our behavior. Rationality is a fetish of the twentieth century; we are not allowed by our culture to admit true irrationality as an explanation of our behavior. Yet the majority of religions and political systems, as well as such aspects of human behavior as loyalty, love, and affection, are all irrational.

In practicing research on human motivations, we feel it to be our duty to get down to fundamental insights, to accept the fact without fear or embarrassment that quite a number of human motivations are irrational, unconscious, unknown to the people themselves. This principle means that most human actions have deeper motivations than those which appear on the surface, motivations which can be uncovered if the right approach is used. No human activity is too enormous or too small to be included in this domain of human and scientific curiosity. The application of this principle also means that easy, superficial logical explanations should be scrutinized with suspicion and should be accepted as the real explanation of human behavior only when all other efforts to explain them in a fundamental fashion have failed.

We make it a practice in our research approach to avoid such lazy explanations as "he did it because he had developed the habit." "He watched the television program because he was interested in it." "He bought the suit because he liked it." All these so-called explanations are in reality no explanations at all. They are similar to the type of pseudoscientific facts assembled over many decades by psychiatry which explained the fear of narrow places as being the result of claustrophobia. Translating this into simple language, the statement would read, "He's afraid of narrow places because he has a fear of narrow places."

Many sociological and market research studies abound with so-called facts by which a buying action or another form of decision is explained as due to habit, or to membership in a social group, or to age or income or marital status. What they fail to do is to ask why the action developed into a habit, what the real reason was for the decision, why other people belonging to the same social or income group did not behave similarly. The mistake made in many of these studies is to confuse a *propter hoc* phenomenon with the *ergo hoc* phenomenon.

Some time ago we conducted the following experiment: several hundred people were asked what they considered to be important in coffee. Aroma, strength, consistency, freshness, and price were all factors mentioned. Through simple laboratory processes we then brewed coffee which contained all these qualities but was colorless. It was actually purer coffee than the normal brew, yet, most people, when offered this colorless coffee in our lab rejected it. The only difference was the lack of color. Yet color had not been mentioned by a single person as being of importance.

In another experiment we displayed twenty-five cakes of soap representing twenty-five different brands. We asked people to pick one of these brands. We had previously asked them what they valued in a soap and received answers indicating that size, odor, personality of soap, and cleaning capacities were all important. Yet when these same people (mostly women) were handed a cake of soup, 70 per cent of them did almost the same thing: they unwrapped the cake of soap, slid their fingers over the surface, smelled the soap, and lastly weighed it in their hands. We took films of their behavior. Later, when we showed them what they had actually done, most of them expressed surprise but could recognize the validity of these observations. They said they had not realized what they were doing. Weight, surprisingly, was found to be a major factor, possibly because it is a vestige of the days when women made their own soap, or because weight, as we pointed out before, is still a value criterion in our modern world. Sliding the fingers over the soap reflected a desire to pre-test the smoothness of the soap. Again this was fairly irrational behavior because no one uses soap in dry form. It is the lather which is soft.

The importance of understanding the fundamental meaning of human behavior has been made clear in numerous findings and observations of anthropologists. Klineberg in his book *Social Psychology* states:

> Just as foreigners object to the Japanese smile as being insincere so the Japanese are surprised at the irritated faces of foreigners which reflect too closely what they feel.

This is only one instance of a misunderstanding between groups who have learned a different language of emotional expression. Kissing appears to us a natural expression of affection. It is unknown, however, in many groups and shows different forms in others: the rubbing of noses among the Maori and the Eskimo, the face rubbing of the Australian aborigines and the nose-to-cheek caress of the Chinese and other Mongolian peoples.

"It may obviously be a mistake," Klineberg continues, "to conclude with Monteiro that affection is lacking when it is not expressed in a way with which we are accustomed." He writes, "In all the long years I have been in Africa I have never seen a Negro manifest tenderness towards a Negress. I have never seen a Negro put his arm around a woman's waist or give or receive any caress whatever that could indicate the slightest loving regard or affection on either side. We find it natural to stand up in the presence of a superior. If Aegeans or Tongans sit down under similar circumstances, the inhabitants of the Friendly Islands would take their clothes off as a sign of respect. Todas raise the open right hand to the face, resting the thumb on the bridge of the nose. To them it means respect, but almost exactly the same sign is used in our society to signify something quite different."

Darwin writes that spitting seems an almost universal sign of contempt or disgust; it represents the rejection of anything offensive from the mouth. The Jaggas of East Africa, however, regard it as a kind of blessing in critical situations and the medicine man will spit four times on the patient or a newborn baby.

I therefore believe that the third principle—the necessity for fundamental insights—is essential to a true understanding of human motivations.

3 ■ COMMAND OR PERSUASION

Once motivations are properly understood, then the strategy of persuasion, the "how to" motivation, can be considered.

The "why" and the "how to" of human motivations are interrelated. I can only then decide on what to do when I have properly understood what the real underlying causes of the present situation are. I have to apply, as discussed in the previous chapter, the principles of functionalism, dynamics, and fundamental insights.

The basic material with which the battle of human progress must be fought is human desires. The social scientist does not have the power to create these desires. He can strengthen them, he can make people aware of them, and he can suggest how they might be satisfied. He can also, temporarily at least, block them.

We all regret that we are often guided by emotions when we should act rationally. Greed is objectionable and many rash acts can be traced back to insecurity and cowardly attempts to provide safeguards. Yet wishing that this were not so does not change our culturally, psychologically, and biologically conditioned behavior. If we want to cure the immaturity of our society we have to devise strategic techniques by which this can be achieved. Even as parents of young children, we are already confronted with the problem of the strategy of desire. We have to decide whether to cajole is more effective than to encourage or flatter when our goal is toilet training or the brushing of teeth.

Decisions of strategy fill our days. Buenos Aires has staggering traffic problems. Yet when normal traffic lights were installed as an obvious remedy, the majority of the people disobeyed them. The lights had to be removed. Now traffic is regulated by the law of the jungle. The stronger one wins and passes, while the others have to wait. How could the people be motivated to obey traffic lights? The answer lies most likely in the necessity of changing the total civic attitude of Argentinians towards authority. No scientific attempt has been made up to now to find out.

Decision-making in many fields was the domain of hit-or-miss procedures. Only slowly are modern scientific concepts being introduced in these areas. Computers and "brain machines" are new developments of the last ten years. A whole new science, referred to as "Game Theory," and a new mathematical approach to decision-making has been developed.

An electric brain machine is a machine containing electrical circuits which permit it to perform operations that are reasonable. This is accomplished by controlling various factors. A flashlight is a simple form of a computer. Every time you push the switch the light turns on or off. By combining thousands of such basic circuits, complicated decisions can be sorted out. In a sense, then, a computer can solve problems. But in order for the machine to function properly information and variables of many types have to be assembled, "fed" into it. This "programming" then becomes the real, decisive task on which the proper decision by the machine depends.

Even in the physical field it is difficult to consider all the eventualities which might have to be considered to arrive at a proper decision. In the psychological and sociological field they are even more numerous. No wonder then that on a day-by-day basis many of our most vital decisions are resolved by hunch or so-called experience. The father who feels that only when he was bawled out as a child did he obey will carry on this strategy over to his children or to his staff. He is convinced that this is the strategy that will bring results.

There has developed, however, more and more recognition over the last decade or so that "wisdom which is only experienced and balanced judgment is gradually being displaced by science in organizational policy-making." (Richard L. Meier, "Explorations in the Realm of Organization Theory," *Behavioral Science*, Vol. 4, #3, July 1959)

The question of how to motivate people is an application of such scientific techniques to decisions of the individual and of management groups. When we attempt to motivate people, we are attempting to introduce such factors into the decision-making pattern as will result in changing the appraisal or the "estimate of the situation" by the decision-maker. Suppose a general of the Korean war wanted to make a decision on whether or not to cross the thirty-eighth parallel. His decision depended on whether or not he felt that the enemy would hit back. Jacob Marschak calls this "subjective probabilities." (Jacob Marschak, *The Social Sciences*, "Probability in Science," Ch. 4, p. 166) A good decision is one that includes a good guess on what the other fellow will do. Through either Communist or UN propaganda these subjective probabilities could have been influenced. The commander could have been subjected to a continuous barrage of statements that the Communists would fight if the thirty-eighth parallel was crossed. Apparently this is exactly what happened.

Communicating with someone, getting him to do something, persuading him, can only be understood by taking a closer look at the psychological processes it involves. You can persuade a guinea pig or a rat to push one button rather than another by punishing and rewarding it in the process of learning. A rat pushes one button rather than the other either to receive the food or to avoid receiving a shock. Human beings, however, are more complex than animals.

During a trip to South Africa I was asked by a government official what motivational research could do to persuade the Bantus not to be afraid of yellow and to remove a taboo from the color yellow. This would have permitted the government to convince the Bantus to plant corn, which is important to their diet. In such a case a persuasion technique may have to be as dramatic and simple as the one that motivated the behavior originally. Another taboo—the threat of punishment for not planting corn—could be the answer.

In studies which we have conducted on voting behavior and on how to get more people to vote, serious discussions were held as to whether the best way to persuade citizens might not be to punish them with a fine for not voting. A good part of our educational system, the armed forces, and our penal system all use such simple and drastic persuasion techniques. We eventually learn to behave to avoid punishment and to reap rewards. To be punished threatens our security, to be rewarded increases it. The simplest persuasion technique, therefore, is to use psychological blackmail. The soldier is motivated to risk his life honorably by being threatened to lose it dishonorably through execution. Heroism then becomes the choice of the lesser evil.

The Naval War College asked me to study the problem of command versus persuasion. It is interesting in itself that a modern branch of the armed services even considers an alternative to a penalty for disobedience. Thirty to fifty years ago it would have been considered sacrilegious even to think in terms of anything else but command. There is growing evidence, however, that unless the soldier or sailor really accepts the command and makes it his inner persuasion, he will fail in any real emergency.

Recently persuasion was practiced with drivers in New Jersey by painting yellow stripes on sections of the roads aimed at slowing drivers at toll-booth approaches. The yellow stripes, which can be seen easily at night and in foggy weather, are arranged to give the effect of closing in on a driver. They are intended to help alert motorists who are going too fast as they near a toll stop. The stripes, painted progressively closer at toll approaches, give the impression that a vehicle is accelerating if the driver fails to slow down. Command is always faster as a method of persuasion, it is more efficient; and what makes it really dangerous is that it often is also much more comfortable. Many young democracies have faltered because people prefer to be told what to do rather than to make up their own minds. Persuasion, on the other hand, is slower, more burdensome, but at the same time also more permanent and healthier. Lowering of prices, special sales, etc. in the merchandising field correspond to command. Building of the personality of a company, the creation of brand loyalty, are closer to real persuasion and are much slower but at the same time also much more permanent.

What are the basic mechanisms of persuasion? In our work we have been able to establish several major effective principles:

1. REORIENTATION

The semanticists, particularly Korzybski, talk about verbal maps. Arthur Korzybski, in his book *Science and Sanity*, states that our languages can at best be considered maps. By showing a person the consequences of his actions and pointing out that he's following a wrong map we can often bring about reorientation. We persuade, therefore, by superimposing the right and adequate map over the wrong or unclear map.

2. ENCOURAGEMENT

Educators often make the mistake of stressing the content of their teaching specialty, be it mathematics, history, or physics. They worry relatively little about the methods of learning. Study hard and you will grasp it, they say. Education that comes easily is rejected. This may be because it took them a great amount of time and effort to reach their own level of education.

In a study for *Time* magazine, we found two major approaches which possibly represent a more modern and psychologically more correct formula for education: a) with each educational attempt, encouragement as to the capabilities of the reader to digest this education was provided; and b) the material was presented in such a way that its structure could be perceived in an easy form. When describing, for instance, the historical development of labor-management relations, the example of a pendulum was used. At first, the pendulum swings from extreme to extreme—from aggressive management to an aggressive union—and over the years the pendulum calms down and a compromise takes place. By the use of such graphic mental constructions, information was much more easily absorbed.

A favorite conversation topic is the failure of American education in comparison with that of the Russians. It is important that we make a distinction between the kind of education that involves facts and the kind of education that involves thinking and more specifically leads us to be creative and to accept a new type of philosophy—a "why not" kind of philosophy. Facts, after study, often are forgotten. Storing facts can be done more efficiently by electronic computers. It is in the development of concepts and structures and, even more, in the courage to think along new lines that the real future of human individuals and a nation lies. In new situations, a conservative, established behavior will not be effective.

We also have to ask ourselves to what extent parents really fulfill their educational jobs. What are we really teaching? Do we repeat the same stereotyped admonitions which in the end the children do not accept anyway, or do we really teach them new ways of adjustment and new ways of thinking which very obviously they will need to cope with the changing world? In our own family, we use the example of the duck eggs. While my children were young we kept ducks. When we had eggs from these ducks, the children refused to eat them. Together we analyzed why. The only reason we could find was their difference in size. When they did not know that they were eating duck eggs, they just as readily accepted them as chicken eggs. This was a dramatic illustration of human prejudice and irrationality. Ever since then, when I find that my children are afraid to do something new and to do it in a different way, we refer to a duck-egg philosophy.

Encouragement to think along new avenues thus represents another aspect of effective persuasion.

3. INSIGHT AS A TOOL OF COMMUNICATION

One of my most dramatic experiences on many trips abroad was the discovery that millions of people lived in enormous cities without my having been aware of them in any conscious way before. I thought of my mother, whose main complaint about America was that it was too big. I had remarked to her, "You don't have to live in more than one place." "But when you know that all the states exist, they represent a challenge and an invitation. You feel you should see them all," she answered.

We are living at a psychological distance from each other, despite modern communications. We are basically alone. This distance is usually shorter between members of the same family, such as parents and children. The shorter the distance, the more successful we are in bringing about insight and willingness to act in a desired direction. Co-operation depends on mutual understanding and respect. If we do not know what motivates our neighbor, we are more likely to be intolerant. Therefore, one of the major psychological problems in democracy is the achievement of insight, the shortening of intra-individual psychological distance. Our goal of "government by the people" can only be achieved if each voting member of this government becomes truly trustworthy in his judgment, insight, and intelligence, and if he ceases to live in selfish psychological isolation.

Insight into the behavior of other people and into one's own behavior leads to balanced personality. A non-neurotic and strong individual is usually understanding and co-operative. At the same time, it is exactly this lack of insight which, so far, has caused failure in bringing about successful democratic co-operation. It may very well be that for a long time to come our immediate aim should be mass education in the discipline of applied psychology.

A study conducted by us at the Brussels Fair with about five hundred people showed that people judge nations not so much by their superiority in one field or another as by their uniqueness. True understanding should result in a strengthening of differences rather than in all being alike.

4. REMOVAL OF MENTAL BLOCKS

A large truck manufacturer in Brazil asked us to find out how he could convince construction companies that it would be advantageous for them to switch to a ten-ton truck rather than to buy two seven-and-a-half-tonners for almost the same price. The truck company's honest judgment was that the larger truck would be more advantageous to the buyer. The mental block which prevented the acceptance of the technical argument was one typical for a young nation. The growth is so rapid, the need for equipment so great, that two vehicles instead of one look like a definite advantage. We helped remove the block by suggesting to the customer a new basis for comparison. The more powerful truck covered three times as many miles in the same time as the two trucks. To pay twice as much for a vehicle that does three times the job is a bargain. To pay twice as much for a vehicle which is actually five tons lighter than two seven-and-a-half-tonners sounded expensive.

Even as social scientists in our individual lives or as parents, educators, or political leaders we have difficulty in freeing ourselves of preconceived notions, superstitions, and fears. As I pointed out before, we are still guided in our daily actions much more by physical concepts than by psychological ones. Much of the resistance to psychological insights comes from this block. In the physical world we are convinced that an object cannot be simultaneously here and not be here. In the field of psychology, however, you can hate someone and love him at the same time.

On a visit to South America, I was struck that even there people spoke about the Northern Hemisphere with greater reverence than about the Southern. What is on top seems to be superior. A dramatic new attitude towards the southern part of the globe might be achieved by printing a globe or a map where the South is on top and the North at the bottom.

We often fail to solve a simple mathematical problem, as tests have shown, if we have been conditioned before to look for a complicated way to discover a solution to a problem. We suffer from illusions of rationality in our motivations rather than accept as a superior form of rationality the existence of emotions. We often replace theological, authoritative goal-setting for realistic, humanistic clinical strategy.

We have been prematurely concerned in the social sciences with techniques rather than with interpretation and understanding be cause we are blocked by our beliefs that techniques alone can provide the answer. We need social inventiveness, creativity in finding answers to our many modern problems of life such as abundance and underdevelopment, nationalism, and unification. Often only by standing on our heads can we find new approaches to the solution of new problems.

5. SETTING OF GOALS

If democracy is brought down from verbal ideal to everyday reality, we see that the tasks ahead in the achievement of democratic goals are mostly of a psychological nature and concern the individual member of the democratic society. Democracy actually operates "by the people" in a scientific and psychological sense. If the people are immature, unhappy, neurotic, and insecure, then the democracy cannot work or is slowed down. Simply putting democratic ideals and *far goals* before the people is not sufficient. It is never sufficient simply to state the desirability of an ideal. It does not help, for instance, to stress the desirability of balanced diets if this is not accompanied by techniques and tactical details which show people how they can overcome practically their tendency to stick to a wrong diet.

Whenever the far goals of democracy are reduced to an operational, clinical, or therapeutic problem, we see that these goals are not as elusive as they may seem to be at first. Suppose we consider a desirable goal, that labor and management co-operate. By analysis we can translate this goal into concrete, specific steps. We know we have first to reduce frustration in order to reduce aggression and to produce willingness to co-operate. Only then will labor and management co-operate if they understand each other. We have developed the psychological techniques which are necessary to achieve such insight. By reducing the goal of co-operation to one of reducing individual anxiety and by developing mutual insight we can persuade effectively.

6. IDENTIFICATION AND ROLE PLAYING

Another aspect of how to motivate is to induce people to play the role of the person they are trying to communicate with. Persuasion is simply a more effective form of communication. One of the cardinal rules of persuasion motivation is to see and understand the attitudes of the other individual.

Some time ago a group of German social scientists visited me. When I asked them how they liked America, they responded: "Do you want the State Department version or our real impressions?" Their real impressions were these: "We were told how wonderful America was and we were also told how backward we Europeans and especially we Germans were, at least by implication. When we came here we were afraid that we would find these statements supported by fact. We geared ourselves, however, possibly unconsciously, to find fault with America. Only if we succeed in this can we go back with our heads erect. We are happy to report that we found many things wrong in your country. We now can feel that we Germans are not quite as backward as all that."

There was possibly still a deeper level of explanation for this attitude in addition to the ego preservation involved. The more damaging things I can find about a country that I may secretly admire, the less necessary it will be for me to change my own country; I can go on in my old habits with the feeling of smugness and satisfaction.

Some of the reactions by Russians to the American exhibit in Moscow and possibly some of the reactions by Americans to the Russian exhibit in New York may have a similar explanation: "Their materials, their atomic reactors, their consumer goods are not any better or different from ours. Russian cars have as much chromium as ours, the Russians are just as emotional and irrational and materialistic as we are."

Arthur Godfrey presents another interesting case. People believe what he says on the air because he behaves the way people would behave if they had to read commercials day after day. He makes fun of them, he does not take himself nor his sponsors too seriously. The audience can identify itself with such a person. In other studies we found the more perfect the diction of an announcer, the less he permits identification on the part of the public. Making a mistake once in a while made him more believable.

7. TESTIMONIALS

Another way in which persuasion techniques can be improved is through testimonials and reference to authorities. "I shall listen to your advice and recommendation when I am convinced that I am not the only one who will be doing what I am requested to do."

A considerable change has taken place, however, as far as the believability of testimonials is concerned. We used to emulate people in positions superior to our own. An interesting example of this change in attitude is exemplified by the following happening: We had done some work for a chewing-gum company. At one point this company used Lady M. as the person whose chewing-gum habits were to be emulated. One nice day, however, Lady M. was arraigned for passing a bad check. The agency became worried as to the possible effect of such lowering of status of the aristocratic lady. We conducted a number of interviews and found to our surprise that the effectiveness of Lady M.'s testimonials had improved. In other words, people were more ready to believe her statements than before. Why? The explanation was a relatively simple and human one. Many people among those being interviewed had passed checks which bounced at one time or another. Lady M. had become more real, modest, and human to the average consumer. She had become one of them. A person passing a bad check was more likely to chew gum.

In a study for Quality Bakers, the organization behind the Sunbeam bread brand all over the country, the problem was how to establish believability for its quality and freshness. The assignment was to find out how various movie stars rated in their ability to convey, at least indirectly, this message. Here are some of the findings which give an interesting insight into the power of identification and role playing by well-known individuals which goes far beyond their physical personality. This study was based on 131 interviews. Of all the stars tested, Gene Kelly and Esther Williams evoked the most positive responses. They were most easily identified with bread. In consequent advertising campaigns, their pictures were successfully used in connection with Sunbeam bread.

In a political study for a candidate, similar findings were made. In one case a candidate for governor had not publicized his physical prowess enough. The public did not know about his travels, his gym exercises, etc., and had the impression that he was too old for the job. Knowing this, he was able to change his image in a helpful way.

The above seven rules of persuasion apply to almost all forms of "how to" motivation. They can be of help in determining which appeals to use in advertising, as well as in teaching and propaganda. There are very few general rules which apply under all circumstances. Rather than answering whether one approach is better than another one, our viewpoint is that whichever approach produces better identification, produces insight, helps remove a mental block, is the more persuasive one. In other words, we suggest that rather than worrying about the techniques employed, the motivational effects of a chosen strategy in the conscious and unconscious layers of the mind should be considered.

Fortunately more and more social scientists and social psychologists are called upon by government, commerce, and industry to lend their scientific training to the investigation of diverse practical problems. These tasks range from finding out why the subscribers to a magazine did not renew their subscription, to an analysis of the psychology of smoking in order to sell more cigarettes. These commercial assignments give the social scientist a unique opportunity and a compelling responsibility to be more than an academician who sells his thinking to advertisers. In a sense, the social psychologist is doing anthropological studies on the American tribe. These studies, disregarding their commercial purpose, provide rich material for an understanding of the psychological basis of attitudes, motivations, and behavior of wide sections of the population. The social scientist, having acquired such an understanding, thus becomes in the truest sense a social engineer. It is not difficult to come to an agreement on the importance of all the therapeutic jobs which must be done to insure the smooth operation and progress of the democratic structure. The blockage occurs when it becomes clear that these tasks have to be achieved with the impact of modern advertising and the mass influence of communication systems which reach large sections of the country. Attempting to achieve these clinical tasks with single individuals or to reach small groups separately will never produce adequate results since each attempt of this type has to compete with the huge influence, often in a negative sense, that mass media can achieve. In other words, in using slow, inadequate, and old-fashioned methods of mass education which, in addition, operate mostly on a verbal level we may make better citizens out of five people. On the other hand, if we use modern media of advertising, radio, or magazines, we exert an influence over thousands of people.

At the moment, therefore, we have the following situation: Advertisers, radio writers, editors, etc. know and use the correct techniques to reach people, but they do not know, or are confused about, the content they should put into their messages in order to be helpful in this therapeutic job of democratic engineering. At the same time, they are forced to use more and more *intangible appeals*. Educators, on the other hand, know to a certain extent at least what kind of influence they want to achieve, but they tend to use ineffective methods because they shy away from "commercial techniques." They too can only be successful by using selling appeals for education.

4 ■ MEASURING HUMAN EMOTIONS

Whenever explanations of human behavior are being offered, the alert audience raises the question: Is it really true, is the finding scientifically proven? "I saw it myself." "I spent three months in Russia," or "I tried it out and it worked"—these are common statements which sound like scientific proof of a sort.

In scholarly reports these "proofs" are broadened. Two thousand people were asked and 70 per cent of them stated the reason why they consumed alcohol was that it was a nice social habit.

In a meeting of the police department concerned with juvenile delinquency, someone scientifically inclined says, "Before we make any wrong decisions, let's get the facts." The "facts" mean to go out and question, observe, and record.

In a discussion in Brussels I was informed by serious sociologists that they had "observed" that there was little freedom in the United States because even picnicking was regulated. They had found in a personal, unprovincial, and factual observation that many parks in the United States contained signs, "No picnicking allowed," or "Picnic here." When I pointed out that this was a form of helping people to find a right spot and to organize such an activity constructively they insisted that this was definitely an infringement of freedom and that in France or Belgium something like that would not be possible. There you could picnic anywhere you wanted.

We all do research of one type or another even as private individuals. Suppose we want to decide on the purchase of a home. We may ask people living in a particular area to tell us how happy they are there. This may sound like a reliable procedure, but very often is not. One can assume, for instance, that those people who were not very happy about a particular living area moved away and therefore would not be found when interviews were being conducted in the homes in this area.

An actual experience of this sort which could have been very misleading occurred to the author. While living in Paris, before deciding to come to the United States, he interviewed about thirty people who had lived in the United States and asked them about their satisfactions and grievances. The majority of these people had very negative opinions about the United States. Only at a later date did it occur to him that he had interviewed all these people in Paris. In other words, these were people who had left the United States after a certain time. The reason for their leaving was dissatisfaction.

The sample used, therefore, for the private research was a biased one. All the thirty people were dissatisfied people. That was the reason why they could be found in Paris. No wonder, therefore, that they all gave negative opinions. As we pointed out in other chapters, in modern life we continuously have to make decisions. They may be simple ones, such as which restaurant to eat in, what brand of merchandise to buy; or more complex ones, such as which type of house to buy and in which neighborhood. It is almost frightening to realize in how many areas of human endeavor we are forced to rely upon public opinion as a basis of our decisions. We select doctors not on their actual qualifications, but on their public appeal. You ask a few laymen, friends you know, how they like Dr. Smith. "He cured me," or "He did not cure me," expressed by a lay person, is then taken as a basis for choosing a man who might have influence over one's life.

How can human behavior be researched, how can we be sure that the motivations discovered for an act of decision are the true ones?

We generally have a choice of two types of research; descriptive research, which tells how many did what; and diagnostic research, which tells why what happened did happen. While there is an interrelationship between the two, it is diagnostic research that provides the tools for creative predictions of human actions in the future and makes possible the correct strategy.

WHEN IS DIAGNOSTIC RESEARCH SCIENTIFICALLY CORRECT?

There are definite circumstances when motivational diagnostic research techniques are the *only* ones which will produce meaningful results. The use of descriptive techniques, under these specified circumstances, may be unscientific and misleading. What are the circumstances?

1. Whenever the data being sought may not be present at the rational or conscious level.

2. Whenever we are dealing with psychological mechanisms and with cause-and-effect relationships.

3. Whenever the person questioned has a chance to produce interference, conscious or unconscious, between the time he understands the question and the time he answers it.

Human motivations are frequently unconscious and represent intertwined and complicated mechanisms. Modern psychiatry and all other social sciences could not exist without the acceptance of this fact. If the existence of unconscious motivations and their basically dynamic and complex nature is accepted, we have come much closer to answering the questions of which research techniques are correct, necessary, and desirable and which ones are not.

It is my view, based upon our studies and experiments, as well as upon the mass of psychological scientific literature, that whenever we deal with human motivations, direct questions are not only inadequate, but unscientific and therefore are to be rejected.

The systematic elements of my argument are the following:

1. *Each individual represents a motivational universe.* In order to be able to record scientifically how a population is motivated in respect to a specific phenomenon, we must first fully understand why each individual, as a member of this group, behaves in the way he does. Unless we have arrived at such understanding, no meaningful statement about the motivations of the group can be made. In other words, I have to be clear at the end of a motivational interview why Mrs. Brown buys a particular brand of coffee. This evidence may include a wide variety of contributing factors.

2. *Direct questioning erroneously presupposes objective insight.* "Know thyself" is one of the oldest goals set for the individual. We have come closer to it but we are still far from achieving this goal. Whenever we are asked why we did what we did, we must analyze our actions and give a correct and insightful answer, often within the

limit of a few minutes. Even if no unconscious factors are at work we are often incapable of choosing one among the various conflicting motivations of which we may be aware, as having been the one which influenced the resulting action.

3. *Rational explanations and rationalizations.* The human personality does not represent a passive observational field You cannot simply consider a question or observation as an objective means of discovering what goes on in someone's mind. Whenever a question is being asked, an active interpersonal process is instituted. An interviewer or a printed form challenges me, as an objective outsider, to give an account of myself.

Psychology has demonstrated that there are several permanent distortion factors which interfere with the objective observation of the motivational field. The most important one is our desire to appear rational to ourselves and to others. When confronted with an investigation of our motives we first search actively for rational explanations. The danger is great, however, that this desire to act rationally results in a rationalized answer, a pseudorational cause for our behavior.

When the communicator wants to be able to predict the outcome of his actions and asks for help, he is asking us to provide him with motivational answers. If he is satisfied with knowing how many people are divorced in a district, or that most people will drink tea when they are ill, that more people have one car than two cars, use one brand of cereal, listen to a particular radio or TV show, then the techniques utilized to approximate census figures should be fully satisfactory to him. If the communicator, however, is not satisfied with such findings but wants to bring about changes, wants to reduce the divorce rates, wants to sell a second car to the family, make them buy his brand of cereal and listen to his TV show, he is invading the field of the social sciences and particularly the field of the psychological disciplines, whether he realizes it or not.

Prediction of human behavior necessitates, first, an understanding of how people behave today. As individuals reacting and at the same time influencing the world within which we live, the motivational researcher and the communicator who applies his findings are at the same time participants and formulators of the future world.

Much of the difficulty which diagnostic research seems to cause stems from the fact that we are dealing with different techniques and even more important with a different form of thinking. Research on a given problem is often conducted in such a way that we worry very much about the number of people who have been interviewed and worry much less about what they have been asked. Too often the problem for which the answer is needed is simply translated into a question and sent out to two thousand people. If it were that simple to solve a problem we would have found the answers to most of our social problems at least by simply asking a correct sample of two thousand to provide us with the answer.

This blind belief that whatever is quantifiable is therefore a scientific fact is so strong that a good part of today's discussion of such new approaches as diagnostic, motivational research is being overloaded with futile discussions of sample size.

Our research, of course, validates, quantifies, and proceeds scientifically. We believe, however, that real scientific procedure follows a three step procedure: 1) formulation of hypothesis; 2) validation of the hypothesis; 3) quantification.

Most of the discussion on sampling concentrates prematurely on the third step without properly considering the need for the first two steps.

It is difficult for some clients to accept motivational techniques because a different kind of thinking is involved. The security that seems to come from being able to point to a study comprising the answers of three to five thousand individuals to a single clearly formulated questionnaire is lacking. The irrelevant doubts raised are expressed as follows:

1. If we run into regional differences, wouldn't the sample be divided into five or six different groups, thereby cutting down the representation in each group to fifty to one hundred case histories?

2. Furthermore, if there were major differences in attitude between men and women, would this not reduce the representation even further?

3. If we find that human motivations are really not all alike, that individuals are radically different in their personality complex, wouldn't the sample's representation be reduced even more?

These questions sound logical and legitimate. However, there are specific scientific answers which indicate that the small sample is not only sufficient, but quite frequently is the only practical method of arriving at answers to "why" questions and an understanding of human motivational patterns.

At this point, we should like to note that the very objections that are raised in regard to the small sample may also be raised in regard to larger samples. No matter how large the sample, is it ever really large enough? Further, in the type of research that uses the large sample, can we be sure that the classification of the population into income, age, and sex groups provides us with insight into the kind of people we are approaching? For example, the so-called $10,000-per-year income category includes many different kinds of individuals and, therefore, different motivational patterns. There are those earning $10,000 per year who have reached the topmost level of income expectation; here we have individuals with one kind of psychology, one level of aspiration. Then there are individuals earning $10,000 who are on the bottom of the ladder working their way up. And there are individuals in this category who have fallen to $10,000 per year. To the researcher, it is important to know whether his $10,000-dollar-per-year man is a dynamic individual who seeks new experiences, a passive individual who is satisfied with what he has, or a disheartened individual who is fearful of losing what he has.

Take the problem of a large milk company. They asked why mothers discontinue using evaporated milk after their babies no longer need a formula. Why don't these housewives use evaporated milk as regular food? Worry about sample size has little value in attempting to find an answer to this practical question. In order to approach a problem of this sort the first need is for intelligent insights and hypotheses. Sampling problems have no place in this first searching for an answer.

When we are interested in finding out how the human heart functions, one of the most effective ways is to look for extremes, for freaks, for very fat people, for very lean people, for very tall people, for very short people. Nobody has the right to question sampling at this stage and to say, "Well, there are not very many very thin people in this world." As a biological and social scientist, I want to look for examples where I can observe the particular phenomenon that I'm interested in—in a magnified, enlarged, exaggerated form. If I think I can discover an answer to my specific problem by examining three very thin people who are a hundred and ten years old, realizing fully that they might represent only one hundredth of a per cent or one thousandth of a per cent as far as frequency in a particular population is concerned, I am absolutely and perfectly justified.

I am first interested in further developing interesting and meaningful new concepts. I don't have to know exactly how they originally were developed. It might be on the basis of previously accumulated knowledge, the accumulation of anthropological data, or pure hunch. At one point we felt that there might be some relationship between evaporated milk and mother's milk. If this were proved, we could understand why there was resistance to evaporated milk related to the odor, consistency, color, and general appearance. This concept had to be put down first in such a way that it makes sense and we can talk to somebody else about it.

Here is how we must proceed further. From anthropological studies, milk is known to have symbolic significance. Add to this a degree of common sense which tells you that milk is one of the first foods that you take in. Furthermore, we know from our own work and other studies that most staple food items like bread, meat, and grain usually take on sooner or later symbolic significance; we can therefore assume that milk is probably more than just milk. It isn't just "a food." Evaporated milk, mother's milk, and milk are all somehow related, there's a symbolic significance to them, there's something emotional about them. This is the first criterion which we had established up to now. The first validation comes from our non-directive interviews where we observed that in almost every one of them people talk about milk in a more or less emotional way. This can be demonstrated either by the fact that the majority of them state that they like milk very much, or dislike milk very much. I can now proceed to go through these first one hundred interviews or so and observe how people talk about milk in general. We might even go beyond that and institute a completely quantitative content analysis; in other words, count the times that certain words are being used. How often do people say, "I just hate milk" or "I love milk"—which is not said about bread, coffee, or tea—in fact, it is said about hardly any other kind of food. We could state that out of a hundred interviews, fifty people stated that they liked or did not like milk. Forty-two of those fifty used emotional language such as, "I adore milk," "I have to have milk," or "makes me throw up," "makes me sick," "nauseates me," "I just can't look at it," etc. They used violent statements of liking or of disliking.

This is one kind of quantification, but it would have not progressed beyond a morphological description of a phenomenon. It would not have explained or assessed, of course. We feel, as social scientists, that we have to go further; we have to ask, "Why is evaporated milk unpleasant to many adults?"

The next more explanatory hypothesis has to be developed. There may be some people who can accept nature in the raw, and other people who have to see it transformed, covered up, changed from its original form; in other words, there may be some people who can handle raw meat, who can kill a chicken and then eat it, while others just can't do it. Now we can go more deeply and hypothesize that this dislike has probably something to do with the number of inhibitions you have, that it may be related to a feeling that you are not allowed to see the forbidden, the raw, the bloody, the inside. Evaporated milk is thick, thus has something raw about it. It is like mother's milk and thus equally disgusting to some people.

We come to the next problem, which is how can we prove or disprove this analysis? We can set up an additional or secondary hypothesis that this acceptance or rejection of nature in the raw might be related to the cultural level. It might be related to income level, education. Low-income people cannot afford to be finicky. They are forced to see things that they are normally not supposed to see. This may be related to housing, to the whole family sleeping in one room. If our hypothesis is correct, then we should find the following things:

On the basis of the milk and mother's milk concept we should find that, in general, men are less shocked at evaporated milk than women are. Our first analysis showed this to be true. We may not even necessarily have to do this research ourselves. At that point, we go back to our client and say, "Do you have any comparative figures between men and women as to liking or disliking evaporated milk?"

We may establish further that there are certain racial groups that are closer to nature. There might be the beginning of an explanation as to why evaporated milk is better liked in southern areas and by colored people. It may be simply that they can't afford any other milk. Yet that is not a completely acceptable answer because the incidence of expensive TV sets, for instance, is higher in certain groups of that population. It cannot be just price alone, because we find that it is not necessarily related to income; if that were the case, then all the poor people would have to like evaporated milk, which isn't true. There are certain racial groups, certain cultural groups to whom evaporated milk is acceptable. In the first wave of interviews we have to have representatives of the psychological universe, rather than of the socioeconomic universe. Simply using the socioeconomic groups in existence—age, income marital status, etc.—means that you are making unjustified or unwarranted assumptions. You're assuming that to our problem the difference between farmers and city people is a relevant one. You could just as well assume that there is a possible difference in attitude towards evaporated milk between mothers who are well-developed and mothers who are not well-developed. I am just as right in stating this from an absolute, purely scientific viewpoint. What I'm trying to get at is that in very many so-called quantitative studies the assumption is that there are only social and economic differences in the population, and as long as you've covered all those in your sample you are right.

The conclusion of this study based on our validated hypotheses and subsequently qualified findings suggested that evaporated milk might be sold to housewives as a food ingredient to make sauces, such as mayonnaise.

The task of changing basic attitudes towards milk was found to be too costly and time-consuming. Instead, the framework of evaporated milk was reduced from an emotionally broadened one to a more sober concept of an unemotional food.

This example shows systematically how we feel diagnostic motivational research must proceed. We want to discuss now in detail these three steps of 1) formulation of hypothesis, 2) validation, and 3) quantification.

STEP 1. FORMULATION OF HYPOTHESES

Since Aristotle we have been impressed with the necessity of scientific procedure and its basis of empirical facts. The modern school of semantics was the first to point out how dangerous such thinking can be.

Suppose I were to observe a stick, such as a pencil, in a glass of water. It appears broken. The difficulty starts with the confusion between the appearance of the empirical observation and its reality. The pencil *appears* broken. Not being trained, however, in the laws of refraction and optics, I could easily make the mistake of talking about my observation as if it *were* a reality. I might say, the pencil *is* broken when put into the glass of water. After having studied some fundamentals of optics I probably will avoid such a mistake, which the semanticists call the error of identification.

The laws of optics are not empirical data, they are abstractions, coming from more complex spheres of scientific endeavor. In everyday life we speak of red, green, and blue; in the science of optics, of different electromagnetic wave lengths.

In the physical sciences and even in the field of biology and medicine we are more accustomed to the necessity of thinking first in terms of hypotheses and abstractions before rushing out to study the facts. In the social sciences however, we have been trapped by our eagerness to copy the outward appearance of the physical sciences, we achieve quantification, even when what is being quantified is meaningless and irrelevant.

Many useless discussions and controversies could have been avoided if greater clarity about real scientific procedure had existed.

HYPOTHESES COME BEFORE THE FACTS

Motivational research deals with decision-making. In order to make a correct decision, one should have all the facts. Facts, however, can be very misleading without an intelligent interpretation and a meaningful hypothesis. More and more modern thinkers come to the conclusion that there lies one of the major problems of social science. C. Wright Mills in his book *The Sociological Imagination* says this: . . . "You seldom get out of any truly detailed research more than you have put in it. What you get out of empirical research as such is information, and what you can do with this information depends a great deal on whether or not in the course of your work you have selected your specific empirical studies as check points of larger constructions." (Dealt with in my chapter on the wholistic approach.)

Researching is a procedure where open-mindedness, the ability to see seemingly unrelated things as related and in a new light, is the major requirement. Without this ability to form meaningful explanations of human behavior no true social science is possible.

We all practice psychology and sociology almost continuously. When we select a marriage partner, when we decide on our profession, when we pick a job or an employee for a job, when we buy one brand rather than another or vote for one candidate rather than another, we are putting the principles of psychology into practice. Contrary to the accusations raised against motivational research, we at least attempt to make people behave more intelligently. This is not possible, however, unless we make people aware of the tricks played upon them by their own faulty thinking, by the distortions caused by emotions or false assumptions.

Most of the people brought up in Western educational systems pride themselves on their ability to think scientifically. However, we often have wrong concepts of what is scientific. What I am trying to clarify is the difference between true scientific procedure and the illusion of it. Next time you are presented with facts on which you are expected to base a decision or accept a point of view, look out for the interpretation of the so-called facts. Even the way statistical columns are put together represents interpretation. Many studies which supposedly prove that one advertising medium is better than another, that television attracts more people than magazines, or vice versa, often can be shown to differ more in the interpretation of the data than in the data itself. It is a little like saying a glass is half-full or half-empty. Countless hours are being wasted in describing national groups by characteristics. Americans are friendly, Argentinians are cold, Brazilians are exuberant, Negroes are inclined to buy flashy cars—these are examples of such meaningless "findings."

Many of our studies have shown that even when the actual figures seem to bear out an interpretation, the introduction of a psychologically more relevant classification changes the interpretation completely. We have found again and again that what might be considered characteristic behavior for Negroes was much more characteristic for certain psychological and sociological groups of people who felt that they were not completely accepted as equals in society. This again did not apply to all Negroes or to all other minority groups. Younger Negroes felt often more accepted than older ones, richer Negroes more so than poorer ones, etc. The very same facts then could thus be interpreted in a completely different fashion, depending on the basic theory or hypothesis which was carried to the facts.

Another frequent error caused by a blind belief in the appearance of a scientific format is the association of two facts which appear simultaneously and are thus seen and explained as being related by cause and effect. For example, a perfect correlation between forays on dark nights and pregnancy of the maidens in a primitive African tribe does not mean that dark nights cause pregnancy.

The apparent preference for the so-called scientific procedure has a motivational explanation of its own. To collect data, to measure and count them, gives the illusion of security, the illusion of tangibility. But in the field of social sciences the phenomena of human behavior are too complex to be immediately translatable into statistical figures.

Wolfgang Köhler stated once in his book *Gestalt Psychology* that the great difficulty with the social sciences is that they have attempted to jump all the historical phases that other sciences had to pass through in their development and in our understanding of the phenomena with which they are dealing. Instead of permitting insights to accumulate and to develop in great detail before they were actually used for measurement and for testing, as was the case in most of the physical sciences, we have expended an enormous effort in the field of social sciences to measure details without first having had the chance to develop over-all systems of understanding for the phenomena of human communications.

It is exactly this need to have the concept first to develop insights, and to use empirical data afterwards to test these hypotheses, that I try to defend. I believe that this approach is an indication that creativeness is a prerequisite for science. We need social inventiveness and social imagination first. True scientific thinking is very close to pure art. The graphic artist, for example, who wants to capture the spirit of a portrait, landscape, whatever it may be, has to be capable of abstractions, whatever the school of art he belongs to. A realistic photographic portrayal of the object is not considered an artistic achievement. Even the photographer produces a really worth-while photograph only when he introduces into his realistic copy of nature an interpretation which is his own. Interpretation, however, is already an intellectual achievement.

The biologist learns to think in terms of biological functionalism. The engineer learns to perceive and understand the soul of a machine, the inner workings of a mechanical structure. The social scientist, similarly, if his training has been correct, should have learned to think in terms of psychological functions. He is, therefore, in a way, a living seismograph that reacts to the slightest psychological earthquake that is observable.

Cohen & Nagel cited the following example of the scientific procedure in their book *Logics and Epistemology:*

> Herodotus, the Greek philosopher and mathematician, considered it his task to find out the real reason why the Nile inundated its shores on a regular monthly basis. At first, he went about it in an empirical fashion, measuring the amount of mud deposited each month, studying the fauna and flora of the Nile. All these observations proved to be of no avail, so he finally stretched out on his back, tired and disgusted, and fell asleep. He woke up in the middle of the night and, looking up at the moon, he had a sudden revelation. It was possible, he felt, that the moon, and its relationship to the earth had something to do with the inundation of the Nile. It is not reported whether he was immediately aware of such things as gravity and the electro-magnetism of the earth and the moon, but what interests us here is how he made this discovery and the fact that only after this hypothesis had been formulated could he proceed to accurate measurements which would prove or disprove his hypotheses.

The discovery itself was an act of creativeness. Does that mean that it was simply a matter of chance? Not at all. Creativeness is a basic scientific ability to see the relationship between seemingly unrelated things. Bertrand Russell says:

> I don't know how other people philosophize, but what happens with me is first the logical instinct that the truth must lie in a certain region and then an attempt to find its exact whereabouts in that region. I trust instinct absolutely, although it is blind and dumb, but I know of no words vague enough to express it. Even in the most purely logical realms it is insight that first arrives at the scene.

Science and creativeness seem to be two diametrically opposed words. Creativeness is a word with both positive and negative connotations. To say that someone is creative, ingenious, an original thinker—these are high compliments indeed. But to say that someone lacks objectivity or operates on hunches and pure guesswork is to make a negative evaluation.

Scientific, objective, well-founded, carefully analyzed—none of these words seems to describe the creative process. One of the reasons for the discrepancy is that we have removed from the word "creativity" the scientific associations which it rightly possesses. Yet creativity is an absolute prerequisite for scientific procedure. There is no field of science where it is not necessary to develop hypotheses before we find proof. It is only because so many people have grown up in the school of empiricism, where only things which are directly observable are accepted as scientific, that we have reached this peculiar impasse. We are dealing here with misunderstandings and difficulties which have damaged the entire field of communications.

In an article in the September 1958 issue of *Scientific American* on the psychology of imagination, Frank Barron makes the following statements based on the report of a number of experiments attempting to get closer to an understanding of what a creative process in a human mind involves:

> The creative individual in his generalized preference for apparent disorder turns to the dimly realized life of the unconscious, and is likely to have more than the usual amount of respect for the forces of the irrational in himself and in others. This respect for the forces of the irrational in himself will generate some ordering principle if it is permitted expression and admitted to conscious scrutiny. To put the

matter more strongly, I believe that the creative individual not only respects the irrational in himself, but courts it as the most promising source of novelty in his own thoughts. He rejects the demand of society that he should shun in himself the primitive, the uncultured, the naive, the magical, the nonsensical; that he must be a "civilized" member of the community. Creative individuals reject this demand because they want to own themselves totally and because they perceive a short-sightedness in the claim of society that all its members should adapt themselves to a norm for a given time and place. When an individual thinks in ways which are customarily tabooed, his fellows may regard him as mentally unbalanced. . . .

In my view . . . this kind of imbalance is more likely to be healthy than unhealthy. The truly creative individual stands ready to abandon all classifications and to acknowledge that life, particularly his own unique life, is rich with new possibilities. To him disorder offers the potentiality of order. They [creative people] have exceptionally broad and flexible awareness of themselves—the self is strongest when it can regress, admit primitive fantasies, naive ideas, tabooed impulses into consciousness and behavior, and yet to return to a high degree of rationality and self-criticism. The creative person is both more primitive and more cultured—more destructive and constructive—crazier and saner than the average person.

Creativity can be engendered and developed if we train ourselves not to be afraid of our own thoughts. Utter honesty and understanding of one's real motivations as far as this is possible are requirements for such an achievement. The desire to be always right often leads to an over-cautious selection of the great variety of ideas floating around in one's mind. By this premature selection process we often lose some of our most valuable ideas. To associate freely, therefore, and permit almost all your thoughts to come out into the open either for yourself or in discussions is one of the prime prerequisites for the development of creativity.

HYPOTHESES MUST BE VALIDATED

It is, of course, not enough to stop with insight. Many of these hypotheses may be and often are erroneous. What is needed subsequently is to introduce a series of validation procedures to make sure that the hypotheses, the hunches, are indeed correct. It is like solving a crime. It could have been committed for three or four different reasons. Which one of the reasons or which combination of reasons actually did represent the cause or causes can only be determined by the proper accumulation of clues and indices.

I will accept the fact that a crime has been committed because of jealousy if I can observe in four or five different and unrelated circumstances that a possible culprit indeed has shown signs of extreme jealousy.

Many of these indices have to be of a circumstantial nature. Validation of hypotheses, however, is not achieved by frequency distribution and large samples. It requires a completely different kind of thinking and a completely different kind of approach. It necessitates the control of variables and the predetermination, as it were, of the type of indices acceptable as proof or disproof for a particular phenomenon.

Encouraged by its success with Wildroot Cream Oil Charlie, the Wildroot Company decided to produce a shampoo for women and call it Lady Wildroot. In a study based on two hundred non-directive interviews, we attempted to answer the question of how this product could be successfully marketed and whether its present name was good or should be changed. We found that the name itself represented one of the major handicaps. Despite its excellent quality, the product could not fully succeed because it somehow clashed with the company image that had previously been established in the minds of the consumers.

Through the resounding success of Cream Oil Charlie, a hair conditioner for men, the Wildroot Company had become a very masculine company. Not only that, but they had established a special type of man as the ideal male. He was forward and aggressive in the minds of women. Our female respondents resented this type of male. They protested against the implication created through Wildroot advertising that merely by having a shock of hair smoothed down with cream oil a man can prevail over them. When, therefore, the Wildroot Company produced a perfectly wonderful shampoo and called it Lady Wildroot, the ladies resented the association to such an extent that they simply did not buy the product. There was nothing wrong with the product which we could discover. Using a form of validation appropriate for the occasion, we tested a group of women with bottles that had the Lady Wildroot label on them, and another group with bottles without the label. The reactions of the two groups were diametrically opposed; and the contradictory reactions were produced simply by the label. Whenever the Lady Wildroot label appeared on the bottle, a number of critical and negative comments were made about the shampoo. But when the bottle was not labeled, the shampoo was accepted as perfect. In other words, we validated our hypothesis that there was something about the product which dominated the consumer's mind to such an extent that it literally transformed and negated the quality advantages of the product.

It is true that the only kind of research "worth doing" is research that meets the most rigorous canons of scientific accuracy and honesty. But it is also true that science in general, and statistics as its handmaiden, offer many different tools for the solution of the different problems of business research.

STEP 2. MULTIPLE VALIDATION OF HYPOTHESES

The second step of our task, then, is to verify these tentative explanations, to find out whether they are true or false, and to study them. To implement this second step, the rigorous statistical testing of our hypotheses, we have a number of avenues open to us. We can conduct interviews and do observational studies noting the actual behavior of people. We set up systems of circumstantial evidence, almost like a detective, stating that if hypothesis A is correct, events 1, 2, 3, 4, and 5 should occur in a particular manner. Then we go out into the field and see if these events do indeed occur, and conclude thereby with adequate scientific justification whether hypothesis A was correct or incorrect.

Parallels to such circumstantial evidence of cause-and-effect relationships are found in all biological sciences and, indeed, in all other sciences. Frequency of the occurrence of a phenomenon, however, does not lead to proof of cause and effect relationships. You cannot jump from knowing that 65 per cent of the people behave in a certain way to an analysis of why they behave in a particular way. The latter requires a different type of scientific argumentation. It is in this field that many of the misunderstandings of motivational research have occurred. It is much more important that the factors be controlled and that intelligent indices refuting or proving the hypotheses be developed than that a large number of people be interviewed. In this field too creativeness is an unavoidable and absolute necessity. Validation of hypotheses has to be done on a multiple basis, and it has to be done in an ingenious way. The development of tests, of continuously developed and standardized techniques, is necessary. It is here that the motivational researcher approaches very closely the experimental laboratory of all sciences and particularly the field of psychology.

The second step, the verification or refutation of our hypotheses involving anywhere from two hundred and fifty to five hundred individual histories, still does not lead us to the same kind of variety and numerical accuracy that two thousand or five thousand interviews would do. However, what we have contributed is a really thorough understanding of a basic motivational pattern among a group of people large enough to indicate that the pattern is significant and lends itself to practical applications. In finding that eighty mothers out of one hundred reveal, in multiple waves and in multiple tests, when talking about food for their babies, that they are as concerned about their own convenience as they are about the nutritional value of the food, we have a finding valid enough to permit any practitioner in advertising or public relations to take advantage of it and act accordingly.

In a study on cosmetics, women would be asked to take off their make-up and put new make-up on. All the details of the performance, the reactions and remarks of the subjects, were noted. We measured the length of time between removal of the *old* and application of the *new* make-up, noting that the old make-up was aggressively removed in a sort of blitz attack. The period of what may be called "psychological nakedness" in between was shortened as far as possible and filled with apologetic remarks like, "Aren't you disappointed?" "What a difference," etc. This period was followed by a carefully worked out facial-engineering technique, wherein each detail had its well-founded, significant purpose. Each one of these research techniques yielded important visual and acoustical appeals of the specific commodities.

In a study on cigarette smoking, our company was interested in finding out what sounds suggest best smoking satisfaction. We took motion pictures of people smoking cigarettes in different situations in order to discover different types of smokers—the oral pleasure seeker, the aggressive type, the fire and the smoke worshiper, etc.

In a soap study, we made tests as to the relative suggestive power of water running into a tub, or the unwrapping of a cake of soap, length of time spent in the shower or tub. We used these observations to prove or disprove hypotheses.

In a car study, I sold cars myself for several days, watched other salesmen, was a car buyer, and pretended to want to trade my car in at different agencies. We went to driving schools and watched people in their first attempt at driving. We went along when new cars were delivered. We went to showrooms and studied layout in a systematic way to discover psychological mistakes in the arrangement of the cars.

Applying these findings to commercials, we found that each commodity thus investigated offers a whole list of more or less significant acoustical appeals that can be incorporated into the commercial. In connection with cars, for instance, we found that the way a car door sounds when it is slammed, the purring of the motor, the quietness of the ride are all helps in making a commercial more vivid.

When concerned with the psychology of odor, we scanned literature for descriptions of food, perfumes, etc., with the accent on smell and taste. The knowledge of such effective taste and odor descriptions is extremely important when taste is being described over the air. Thus, in a whisky survey, we studied novels and short stories to find taste descriptions of food in general, and alcoholic drinks in particular. Often we used biographical methods, going back to the very first car somebody owned, and following up the connection between cars and life periods. We went to art museums to find out how artists had treated the theme of bread. We have used clinical material on cigarette smoking, based on the reactions of neurotics to smoking. This approach has proved very helpful in arriving at an understanding of the *guilt feeling* in smoking, a fact that may determine the acceptance or rejection of actual health claims.

While these examples describe the methods in a rough way, they are not new at all and are quite commonly used in psychology. What we attempted to establish in the first place was the significance of the causal relationship and not necessarily the frequency of its occurrence. In establishing this causal relationship we bring to bear on the problem not only the findings of the individual study, but also the findings of all previous relevant studies, plus the accumulated knowledge developed by the social sciences.

CULTURAL NORMS

The establishment of causal relationships is governed by a different set of scientific rules from the establishment of frequency of occurrence.

Motivational research tries to determine how certain psychological laws manifest themselves within a given culture. In all societies there are certain norms which characterize the behavior of the overwhelming majority. If five hundred people react with horror and revulsion to the thought of eating human flesh, you may rest assured that you speak to the members of a society where cannibalism is taboo. If as many people speak of human flesh with longing, you are pretty sure you have been interviewing cannibals. This is, of course, an extreme example, but it applies to every phase of human life down to the humblest attitudes and reactions.

When you read Fielding's *Tom Jones*, you have the impression that you have a good picture of the mores, the prejudices, the habits of eighteenth-century England. If you wish to make sure that your hypothesis as to British life of that era is correct, you go on reading a number of contemporary documents, memoirs, letters. Gradually a pattern emerges, details are clarified, and everything falls in place. The irony, the exaggerations, the symbolism of *Tom Jones* make complete sense. After you have read a few hundred documents you don't need to go on.

SOCIETY AND INDIVIDUAL

The imprint of his society is unmistakable on the individual. It is so today and it was so yesterday. Take a Louis XV chair. You can look at it and say: "These are the lines, the forms, the decorative elements which characterized the aesthetic norm of the Frenchman two hundred years ago." If you are very cautious and very scientific-minded, you may not be satisfied. In that case you may line up another 499 chairs taken at random from homes and castles of that period to validate your thesis. If all of them show identical features, whether they come from the north, the south or the center of France, you will have no more doubt that you are facing an authentic expression of a cultural trend.

But why did Frenchmen prefer this complicated, ornate furniture two hundred years ago? Why did they not furnish their homes with straight and spare Early Renaissance chairs? Clearly because the latter were not in tune with the times of Louis XV. But if you had gone up to individuals of the era and asked them this question, they would not have known what exactly to answer. I am certain no one would have said, "We prefer these chairs because we are more frivolous, more addicted to sensuous pleasures and ostentation than our ancestors were." And yet, if depth interviews had existed at that period this is probably the finding we would have made—on the basis of responses to five hundred chairs selected at random.

The same principles apply today, let us say, to a package. Suppose for argument's sake that a firm puts on the market a cigarette lighter in a heavily ornate case embossed with all kinds of Gay Nineties motifs. It does not sell well and we are called in to investigate. What we must find is the psychological pattern of negative reactions.

As we go along, respondent after respondent reveals his own reasons for not buying the lighter. One says it's too heavy. Another that it doesn't function well—although we know that it does. A third one gives a third reason, and so on. But underneath it all, we find a constant theme which is often masked by the logical reasons advanced, but which in reality is dislike for the ornate decorations of a bygone age.

At this point, along comes a respondent, the representative of a minority, and declares: "This is a perfect lighter. The best I ever had." And when we probe his habits, his taste, his preferences, it turns out that in everything he does or buys he is an escapist from the realities of contemporary life, a trait whose esthetic manifestation is a characteristically old-fashioned taste.

According to modern science, human behavior is determined by instinctive responses and social norms, or cultural values. What is of interest to us is to determine how, under the pressures and within the value system of our own society these basic motivations influence man's relationship to a given product. Will it enhance or menace the consumer's image of himself as a male? Will it enhance or menace the role he would like to play in society? Does it give him a feeling of security (the feeling that he knows how to handle the product, what the product will do to him, etc.) or will it make him feel less secure?

To find the answers to these paramount questions we must find the social norm. And the norm is exactly what it says: the contrary of exception, the ruling pattern of behavior.

STEP 3. THE FREQUENCY OF MOTIVATIONS

We proceed, in many instances, to a third step when we are interested in regional differences or in any form of more complex segmentation of the market and the problem with which we are dealing. It is at this point that we use a quantitative approach, not to determine the motivation—which we have already established—but to determine how often something occurs. Even in this third step where we are dealing more specifically with quantification, inventiveness and imagination are indispensable. The introduction and utilization of socioeconomic groupings, as they are being utilized in a vast majority of market-research studies, has become highly questionable. We have no real justification for the assumption that age, educational levels, marital status, and similar data are in truth relevant factors that determine and differentiate human behavior. In many of our studies over the last few years, we have introduced more and more frequently psychological segmentation by types, by degrees of security and insecurity, by various forms of adjustment, and by the role that a particular product or service plays in these types and forms of adjustment.

The large sample is a function of the number of variables that you have under control. Not only do we have to watch out for socioeconomic factors; psychological factors have to be considered as well. Just because educational grade, income group, sex are usually included in a socioeconomic scale, it is wrong to assume that they are relevant functions of a particular problem.

In an assignment for a greeting-card company we were told that married, middle-aged women were their main market for recruitment of saleswomen for their greeting cards. People are invited to buy a box of greeting cards for about fifty or sixty cents and then to sell it for a dollar. This is often done by church groups or by individuals to make some extra money in an easy way. The company told us that there was no sense in interviewing anybody else outside of this market. This was the universe they were interested in. Nevertheless we felt that it was part of our task to go beyond that and not to restrict ourselves; we wanted to find out what it really was, psychologically, that makes these women sell greeting cards. One of the motivations we found was a desire to be financially independent. They were not just middle-aged women. Often they were women whose children had gotten married. Very many of them were widows, or they were women who did not want to be dependent on their husbands' salaries, whether the salary was big or small. In other words, the real psychological motive was, "I want to be independent." Then we asked ourselves, "Well, if that's so, there ought to be other people who also want to be financially independent." We included these other groups, such as school teachers, and students in our sample and found that indeed they were interested in selling greeting cards as a means to make extra money. We used a real functional classification rather than a mechanical one. Therefore, the so-called socioeconomic representation of a universe is often only an assumed list of irrelevant variables; it is not per se a scientifically established categorization of human beings.

PSYCHOLOGICAL FACTORS IN SAMPLING

Sampling in itself is a research task. We cannot assume that as long as we have correct representation of all the parameters of the socioeconomic strata we are doing all right. The more relevant variables we have in our sampling procedure, the more the necessity for a large sample is reduced.

An example of wrong sampling based on assumed groups was encountered in a study for a southern brewing company. They were very much convinced that the Negro consumer, particularly as far as beer is concerned, represented a group by itself. They seemed to have proved this to their satisfaction by the fact that the same appeal would not work on a program reaching white people. In assuming, however, that color was in itself a sufficient sampling category, a major error was being made. The emancipated colored person represents a completely different group from the unemancipated one. Young Negroes are different from old ones. The young colored person is much more like the young white person. In other words, when we were asked, "Whom shall we reach, who is our market, what media should we use, which is the market at which we should aim our most powerful appeal?" we said "Forget about color per se as a classification. Distinguish between young beer drinkers and old beer drinkers and divide possibly each one of these groups into emancipated and non-emancipated Negroes."

In another instance, a finance company came to us and said, "Look, we're really in need of a very sharply defined sample which will give us the answer as to why people on the west coast are more readily borrowing money than people on the east coast or in certain other regions." Regional differences seemed to represent important sample considerations. We found, however, that west coast people worry less about what their neighbors would think and borrowing money. This same behavior would be a very unconventional thing in a small community in, let's say, Pennsylvania. Therefore, borrowing money is less endangering to the ego of a west coast person, perhaps because he wasn't brought up there. But it isn't the region. The region is only a secondary thing. Knowing this you can hypothesize in a completely different fashion. You could assume that any region where people have moved from somewhere else should show the same kind of phenomenon. In Florida, for instance, we may find that the same holds true.

Many other of the customary classifications are similarly outdated where motivations are concerned. Instead of asking, "How much rent are you paying?" it is more relevant to ask, "Are you paying the right amount of rent, are you paying too much, are you paying too little?" Almost every one of our quantitative surveys could gain from revising the face sheets in a really modern way. A lot more intelligent questions could be asked and the answers used for a more relevant sampling approach. Just on the basis of common sense, it must make a lot of difference whether I'm making less money than I used to make, the same amount of money, or more money. This is much more important knowledge than absolute income groups.

SUCCESSFUL PRODUCTS SATISFY THE "TENSION DIFFERENTIAL"

If a man or woman is completely satisfied, he or she will not seek to acquire anything more. In fact, without tension, without the arousal of an unfulfilled need, human beings, living things in general, would not act, do, think, behave at all.

The socioeconomic descriptions can be invaluable if, in addition to knowing what a person's age, sex, income, and occupation are, we also know whether or not he is satisfied with his present age, whether he accepts his sex role, whether he is content with his educational and occupational level, whether he is relatively happy with his income, or what income he thinks he would need to be happy. Do the older people in a given group want to be younger or are they satisfied with their present ages? Do the younger people want to be older? Does a given product relate to the acceptance or rejection of one's age? Do the women in a given group accept their role as women or are they trying to emulate and compete with men? Do the men of a certain group accept their sex role or do they envy some of what they consider the advantages of women? Do the married people want to be single and the single people yearn to be married?

Knowing where a group stands in the level of its aspirations in regard to socioeconomic categories can supply far more vital information than merely knowing how many people fall into each category.

THE "TENSION DIFFERENTIAL" LEADS TO ACTION

When a single man wishes to be married, when a housewife wants a career, when a member of the middle class dedicates himself to becoming a member of the upper classes—whenever a person in one socioeconomic category aspires to a different category, a "tension differential" is developed within him and this leads to frustration and action. Where a product promises to help a group overcome this tension, achieve its level of aspiration in whatever area it may fall, that product has a chance of success.

5 ■ THE SOUL OF THINGS

"Our life is becoming too soft. We are too much interested in material things." So goes the lament. Few who seek easy applause with such statements have bothered to tell us what they really mean by material or by spiritual values. We are faced here with one of the real conflicts of modern life. Several thousand years ago we lived in a world where the real values and the real aspects of everyday life were pretty much in line with the ideals and tenets as set forth by religion or philosophies. A religious leader and his followers believed that possessions were immoral and that they should get rid of these possessions and live in poverty. Today, we might go to church and deny the materialistic world and decry it as immoral. At the same time, however, in the remainder of the week we would subscribe to and live in a realistic world of possessions, goods, and materialistic desires. Even if we agreed that people should change their values and become more interested in spiritual goals, a conflict which has to be clarified in itself, we are still confronted with the question of strategy. Agreed, we should drop our concern with worldly possessions. But how do we go about changing this apparent, only too human desire? If we want to elevate humanity to the lofty heights of idealistic concerns, we have to start with them from their present level, which we complain is materialistic. The world in which we live is crowded from morning to night with tangible objects and products. It is possible that much of our frustration and our contemporary neuroses stems from the fact that we still steadfastly refuse to accept ourselves the way we actually are. Our modern world, with daily increasing achievements in the world of missiles, atomic energy, and in electronics as well as biology, is becoming more and more absorbed in expressing itself by physical means.

To want material things, then, is a natural human desire, engendered partly by biological forces, the wish for security and protection, and reinforced by our contemporary culture. In order to change human desires, we have to have a strategy. Strategy requires correct appraisal of the problem. First, the division itself between materialistic goods and idealistic goals is an erroneous one. What we need is a re-evaluation of all our values. There is no sharp dividing line between materialistic and idealistic values. To make such a distinction is unscientific. It is cheap moralistic hypocrisy. Let's look at the amoral facts of human behavior. Doing so does not mean we approve of it. But even to think that nature needed our approval for the way we are put together is blasphemous and arrogant in itself. How do we behave always comes before how should we behave.

I buy a book. Is this materialistic or idealistic? A book offers opportunity for new adventure, education. Raising vegetables, taking a trip, the child's thrill with a new pair of shoes, the new Broadway shows, what are they all? What values do they represent? We still want suds in detergents, not being able to forget the stereotypes of soap; we judge tools by their strength, we can't conceive of aluminum being as strong as steel. In all these cases ideas contaminate material things.

Cultures where the individuals do not wear shoes are not considered completely civilized even if their social organization is ahead of ours. We judge nations more by the kinds of products they produce than by their ideals. In the "affluent society," as John Kenneth Galbraith calls it, the world of things seems to be in conflict with the world of ideas.

In many of our studies, we could demonstrate that the old proverbs "Clothes make the man," "Tell me what a man eats and I'll tell you what he is" are not too impractical and are not empty statements. Modern psychology has overlooked to a very large extent the real expressive powers that objects have. Objects have a soul. People on the one hand, and products, goods, and commodities on the other, entertain a dynamic relationship of constant interaction.

Individuals project themselves into products. In buying a car they actually buy an extension of their own personality. When they are "loyal" to a commercial brand, they are loyal to themselves.

In turn, products have specific psychological effects on respondents. The cars respondents owned or wished to own decisively influenced their pattern of behavior. Inanimate objects also deeply influence interpersonal relationships. It was found that specific products an individual possesses often influence the reactions of other individuals toward him in a specific way. Inanimate objects thus possess a definite psychic content, a "soul" which plays a dynamic emotional role in the daily lives of individuals within the context of their social value system.

Take fur for example. In a study conducted for the fur industry, the problem was, in addition to the commercial one of helping to sell more furs, to also understand what the "soul" of the fur is. Few people today buy fur coats in order to keep warm. There must be other deeper reasons. We found that expensive fur coats are often being bought by men for their wives or girl friends. Mink stands out in this respect. Mink and most other fur coats are not logical buys, they are based on emotions, on the "ideological" meaning of these furs. In order to understand this meaning fully, to find the answer to this why problem of human behavior, we investigated the cultural anthropological meaning of fur. Originally it was the warrior of the tribe who brought the fair maiden a skin, the trophy of his hunts and the proof of his prowess. The rarer and the more dangerous the animal, the more it served as proof of the skill and virility of the warrior. This is replaced in the modern world by price. The more expensive the fur, the more it proves the earning power of the male giver of the fur coat, his earning virility. Fur, hair, sex, are of course all interrelated. The famous paintings by Dürer, entitled the "Furlet," and the painting by Botticelli, "The Birth of Venus," show that many hundreds of years ago the real artist intuitively felt this relationship.

From a practical viewpoint our findings were developed for the fur industry in the following way. We found that a fur hierarchy has developed wherein furs are seen on a descending social scale on which each fur is assigned a rigid place related to the age, type and status of the woman who wears it. At the same time mink has become a too obvious status symbol. In general a new trend is developing, particularly in the United States, to be more subtle in one's conspicuousness. We are becoming more interested in keeping up with the "inner Jones," than with the too obvious outer one. We want the neighbor to guess at our wealth and status rather than to display it too openly. At the same time we have learned that an easier way to stand out and to buy status is to resort to individuality and to be different.

From this different and new viewpoint which we found to be operative in the psychology of fur buying, we found that mouton was seen as a fur for typists, sales clerks, and college students; beaver for suburban housewives and professional women; persian lamb for elderly spinsters; and mink for society women, chorus girls, and movie stars. Our advice thus was to develop specific personality profiles for non-mink furs. We suggested that furs be pulled down from their psychological pedestal and be promoted as fashion items rather than as status symbols. Wearing a fur coat would thus lose its blatant conspicuousness.

In attempting to adjust ourselves to the exigencies of modern life, we do not pursue the psychological goals of security, happiness, or social recognition as such. That is, hardly ever are we consciously aware that we want to feel good or secure. We do, however, strive to conduct our lives every day in such a way that we feel a vague emotional balance at the end of the day, which we usually refer to as security and happiness. During our day, we do a great number of things which in their turn help to build up this final feeling of satisfaction. After a sound sleep we may enjoy a favorite coffee and follow a certain breakfast routine. Should this routine be disturbed, or should the coffee not be quite as good as usual, a fraction of our final daily happiness will have disappeared.

We may fulfill a long-dreamed-of desire to buy ourselves a new electric shaver. For a few hours we very proudly display this newly won acquisition, and we look forward impatiently to using this gadget at the first possible opportunity. The shower we take in the morning also will add another particle to our total balance and our feeling that life is good. The lunch, the food we select, the diet we follow, the cigarette or pipe which we enjoy, the new typewriter which functions smoothly, all of these apparently completely material and minor enjoyments of life somehow spell in the end this tremendous word, *security*.

The same thing is true of other mysterious and intangible goals we may set for ourselves, consciously or subconsciously. A feeling of security is a conglomeration of innumerable little details. Let the roof leak, and whether you admit it or not, you are slightly disturbed. The feeling of shelter and security your home offered you is not as strong. A scratch on a new piece of furniture may, in a psychological sense, often make it worthless to the owner. There is some peculiar attraction in new products which one owns. They also give you a feeling of security. Any kind of possession really functions, in a sense, as an extension of our personal power. Therefore, it serves to make us feel stronger, and compensates to a certain extent for our inferiority feeling toward the world which threatens us. It is not astonishing, therefore, that in many research studies which have been made, it is found that shopping as such has a tremendous therapeutic power. It actually can help relieve a feeling of blueness and depression. Often when we are down and out we count up all the possessions we have. We cling to them as tangible expressions of our anchorage, for they help give us a feeling that our basis of existence is more than the narrow scaffold of our naked self. When you watch a small child cling to a piece of toy or a doll with all its power, you may begin to understand the power of ownership.

Social recognition is but another variation of security which we can distinguish as helping us to adjust ourselves to life. It also is infrequently thought of or strived for in a consciously formulated way. Few people will say: "Tomorrow I am going to get more status." You will find, however, many people who will tell you with pride that they have finally been admitted to the club in their community. We can only keep up with the Joneses in some very tangible and concrete way by pursuing a very definite "near goal."

Such near goals of social recognition may be the fur coat you own, the brand of fountain pen you buy, or the hat you are wearing. We often overlook the fact that in America the brand of merchandise purchased has become almost a substitute for nobility and a family tree. Wearing a Stetson hat puts you in the same class with all those men who wear hats of the same class as Stetsons.

In a study made by the author on whisky, it was found that we buy whiskies according to a very strict class system. One of the first things we do, again not too consciously, is to peg a brand as being a legitimate member of a certain class. We permit substitution within that class, but never with a brand that belongs to a different "social sphere." Price is not necessarily the most important determinant of such a class.

Until the time of World War II, at least, the ownership of a Ford, a Plymouth, or a Chevrolet stamped us as belonging to one and the same social class much more so than did belonging to the Republican or the Democratic party.

All men smoking the same brand of tobacco or one which belongs to the same accepted class category feel like brethren and members of an inner circle. In pipe tobacco, certain factors of aroma and spiciness are psychological determinants in helping to classify men into certain groups. Certain products lend themselves more than do others to a descriptive function as far as social recognition and "class consciousness" are concerned. Cigarettes, for instance, are one of the most democratic products. It is quite insignificant whether you smoke Lucky Strike, Old Gold, or Camel as far as your social status is concerned. In other countries, like Germany, cigarettes still have a class symbolism. Filter cigarettes are more elegant, certain brands more sophisticated. Restaurants, on the other hand, are quite clear criteria and expressions of the social factor and thus of security.

The human mind can be seen as a projector and a receiver of the things which surround it. Growth of life can be understood as an ever increasing variety of objects that we come in contact with and an ever increasing intimacy with these objects. Dealing with stones in the Stone Age must have contributed to a large extent to the formation of a corresponding mentality. Since we are surrounded now by more and more electric and electronic gadgets, some of their patterns of operation and functioning must leave their mark upon our mentality.

Occupations differentiate people to a large extent from the viewpoint of the kinds of mental patterns that are created by the materials and objects and functioning principles which govern their particular trades. The cause-and-effect patterns differ in the biological field as compared to the electrical, mechanical, or psychological fields.

The objects which surround us do not simply have utilitarian aspects; rather they serve as a kind of mirror which reflects our own image. Objects which surround us permit us to discover more and more aspects of ourselves. Owning a boat, for example, for a person who did not own a boat before, produces new understandings of aspects of his own personality; and also a new bond of communication is established with all boat owners. At the same time some of the power strivings of the individual come out more clearly into the open, in the speed attained, the ability to manipulate the boat; and the conquest of a new medium, water, in the form of lakes and rivers and the ocean, becomes a new discovery.

In a sense, therefore, the knowledge of the soul of things is possibly a very direct and new and revolutionary way of discovering the soul of man. The power of various types of objects to bring out into the open new aspects of the personality of modern man is great. The more intimate knowledge of as many different types of products a man has, the richer his life will be.

At the same time, the development of this new approach might well lead to new possibilities of therapy. A mentally diseased person, a person who has lost contact with the world of things, is self-centered, not interested in what goes on around him. Re-establishment of contact with the essential elements of the things surrounding him may represent a new therapeutic approach. When mentally ill women start applying lipstick again it is a sure sign that they are on their way to recovery.

The artist has been attempting to capture the soul of products for several thousand years; the novelist and the poet have attempted to establish this contact with the inner meanings of objects in many different ways; so does the modern script and copy writer.

When we buy something are we simply buying the technical functionality of a product? Or are we not making an attempt to establish a close contact with a new object? A friend once told me that building his house with his own hands had been one of the most soul-satisfying things he has ever done in his life. It acted in this specific case directly as psychotherapy and helped him cure his neurosis. Scientific effort, in all its forms, could very well be nothing else but another aspect of buying this intimacy which is not openly visible and available on the surface, by working with a machine, by manipulating an invention, by playing with chemicals and medical pursuits.

The things which surround us motivate us to a very large extent in our everyday behavior. They also motivate us as the goals of our life—the Cadillac that we are dreaming about, the swimming pool that we are working for, the kind of clothes, the kind of trips, and even the kind of people we want to meet from a social-status viewpoint are influencing factors. In the final analysis objects motivate our life probably at least as much as the Oedipus complex or childhood experiences do. On the other hand these childhood experiences themselves are very likely reactions to objects which have surrounded us. The objects, then, within the sphere in which we live, exert a great influence upon us while, at the same time, in buying, acquiring such possessions we express ourselves. There is a process of intercommunication taking place between thc individual and the world within which he lives. He shapes his own world and the world shapes him.

If I can describe a cake, a cigarette, a fishing rod, or a bottle of whisky in such a way that its basic soul, its basic meaning to the modern man, becomes clear, I shall have at the same time achieved direct communication, I shall have established a bridge between my ad and the reader and come as close as possible to motivating the reader or listener to acquire this experience via the product which I have promised him.

In his book *Existence*, Binswanger says that one of the fatal effects of psychology has been the theory of a dichotomy of world into subject and object. We fully agree, and in our practical work we see again and again how much difficulty has been created and most of the time unnecessarily by maintaining this differentiation. J. von Vexküll the noted German scientist specializing in research on environments, in a number of his books, makes the point that each person lives within his own environment, has his own world which surrounds him. What we have been attempting to do in many of our studies is to find out exactly how a particular product or service fits in with the personality of the individual, what role it plays in his particular world. This reorientation and new form of thinking has many applications.

Suppose we study furniture. In order to understand what motivates people to buy furniture, we have to know first what furniture means in human life. We almost have to know why there is such a thing as furniture in our human existence. Putting it differently, we want to know how we can read into, understand, and interpret the human quality that exists in a piece of furniture. All objects which surround us have souls of their own, have human qualities because they only exist in a human world. There are really no objects which man perceive. There are no raw inhuman objects. The moment furniture, houses, bread, cars, bicycles, or other products appear in our life, they are related to us, they are human.

One of the prime rules, therefore, of motivational thinking is to attempt to understand the why of the existence of a particular product. The moment such questions are being posed we see that furniture has much more than the utilitarian connotation of table, chair, bed. The size of a desk in an office is one of the most clearly understood prestige symbols in our modern culture. Round tables are different from square ones. Considerable time was devoted during the 1959 Geneva Conference to the question of whether the delegates should be seated at a round or square table. A chest of drawers is used to put things away, but also to hide things. Not only are there special relationships, but also timely ones. You put things away in your chest of drawers that you do not need at the moment. It's related to the past, but it is something that I may want to use or intend to use later on. The chest of drawers, therefore, somehow has something to do with the continuity of my existence. The desire for closet space in homes—a desire that seems to be never satisfied—has a deeper psychological meaning. Closets are the time capsules of the family life. This is seen in the famous closet of Fibber McGee: each time the door is opened, all his possessions, past and present, fall out. The throne, the stool, the high chair, the low chair, all these are variations of an important psychological meaning of the simple utilitarian aspect of a chair on which one sits down.

The Japanese have practically no furniture, in many societies people sit on the floor. These habits may result in radically different cultures. In India I observed that much of life takes place in the streets; for a Westerner, such habits seem to restructure the world.

They may lead to greater humility, a narrower viewpoint, a more upward view.

The visibility of the content of a cabinet or a closet may make a difference. In a study for a branch of a medical association, we found that the glass cabinet showing surgical instruments played a very interesting psychological role. It displayed, on the one hand, the professional skill and the tools of this skill to the public; at the same time, it acted as reassurance to the doctor himself of his own professional achievements, as did the books on his shelves. An invitation to hide these instruments behind opaque doors encountered considerable resistance, even though we could demonstrate that by giving it up, fear reactions could also be avoided.

How much soul is there, for example, in a cigarette lighter? All it is supposed to do is work, to do its job and light the cigarette. Yet some study of the meaning of lighters show that there is much more to it than meets the eye. It makes fire. Fire has symbolic meaning. You create a flame. A large lighter company discovered that the sales for one model slipped when they changed the design. Why? The new design did not show the "plumbing"; it was simply good-looking, the functionality had disappeared, the inner workings of the lighter were not visible any longer. But why should this make any difference? Because a lighter, as our depth interviews with several hundred people showed, is a very special kind of product. You expect a lighter to work and yet you do not assume, or even desire, that your lighter would admirably perform under all circumstances. A good part of the fun would be taken out of it if this were the case. It is almost as if love-making were infallible. There would be little room left for masculine pride. The fact that we fail once in a while makes the perfect performance worth boasting about. Hiding the plumbing of the lighter and stressing the good looks made this model less desirable for men.

Some readers may consider this analysis as farfetched. What proof do we have that any other kind of explanation would not serve as well? We conducted several hundred interviews, we used projective tests where people could freely associate with the designs or with real lighters of different designs. This approach then approximated a controlled experiment Changed advertising copy produced improved sales. But even if all these facts could be rejected, another interesting storehouse of materials of an anthropological nature can be brought into play as additional evidence. As reported by Bernard Gotz, in the *Archiv für Frauenkunde und Konstitutionsforschung,* Band 19, Verlag von Curt Kabitzsch, Leipzig 1933, under the title "Erotische Heilszeichen an altem Gerät," (erotic symbols on old equipment) fire-making equipment has had erotic significance in several different cultures: Lighters of a clear phallic form come from Australia and from the African grasslands of Cameroons. The Australian lighter is further characterized by the similarity of the red "head" with the fire red of the flame.

Prometheus as the god of fire, and fire itself as the greatest gift of mankind, the identification between Eros and the dawn, the glowing of the rising sun, the fire worshipers in various tribal religions—all represent further interesting validations of the meaningfulness of our hypothesis. Its confirmation by systematic interviews and special tests showed the existence of a similarity between the nature of fire and cigarette lighters even in our modern, sophisticated world. This then led us to the practical recommendations discussed before.

In an interesting report and study made on South African urban and rural Bantus by Waldo Langschmidt, it was found that the majority of Bantus normally work in mines for one or two years and then they go back to the kraal. They arrive at the mines owning a pair of torn pants, a shirt, and a blanket, and go back home with three blankets, three shirts, two pairs of trousers, a brightly colored trunk, a phonograph with records, a massive pair of miner's boots, an elementary first-aid certificate, and enough money to buy a wife. On a recent trip to South Africa, I was also told that it is common practice for Bantus to buy the cap of a Parker "21" fountain pen and display this as a symbol of civilization, without being able to write or without having even found it necessary to own the other part of the pen.

Anthropological literature, when it concerns itself with objects and their symbolic meaning in various cultures, often enters into the field of the soul, the meaning of objects.

Arrows can also be seen as erotic symbols, particularly as in a number of cultures the bridegroom is asked to send an arrow three times into a chimney. The wedding ring can likewise be understood as a sexual symbol.

We found in many studies that products can have a gender. Our tea research showed that tea in our culture is a symbol of femininity, weakness, and sissiness. Our recommendation, therefore, was really one in the direction of changing the sex or gender of tea, making it masculine.

Most people, when being asked when they drink tea, answered very easily that they did so whenever they felt ill, had chills, or felt irritable and nervous. To produce an advertising campaign based on these responses turned out to be what I call a subversive kind of approach—subversive because it sold coffee rather than tea. People looking at these ads acknowledged their truth and said, "Yes, it is true. I too drink tea when I am chilled, nervous, and irritable. Next time I am in a similar dilemma I shall reach for tea. In the meantime, however, I do not feel quite as bad as all that. I shall therefore continue to drink coffee, which is my preferred beverage." Even when we attempted to get fifty women to promise us to serve tea during the following week, we discovered that when we returned hardly one of these women had kept her promise. The reason for it was that their preparation of a hot beverage had become so routinized that they automatically served coffee when it came to the moment of making a decision.

Our advertising approach then had to be a completely different one, not one that emphasized the desirable aspects of tea, but one that concentrated on breaking this almost conditioned reflex, tapping the woman on her shoulder, as it were, at the moment when she was about to make a decision and inviting her to prepare tea instead of coffee. This was accomplished by such phrases as, "Take Tea and See," developed by the Leo Burnett Advertising Agency, and the introduction of a symbol of a red teapot which became psychologically associated with the actual teapot in every woman's kitchen. The idea was that every time the woman saw this real teapot she would see at the same time the red symbolic teapot with the phrase printed on it, "Take Tea and See." Thus her teapot became the basis for a poster planted right in her kitchen. Tea sales have been continually increasing. Whether this was due to any one of these factors or a combination of them is, of course, almost impossible to determine. But it does seem to make sense that abandoning this division between product and the consumer and concentrating on the bridge of relationship, the arch, as it were, between the product and the consumer, produced better results than the previous erroneous assumption and procedure.

It is probably no coincidence that those languages that distinguish dramatically among masculine, feminine, and neuter in the articles have done so out of psychological reasons. Even in the English language, where this possibility does not exist, it is common knowledge that cars and boats are usually referred to as "she." I found posters in Buenos Aires which referred to wine as "Señor Vino." Mr. Wine would seem to be a misnomer in other countries. It is a little less understandable why operators of bulldozers and huge caterpillars and grading machines also have the habit of referring to their machines as though they were female. In one of our studies, we concerned ourselves with the reason for this and found a desire to take possession of the big machine, to have it under your control, to be the explanation of this attitude.

In a study on gloves we found that the so-called short glove really had the function of a décolleté, exposing a small part of the wrist. It was further interesting to see that whiteness of gloves had something to do with social status. During the Middle Ages laboring classes and serfs were not allowed to wear gloves. This was a privilege reserved to the aristocrats and knights.

With a few exceptions, such as J. C. Fluegel's *The Psychology of Clothes*, there is very little in the literature of the social sciences that concerns itself with the objects that surround us. In 1959 we had in our library over twelve hundred studies concerning the phenomenology, the psychology of such diverse objects as cars, soap, toothpaste, toys, dictating machines, surgical supplies, the meaning of lawns, electrical kitchen appliances, baseball gloves, weed killers, cigarettes, cold remedies, pencils, television sets, books, telephones, shampoo, all aspects of clothing, shoes, hats, sweaters, dresses, coats, bras, girdles, farm machinery, furniture, silverware, and doilies. Literally each one of these studies and others not listed show again and again that products are not inanimate objects, that to separate or neglect them as objects of scientific analysis is a major oversight on the part of the social scientist.

Our daily life is full of objects, made of different materials. Not only clothes make people. We relate to objects and they to us.

We touch, feel, smell them, daily, hourly. A man shines the bowl of his pipe against his nose. A woman crosses her arms and rubs her hands on the fur sleeves of her coat. An Italian mason deftly and quickly sets one irregular stone after another into the wall he is building and in his hands the stones seem soft and pliable, almost alive. What is the relationship of man to materials that calls up these responses?

The question is of importance for more than mere reasons of curiosity. The furniture producer sells wood, metal, plastics, as well as tables and chairs. Shoe and glove makers sell leather as well as shoes and gloves. And the relation of the consumer to the material of any product is part of his basic relationship to the product itself. We are, in other words, confronted here with a hidden aspect both of appeal and of resistance to nearly all products.

Here is how we reported on the studies conducted by our institute in the psychology of the following basic materials. Samples of wood, stone, glass, metals, and leather were shown to respondents and our trained interviewers then probed for the entire range of thoughts and feelings that arose as the respondents picked up each object in turn.

WOOD

In all cultures the tree is a symbol of life—with its roots nourished in the mother earth, its great trunk thrusting upward toward the realm of light and air, its leafy crown bursting forth in the bright sun above. Psychologically speaking, wood retains life after its biological death. Moreover, wood does not merely *suggest* life. Rather, people feel very strongly that life is deep *in* the wood itself. A housewife said, "Wood breathes under you as you polish it." A science writer said as he fondled a piece of polished wood, "There is a thin borderline between the animal and vegetable that disappears with wood like this. These things attain personality—living, throbbing warmth. Of course, I know that this is dead and inert, but I can't accept that rational knowledge."

A photographer whose hobby is cabinet-making said, "Wood is like the stars instead of like a planet—I mean it has an inner glow of its own—it doesn't just reflect light like glass. A good workman can always bring that glow out of a piece of fine wood." The movement of the grain of the wood also evoked expressions of orderly life. "It's like the pushing out of ripples, like years, layers, growth. But with a feeling of calm and order—security—relaxed."

A fifteen-year-old girl said, "When I hold this piece of wood I feel its strength and I think of my own big tree when I sit under it and feel protected and safe." And another respondent said, "Wood—woods—great trees. Staunch and true like a tall pine tree. Stout-hearted like an oak. That's how my mind goes when I think of wood. There is never anything in wood that makes you fearful. You trust it." Even the smell of wood is sensuous: "The smell makes me feel—oh kind of excited inside if you want to know the truth."

THE EMOTIONAL FACETS OF GLASS

In contrast to wood, the story of glass is a story not only of appeals but also of dangers and pitfalls.

Wood proved to possess a hitherto unrevealed wealth of richness and depth of positive qualities which the maker and the advertiser of wood products can draw upon and put to use. Glass is an ambiguous material and ambiguity leads inevitably to ambivalence.

Glass is tantalizing. Frustration is defined by modern psychology as the emotional reaction that occurs when a barrier stands between an individual and a goal. Glass, which permits us to see but not to touch, is the perfect symbol of frustration. Said one respondent: "Glass is something that keeps something from you. Like the emotions of some people. You see but you can't get through. The only way to do that is to break it—to smash it." Here is the reason that rebellious, frustrated boys smash windows, why the frustrated child drops the glass he drinks from. Smashing glass is the perfect symbol of the bursting forth of pent-up emotion.

Glass has mystery. The emotional atmosphere of crystal is a rarely complex one among materials. It fascinates the senses by its smoothness, symmetry, and brilliance. At the same time it evokes deep, strangely pleasurable, yet disconcerting feelings of mystery.

An office manager, peering into a crystal goblet, said: "It gives me unusual feelings when I look deep into it like this. Just look at it when I turn it. See how it keeps changing—the light and all the patterns and shapes, I mean. They say that architecture is frozen music. I keep feeling that crystal is frozen intellect."

This respondent has touched upon the secret of the fabled crystal ball—we expect that somehow it will reveal answers to great mysteries. Crystal gives this effect to an especially high degree since its surface is so precise and definite in its orderliness. The hard, cold, and impersonal quality of such surfaces clashes with the fact that we can see into them. We feel that we are looking into something at once close and alien to our own nature. Crystal is like a translucent precious gem in this respect—both are hard, cold and foreign, yet we can peer into their "hearts." Small wonder that superstition has sought the answer to the unknown in such objects.

Glass can be malicious. "Glass is treacherous. One minute it is soft, delicate, fragile. The next minute it is sharp, penetrating, dangerous. You always sort of anticipate this splitting and breaking. You think of wounds, blood."

Hans Christian Andersen, in his tale of the glass sliver that pierces the heart and leaves the victim not dead, but cold and emotionless, captures perfectly the quiet terror that always lurks in glass.

Glass is liberation from matter. Here is the strongest of all the appeals of glass—an appeal that no other material seems to possess to the same degree. An engineer said: "Glass means ice, but ice is water, and water can become a part of the air. Glass is dematerialized matter, lightness, a transparent ghost. It is like radio waves, electricity—there and not there. Glass promises a kind of freedom that you associate with air and light. I think that's why this damn thing fascinates me so if I let it."

Our science writer should perhaps have the last word: "Glass is modern, progressive. It belongs to the twentieth century—to the future. Glass is a way of having our cake and eating it—of having the advantages of the controlled environment of indoors and the wonders of outdoors at the same time. I think of men in glass helmets on a strange planet exploring a new world but safe in their own world at the same time."

When we say that a product or a brand has a personality we are really saying that the public attributes to it various human qualities and characteristics.

In fact, just as the ancient Greeks consciously attributed human qualities to trees and bushes and flowers, we unconsciously attribute various human characteristics to the products we buy or don't buy. It has been proved that advertising and merchandising promotion become vastly more effective when they possess full and conscious knowledge of this intimate emotional relationship between the product and the buyer—of this anthropomorphic process—and build their appeals on this firm knowledge.

THE SECRET LIFE OF A FRUIT

We had occasion to analyze the personalities of the orange and the grapefruit in a study devoted to the promotion of citrus fruits. Our assignment was to establish in detail their current perception by the public as a guidance to psychologically correct copy, art, slogans. In trying to discover the personalities of the orange and the grapefruit as they are established in the public mind, we used a number of projective tests, each devised to throw light on a specific facet from "gaiety," "sociability," "reliability," etc., etc. to "family feelings" and "social status." As an example, here is how we investigated that last point.

First, we described four people as follows: Mr. Jones is a deep-sea diver who breakfasts at 5 A.M. Miss Vanderbilt is a debutante who breakfasts in bed at 11. Mr. Cannini is an orchestra conductor who breakfasts in his study at 9:30. Mr. Nash is a clerk who breakfasts at 7:00 at the corner diner.

We then asked a sample of two hundred respondents: "Which of these people will order orange juice? Which of these people will order grapefruit?" Here is the result of the test:

	ORANGE	GRAPEFRUIT
Jones	76%	24%
Vanderbilt	38%	62%
Cannini	29%	71%
Nash	85%	15%

There was thus substantial agreement to the effect that orange juice belongs in the life of the working men Jones and Nash, and grapefruit in the life of debutante Vanderbilt and orchestra conductor Cannini. This agreement permitted us to define with fair accuracy the "social status" of each of our two citrus fruits.

In another test, we asked our respondents to assign one of two opposite qualities respectively to oranges and grapefruit. This procedure allowed us to observe further the differences in the perception of the two citrus fruits, and brought out many qualities which had to be reflected in advertising so as to awaken positive responses in the viewer. Here is a partial table of this test:

	ORANGE	GRAPEFRUIT
Sunny	88%	64%
Cool	12%	36%
Old	38%	76%
Young	62%	24%
Fast	78%	28%
Slow	22%	72%
Gay	74%	68%
Sedate	26%	32%
Many	93%	18%
Few	7%	82%
Dynamic	78%	44%
Static	22%	56%
Friendly	94%	42%
Reserved	6%	58%
Intellectual	42%	82%
Emotional	58%	18%

Using such findings, combined with the analysis of depth interviews, in the end we were able to offer a great amount of detailed information to be used by promotion and advertising, by copywriter and artist. It was certainly pertinent for them to know that oranges are visualized in quantity but grapefruits singly, that the orange evokes the association of friendliness and the grapefruit that of elegant reserve; that both of them are believed to be sunny; that the orange appeals to the emotions but the grapefruit to the intellect. It is after assimilating such data that creative imagination may soar purposefully and come up with a winning advertising formula.

What has been done with the grapefruit and the orange may of course be done with every other fruit, and with every other product, as a matter of fact. For the anthropomorphic tendency of the human mind is universal and this applies to everything with which it establishes any kind of relationship.

THE SOUL OF METALS

In our study of the sales potentials of an aluminum boiler we found that the aluminum alloy was chosen because extensive research showed it represented the most suitable material for the purpose. Yet when the product was introduced, many engineers rejected the aluminum boiler because they felt it was too light, too insubstantial.

No demonstration or documentation was able to overcome the prejudice caused by this purely emotional judgment. In the end the original product had to be replaced by one made of another metal.

If experts and technicians betray such irrational attitudes, it is not surprising to find that the choice of a metal product by the general consumer is quite often made first of all by his subconscious feelings about the material itself.

The impact of metal on man is probably rooted in the fact that the ever-changing artificial world which is the habitat of the human being is nearly always built on a foundation of metal. So basic are the metals to the character of a civilization that whole historical eras are named for the metal of which they were built: the Bronze Age, the Iron Age, the Age of Steel.

Of all materials, then, metals are the most intimately related to the saga of the civilizations of man. Every metal carries with it an aura of a historical time, an aura which colors man's feelings about the metal. Bronze is ancient—bronze has roots deep in human history. A bronze piece is always a piece of ancient history—a bit of another era brought into the modern world.

Copper, on the other hand, is seen as ageless, rather than as old—psychologically it is the most primitive, the most "natural" of the metals.

Iron belongs psychologically to the period from the early days of the industrial revolution to the beginning of the era of the automobile. It is "old-fashioned" in the sense that grandmother is old-fashioned.

Steel and aluminum are modern. Steel, however, has a past which reaches back perhaps seventy to eighty years, while aluminum is seen as having no past, but rather as the metal of the present and of the future.

Next to the aura of time, the element that most forcefully seems to influence subconscious reactions is the process by which a metal is obtained. The process, in fact, represents the contest and the struggle (in some cases violent, in others mild and friendly) between man and metal.

TEXTILES—THE FABRIC OF LIFE

Every undergraduate student of economics is taught that such industries as steel and power are "basic" while such other industries as textiles are not. There is no better indication of the great gap which so often appears between social truth and psychological truth. For, although steel is indeed basic to the functioning of our society, it is not basic to the functioning of human life itself.

Textiles, on the other hand, are as psychologically basic to human life as food. Biologically, man is a naked creature—"naked" in the full sense of "standing unprotected and exposed to the world." All creatures need a barrier which enables them to resist the changes in the environment to which they cannot adjust. But, alone among the animals, the human species has no such adequate natural barrier between itself and the world. Only in the context of this basic situation of humankind can the psychology of textiles be understood.

"Cloth"—a synonym for textile—has the same meaning as "clothe" —to cover. Naked things, like naked people, demand to be covered. In covering nakedness, whether of people or of things, we accomplish these five basic purposes: we protect and insulate; we facilitate contact with the world; we hide defects and weaknesses; we give the appearance we wish to give; and we decorate.

Man's basic need for a barrier between his nakedness and the world is met by his use of textiles. In all the thousands of years since the first appearance of the arts of spinning and weaving to produce cloth, no better solution to this basic human problem has been found.

How do textiles protect? To some degree, textiles "ward off" physical dangers to both people and objects. But their main purpose as protectors is *to insulate—to prevent contamination* of one thing by another. Clothing, for example, doesn't give warmth of itself. It wards off cold and holds in the warmth we ourselves generate. Bandages have no healing power of their own. They keep out "bad" bacteria and allow the body's own curative powers to work. Similarly, sheets on a bed, undergarments, table linen, all serve this same basic function of acting as a barrier to contamination.

This function is psychological as well as physical. Proper clothing, people tell us, permits them to keep their psychological balance as well as their temperature balance. White lace curtains at the window are a symbolic barrier keeping the home atmosphere uncontaminated. Appeals based on these factors will be powerful motivators for they touch upon fundamental relationships in the web of human life.

Because textiles insulate—prevent contamination of one thing by another without hampering freedom of action—they also facilitate contact between people and people as well as between people and things. Fresh sheets allow us to sleep in a bed that others have occupied. Fresh tablecloths renew the dirtied table. Clothing, similarly, not only insulates us but promotes social contact at the same time.

We find that the protecting barrier of textiles softens as well as insulates. The hardness of the chair is softened by its covering. Similarly, our respondents speak of the inner hardness of a person as softened by his clothing or the hardness of the bare window as softened by draperies.

The ancient Bible story tells us that when Adam and Eve ate the fruit of the tree of knowledge, they looked at their nakedness and were ashamed. Ashamed of what? Not, we may be sure, of the exposure of their sex organs. We now know that this kind of shame depends solely upon social conditions. And in any event, such biblical allusions always refer to far deeper human forces than mere embarrassment.

Man's shame at his own nakedness to which the Bible refers is a shame arising from the awareness of being exposed in the fullest sense: exposed to the world as a creature of weakness. No force in man is more basic than his need to maintain his inner privacy—to prevent the exposure of his naked thought and his inner weaknesses.

But the great *strength* of human beings lies in the fact that they can become aware of their weaknesses—and do something about them. (The essential meaning of the Bible story then can be schematized like this: Discovery of knowledge—awareness of weakness—shame—action to overcome weakness.)

Against this background of basic functions we can now analyze a few of the basic textile materials and understand their particular appeals and lack of appeals.

Cottons, women tell us, seem "chaste" and "innocent"—"fresh, clean, cool." They give an appearance of "inner calm" and "unostentatious confidence." On the other hand, they speak of cottons as "very feminine," "attractive," "sexy in a quiet way." The "purity" appeal of cottons is enormously enhanced by the fact that women see them as wonderfully easy to launder, to starch and iron, to keep clean.

Cottons are "soft and friendly," our female respondents say, yet even for the most intimate clothing are "kind of impersonal."

Curiously enough, men don't share this enthusiasm for cotton, but on the contrary have a strong prejudice against the idea of cotton fabrics. Even though in practice they find cotton shirts, skirts, blouses, etc. quite pleasant, in principle cotton connotes to men "cheapness," "shoddiness," "lack of durability." Partly, we find, this stems from a lack of awareness of the advances made by the textile industry in improving styles of cottons, and of the durability of this material. Partly, the prejudice comes from the fact that where women think of cottons as soft and yielding, men think of them as a neutral material—neither soft enough for the intimate, nor "hard" enough for the impersonal functions of everyday work life. A major task of advertising for cottons in the immediate future will be to overcome this strong male prejudice.

Wool, in contrast to neutral cotton, is seen as strongly male by men and women alike. To be "male" in our society means, among other things, to be "without inner weakness"—and wool almost perfectly conveys this impression. As a result, wool, above all the materials which we tested, fulfills best the function of hiding inner weakness, is best for presenting the impression of unquestioned ability to withstand and deal with the rigors of the world.

Wool, our respondents say, is "out-doors," "belongs in the woods"; "pipe, fire, lodge, rich pine smell, man in a red check wool shirt." Thoughts of a rigorous environment make respondents think of wool and vice versa. The two belong together, as "Children playing in the snow, clad in wool snow suits."

While wool itself is not personal nor intimate, it is a shield to the personal and intimate—a protector that permits personal and intimate things to happen. One of our respondents from Maine said, "I never seen it to fail. Get a man and woman together in a sleigh wrapped around with the same wool blanket and you can't keep 'em from getting all over one another." Several of our respondents had a train of thought like this—"Cold night, warm wool blanket, warm and cozy inside and umm . . ."

Yet wool itself is sedate, conservative, refined despite its rough ruggedness. Nearly every respondent thought of English tweeds in a setting of old ivy-covered buildings—the English country squire, or the American college professor.

Because of the impersonal quality of wool, it serves perfectly to symbolize the group membership of its wearer—tweeds for university people, gray flannel for Madison Avenue, olive drab for the military.

Men relate to wool with strong emotions—it expresses exactly the qualities they wish to possess. Women, too, respond to wool warmly.

Silk is at the opposite pole from wool. It is as feminine as wool is masculine. It is as intimate and personal as wool is impersonal. Wool connotes rugged gentility; silk is refined, delicate, and tenderly gentle. Wool belongs in the rigorous outdoors; silk belongs in the "inner chamber." Wool conceals; silk reveals.

Silk is sexually exciting. For many men, far more exciting than the woman in the flesh. Again, the Bible story comes to mind—man's shame at the appearance of his nakedness. Silk, however, enhances all the personal, warm, tender qualities of the wearer, while at the same time causing the "animal" side of nakedness to disappear.

Clinical psychologists have long known the role of silk for those whose fear of the "animal" side of their nature inhibits their sexual responses. Silk can become a fetish for such people—silk "worship" is, in fact, a surprisingly frequent "secret vice" in our society and is found in a great many otherwise well-adjusted people. Many, many children are ardent silk fetishists and cannot go to sleep without a "piece of silk" to hold and rub between their fingers. (This behavior does not, of itself, indicate any serious psychological disturbance. Usually, it is merely compensation for some slight lack of mothering or indicates some degree of lack of assurance about the real depth of mother's love.)

Where the fear of the intimate, the personal, the "naked" becomes really strong, however, it extends to silk itself and there are many men and women who for this reason violently dislike silk.

In spite of the passionate references to silk, silk itself is "cool—like soft skin." It is "elegant," "luxurious." Everyday speech acknowledges it as a standard of excellence—"as fine as silk." A special value is attached to hair which is "silken." In other words, silk is seen as the ultimate in refinement. Silk evokes images of palaces, of kings and queens and princesses, images of "graceful oriental luxury."

A fascinating series of studies on the nature of love was reported for the sixteenth annual convention of the American Psychological Association, August 31, 1958. In an address by Professor Harry F. Harlow, University of Wisconsin, he stated that neonatal and infant macaque monkeys were used as the subject for the analysis of basic affectional attitudes. Real monkey mothers were replaced by wire and cloth mother-surrogates. The almost frightening conclusions of these studies were that the baby monkeys developed strong affection and love for the artificial cloth mothers. Further detailed experiments showed that while these cloth mothers could be made to provide milk to the infant monkeys, it was not the lactation, but almost exclusively the softness of the cloth that appealed to the infants. The experimenters talked therefore about the "contact need," which apparently operates as well in these mother-surrogates as it does in the attitudes of people toward their pillows, blankets, and soft, cuddly stuffed toys. As Professor Harlow says: "We were not surprised to discover that contact comfort was an important basic affectional love variable, but we did not expect it to overshadow so completely the variable of nursing; indeed, the disparity is so great as to suggest that the primary function of nursing as an affectional variable is that of insuring frequent and intimate body contact of the infant with the mother."

In one of the delightful poems accompanying this article, the following struck me as particularly revealing: "The rhino skin is thick and rough/ And yet the skin is soft enough/ That baby rhinos always sense/ A love enormous and intense."

The point of this chapter then is that to separate materialism from idealism, one with a negative, the other with a positive and more desirable connotation, is naïve, to say the least. What we do day after day has to be the staying point of any strategy for change. We have to accept the realistic behavior of people and eliminate morality judgments in a scientific approach.

Our problem is always how we can get people to behave the way we think they should. The discussion of the desirability of material goods and the need to turn our interests more in the direction of ideals can only be solved if we drop this superficial distinction. There are ideals that are good and those that are bad, just as much as there are good and bad possessions. What makes either one of them good or bad? To answer this, we have to go back to the problems of human goals and purpose. As I shall state in a later chapter, these goals are growth and self-realization. A product whose possession does contribute to growth, new experiences, and dynamic forms of happiness, one which opens up new horizons, I would consider good. The word "good" has to be used in the human, clinical sense; that is, good for human beings, their final goals in life, contributing to a richer rather than poorer life in the psychological sense.

If you keep on buying new cars, new clothes, in order to impress your friends or to follow the crowd, it is the object that possesses you. You are not getting psychologically richer. If you, however, only choose those tangible things that permit you to express yourself in a wider way, providing you with self-realization, then the object is being mastered by you.

The real role of motivational research and strategy of desire, then, in the ideal sense should be one where only those goals and objects are being praised that permit new discoveries, new experiences, self-realization. Of course, we are far from such an ideal stage. But the motivational researcher in advising the communicator, the educator, and the advertiser to stress the new horizons opened by his ideals or products would at the same time help the advertiser not only to sell his product but also to reorient, re-evaluate the value system prevalent in our society. Even buying of tangible goods, instead of arousing guilt feelings, could very well then be interpreted as one form of translating aspects of your personality into tangible form.

6 ■ WE THINK AS WE PLEASE

Homo sapiens, the rational man, has been the dream of humanity. If we could only utilize to the fullest our rational powers we could solve most of our problems.

Yet when we seem to get closer to this goal in our thinking machines, our computers, we get frightened. It could be that what we fear is the fulfillment of our wish. The ultimate in rationality is at the same time the ultimate in inhumanity, the machine-monster.

The strategist of human behavior has to concern himself, of course, with this problem. Although I believe in rationality as the goal of man, I have to look at the real man, and real man is both rational and irrational.

Much of the discussion of the use of motivational research centers around the idea that in utilizing irrational or unconscious motives, the motivational communicator frustrates rational behavior. This kind of opinion is based on a complete misunderstanding of the basic dilemma or problem of rationality versus irrationality.

To begin with, there is a silent assumption that rational motivations, such as spiritual values, are somehow more moral, more acceptable than irrational ones. Academic psychology often talks about cognitive versus emotional or affective behavior. I suggest that these divisions are in themselves wrong and irrelevant.

In work done for a large industrial company, we found that engineers who, one would presume, absorb information rationally, when being asked to describe what an alloy was, came forth with all kinds of symbolic and allegorical parallels such as two metals joining hands, two or three hot liquids being married in a big vat, etc., in addition to chemical or mechanical explanations of an alloy.

In other instances we found that very many, if not all, of the so-called cognitive processes by which professional or occupational knowledge is being absorbed at one point or another are being aided by non-cognitive emotions. Engineers describe the size of a turbine not only in cubic feet but in a more human way by stating that "you could put one, or two or three of the houses that I own or live in, into one of these turbines."

Rapaport, in his book *Emotions and Memory*, demonstrates that we remember faces of people we like or dislike better than those towards whom we are indifferent.

We should really be talking about the factors of awareness and unawareness in our motivations, rather than about rational and irrational aspects.

If I buy a boat, aware of the emotionality of my motivations, this is not irrational behavior—this is awareness of my emotions. It is equally likely that many of my actions are being guided by emotions that I'm not aware of. Similarly, I may have learned things in a cognitive sense and I may be aware of this learning process or may be unaware of it. One could almost state that there exists a higher degree of rationality in an individual if he is aware of the irrational streak in his personality.

A number of conflicts arise out of this subconscious value system that applies to reason and irrationality. It is the leftover of the value systems discussed by Greek philosophers such as Plato. It has been taken over by many religions, particularly the Christian religion and such sects as the Puritans. In many ways, it is the explanation for the way we feel in our modern world about sex, considering it as an animalistic, undesirable, dirty emotional business that one has to live with but that should be controlled as much as possible. It is possibly based on a fear and an anxiety that emotional aspects of the human personality cannot be controlled because they are not too well understood. We are dealing with the fear of the unknown in man.

Bertrand Russell says in an article on emotions in *Two Modern Essays on Religion:*

> These considerations bring us to the sphere of feeling. It is feeling that determines the ends we shall pursue. It is feeling that decides what use we shall make of the enormous increases in human power. Feeling,

like the rest of our mental capacities, has been gradually developed in the struggle for existence.

He states further:

> Two nations which cooperate are more likely to achieve economic prosperity than either can achieve if they compete. Competition continues because our feelings are not yet adapted to our techniques. It continues because we cannot make our emotions grow at the same rate as our skills.

Our newspapers are filled every day with high-sounding requests made by the representatives of goal-determining groups, such as churches and political parties. They set up various demands. We are told to be good, to drive safely, to concern ourselves with education, to be better citizens. But we have to discover for ourselves how to go about reaching these lofty goals. Being human, being involved in irrationalities and emotions, being only half-aware of his own motivations, the citizen gets caught in many snares and pitfalls of everyday life and thus lives almost continuously with a feeling of guilt. An interesting comparison is the following:

During World War II, the German Army told its soldiers, "No German is a coward. We are all heroes." The German soldier discovered in contrast to this glorious description of himself that he personally and individually did have cowardly feelings like everybody else. Inasmuch as he was told that he was not supposed to be yellow, tensions and guilt feelings about his shortcomings built up in him. The American Army instead used a much more intelligent approach: "Every human being is basically a coward," it told the G.I. "You would be abnormal if you did not have fear in the face of enemy fire." Despite this fear and this cowardice and the desire to run away, to stand your ground and fight is real heroism. Without attempting to evaluate the contribution of these different attitudes to the fighting spirit, it is obvious that from a psychological viewpoint, the American approach was the sounder one.

In a study we did several years ago during the Kefauver hearings, we found that when people were being questioned as to their reactions to the various political actors in this drama of reality, the most disliked person was a pious senator, while those who had more influence on the audience seemed to be the ones people could identify with, who were the weaklings, such as a union chief.

The reason for this different attitude was that this senator put himself on a pedestal, quoted the Bible literally every two or three minutes, and made unfulfillable demands, according to the reactions of the audience. He reiterated the Ten Commandments—thou shalt and thou shalt not. When he asked, for instance, "What have you ever done for your country?" and one of the people on trial said, "I paid my income tax," the reaction on the part of the listener was, "That's true, what else could he have done?" Rather than feeling annoyed and enraged by such a statement, the listener identified himself with people who had gotten themselves into trouble. When one or two of them described the great difficulty of making a living and staying honest at the same time and said also that they were trying their best to keep unethical behavior down to a minimum, they succeeded in describing an attainable goal. They produced a more salutary effect from a therapeutic viewpoint than the high-sounding senator.

Many of the contemporary religions make the same mistake. When they ask, as they have done in studies conducted for them by our Institute, "Why don't Americans come to church more often, why are they not more truly religious?" the answer usually is that too many churches use their influence to describe lofty goals rather than to teach people how to get there. Heaven is wonderful, but for most of us too far off.

We have reached the point today where no leadership of any kind can be practiced without a clarification of some of these problems of human goals and of how to reach them. There are literally thousands of people every year needing the help of therapists because of this confusion between the realistic behavior that governs their everyday life and the demands made upon them by the groups and people who simply wave the flag of desirable goals. They know they ought to be reasonable, work hard, avoid temptations (drink, cigarettes), and yet they know that in their daily lives they succumb continuously. It is out of this dilemma that many neuroses are being born of failure to accept oneself the way one really is.

THE ILLUSION OF RATIONALITY

A few weeks ago, when we were sitting down at home reviewing how we came to buy our first house and change our rental arrangement into a purchasing agreement, we recalled that we had planned to put a pair of doors between the living and dining rooms, in order to get more privacy for ourselves. That would have meant an expenditure of $30 and we felt it was unreasonable to spend $30 on a house that did not belong to us. Thinking ourselves to be rational human beings, we did the most irrational thing we conceivably could have done: we bought the house and spent several thousand dollars on it in order to avoid an expenditure of $30. As we looked back on it, we could not help laughing at our own irrationality.

This is only one personal incident, but in our research work, we have constantly come across similar examples, many of them even more irrational, if that is possible. Not everyone will admit, however, as readily as we did to ourselves, the irrational nature of a decision.

In an analysis which we did for a large mail-order house, a merchandising club, which used several thousand agents to sell its merchandise, we found the following situation. As long as this company referred to the selling of its products as a selling procedure, speaking the truth, they ran counter to the irrational tendency of these agents not to admit that they were selling in order to make money. The moment the mail-order house changed its approach to telling the agents that the company knew they really did not need any money, but were selling as a sort of pastime, a much larger number of agents was acquired. All of this was accomplished because they helped people to keep up their illusions. In other words, in many selling activities, when you are confronted with the problem of irrationality, the illusion of rational behavior must be kept up at all costs.

In another business analysis, where we attempted to find out what types of flowers women preferred, the answer we received was one that seemed to indicate that the most beautiful flowers attracted the greatest attention. Yet when we checked on actual purchases, we found that the majority of women bought the kind that needed the least care. This is just another example of the fact that we kid ourselves trying to keep up an illusion of rational behavior, in this case in the form of aesthetic appreciation. Actually, these women, like most women, turned out to be very utilitarian; their real behavior had little in common with their professed beliefs.

Our daily actions are full of such examples of irrational behavior. In one incident, we found that a man had been buying the largest cars on the market, and he himself did not know what could explain this kind of behavior. A more thorough analysis of his motivation brought to the surface that he had during his entire life attempted to compensate for a childhood which was marked by narrow living quarters and restrictions of all kinds. Not only did he buy the largest cars he could, but he also lived on Park Avenue in a very large apartment, and tried to have the largest and best of everything. It was fortunate for him, of course, that he happened to be in a position to afford this. But even without such financial blessing, we very often behave in a peculiar, irrational, extravagant fashion while not quite realizing why we are doing so. All of us can quite easily discover in ourselves inexplicable preferences for certain types of merchandise, and a thorough psychological analysis reveals the real reasons behind this.

There are also examples for mass behavior of this sort. During one specific year, one of the new car models happened to have a very blunt front end, and this particular model turned out to be a complete flop. For a long time, the reason for this flop was attributed to purely technical reasons. Actually, what had happened was that this car manufacturer had run afoul of one of the irrational factors at work in human nature. The normal shape of a car has a lot to do with its symbolic significance, that of a penetrating instrument. It symbolizes speed and power, it has, furthermore, in a psychological sense, considerable significance as a phallic symbol. In a sense, therefore, when the model with the blunt front end came on the market, it violated this symbolic significance of the shape of the car, and it was rejected instinctively by people who did not quite know why. In other words, to them it lacked a certain sense of potency and penetrating power. From an engineering viewpoint there was no truth to this. It conceivably was more streamlined and had better flow of air, and therefore guaranteed better speed than did other models. Yet, as this example showed, technical and engineering facts of that sort cannot stand up against psychological and emotional considerations. It is very important that the man whose job it is to persuade others be aware of this peculiarity of human nature. If he is not, he is bound to make tremendous mistakes. The recent example of the Edsel failure has a similar explanation. The shape of the front end aroused ridicule and became a target for the sharp-witted American consumer. "Rational" market research conducted before the introduction of the Edsel had overlooked this psychological factor. Furthermore, Ford had made the mistake of discounting the consumer, similar to the one Dewey made in the Truman-Dewey election fight. The voters' and the consumers' reaction was an emotional one. They instinctively decided to show how important they really are. Our Institute demonstrated these facts in its motivational study which was conducted *after* the failure had become obvious.

In numerous studies on many subjects, we found over and over again that all types of readers, listeners, and consumers are inclined to base their feelings toward products, people, books, plays, or messages of any kind on the amount of personal reassurance and self-satisfaction they were able to get out of them. The "objective" value of the product, so we found, was definitely of secondary importance.

An illustration of this basic reaction is provided by a study we conducted for the manufacturer of a well-known dictating machine. In spite of the acknowledged quality of their machine, the company had encountered increasing buying resistance. And what was even worse, salesmen returned with reports of dictating machines idly sitting in office corners. Instead of being appreciated as the time-saving and economy devices for which they were advertised, they were called "monuments to a sucker," in a typical and revealing remark by the man who had purchased them. Deeper analysis brought out what was hidden behind that resistance. The machine had been advertised as a means of economizing, and soon the executives who were using it felt humiliated; weren't they worthy of having a real secretary anymore? They felt as if they had been degraded. Small wonder that their hatred against the machine bred every type of complaint—complaints that sounded very "objective"! Small wonder it finally put the intruder out of use. However, removal of the economy angle from the advertising copy, replacement by less "objective" appeals, plus new instructions to the sales force, eventually succeeded in turning the tide.

The psychological force of ego-involvement is hardly considered in any field of education. Students and audiences are expected to "buy" knowledge and ideas because they are valuable, or interesting as such, not because of the ego-gratifications they might be eager to draw from them.

THE SYMBOLS AROUND US

Symbolism is fundamental to our very existence as men. Man has always used symbols in every form of self-expression and communication. Words, shapes, colors, designs, forms are the basic materials to which man attaches meaning and uses for communication both within his own psyche and as a vehicle for reaching other individuals.

A. N. Whitehead, in his book *Symbolism, Its Meaning and Effect,* states:

> No account of the uses of symbolism is complete without this recognition that the symbolic elements in life have a tendency to run wild, like the vegetation in a tropical forest. The life of humanity can easily be overwhelmed by its symbolic accessories. A continuous process of pruning, and of adaptation to a future ever requiring new forms of expression, is a necessary function in every society. The successful adaptation of old symbols to changes of social structure is the final mark of wisdom in sociological statesmanship. Also an occasional revolution in symbolism is required.
>
> There is, however, a Latin proverb upon which, in our youth, some of us have been set to write themes. In English it reads thus: Nature, expelled with a pitchfork, ever returns. This proverb is exemplified by the history of symbolism. However, you may endeavor to expel it, it ever returns. Symbolism is no mere idle fancy or corrupt degeneration; it is inherent in the very texture of human life. Language itself is a symbolism. And, as another example, however you reduce the functions of your government to their utmost simplicity, yet symbolism remains. It may be a healthier, manlier ceremonial, suggesting finer notions. But still it is symbolism. You abolish the etiquette of a royal court, with its suggestion of personal subordination, but at official receptions you ceremonially shake the hand of the Governor of your state. Just

as the feudal doctrine of a subordination of classes, reaching up to the ultimate overlord, requires its symbolism; so does the doctrine of human equality obtain its symbolism. Mankind, it seems, has to find a symbol in order to express itself. Indeed, "expression" is "symbolism."

In our verbal logical culture we are too prone to reject symbolic non-verbal forms of communication. Many hours of discussion are being wasted on trying to determine whether to help combat juvenile delinquency or improve intergroup relations via comic strips or records, or whether it would be better to sell a product via radio or TV. While it is true that the same message presented via comic strips or via a book will change to some degree its meaning, this is not due to the technical format used, but to the psychological aura surrounding these particular media. What we are to concern ourselves with, however, first are clarifications of some of the basic processes of communications.

There are a number of such principles which we have learned in our practical task of examining the comprehensibility, the effectiveness of messages via all types of mass media.

1. THE MELODY OF HUMAN UNDERSTANDING

Understanding is not an atomistic registration of single words. In order to understand orally or visually, we have to perceive whole meaningful units, the melody of a message. It is thus misleading to concern oneself too much with individual words and terms in an advertisement or any form of message. When *Time* magazine attempts to end each story at the bottom of the page, this is more than a clever trick. It helps to establish a structure in the mind of the reader and thus helps comprehension. In many instances, when a story is being understood, an event or development grasped, we find that what exists underneath the actual understanding is a graphic underpinning which serves as a structural organization of the message which has been understood.

By the same token, comprehension is disturbed, delayed, and sometimes even made impossible if the wrong graphic structure is carried into the message. One such wrong concept concerns progress. Whenever we think of progress and growth, we often have a graphic picture of an ascending line. In reality, growth is much more realistically symbolized by a spiral development, where often the real development is one of thesis-antithesis and finally synthesis. In a chapter called "Human Behavior and Personality Growth" by Harold H. Anderson, appearing in the book *An Introduction of the Different Techniques of Communication*, edited by Harold H. Anderson and Gladys L. Anderson, growth is defined as at once a creation of differences and an integration of differences. This is illustrated by an example taken from biology in the process of fertilization. The egg is different from the spermatozoon—each has an individual organism. In the process of fertilization, the egg abandons its structure and its function as an unfertilized egg for a new and emerging function. The spermatozoon also abandons its structure and function as a spermatozoon for a new and emerging structure and function. Growth, therefore, Anderson says, comes about through an integration of differences. The graphic presentation of this process is certainly not a straight ascending line.

A cereal company, which was using as a model for its development of new products such a concept of an ascending line symbolizing progress, felt that its future market could best be reached by developing more and more instant-type cereals, more and more machine-made type cereals. If the cereal of today was one that was "shot out of guns," the cereal of the future must be one that would be made with atomic energy. The space cereal, as it were, seemed to be the logical development. Substituting, however, as we did, for this erroneous straight-line concept one which saw progress as a spiral development, we could demonstrate that the cereal of the future would resemble much more the old-fashioned cereal in its basic classifications. It would be warm, relaxing, providing a feeling of leisurely breakfasting and security. Because this new cereal would find itself, however, on the next layer of the spiral, it would have to be easily preparable and contain all modern advantages of nutrition and speed.

Not long ago, we were asked by a meat company to find out what new uses of meat could be discovered. Again, rather than thinking of progress as a straight line, we considered the possibility of a return to many previous habits in the meat field. This permitted us to come up with some ideas of meat for breakfast, in the forms of small cubes, meat snacks as pick-me-ups in mid-morning or mid-afternoon; the possibility of combining different types of meat, such as pork and lamb, beef and pork, serving meat in different fashions, such as meat twists, where each strand would be meat of a different type. Many such recommendations come out of a research approach which permits a tracing back of a modern attitude towards historical development in the layers of the spiral that came before the present attitude.

When we studied for a financial institution whether or not the message "Common Sense Can Beat Inflation" was understood, we found that in the pure grammatical sense almost everybody knew what was meant. There was, however, a tremendous difference between this logical, grammatical understanding and a real understanding. We saw that very many people attempted to introduce a series of translations, when pushed into the necessity of really explaining what the message meant. They said, "Well, 'Common sense can beat inflation' means everybody can beat inflation." When urged further, they substituted for the word "everybody" "you and I can beat inflation." At this point, it became fairly obvious that the copy "You and I can beat inflation" is, of course, much better than the one "Common sense can beat inflation." We reduced the abstract statement to one that could be demonstrated by pointing to concrete situations, and thus could be understood in the true sense of the words.

In a study conducted for a greeting-card company, it was our assignment to find out more about the psychology of sending greeting cards. A fact which seems fairly obvious when pointed out but which had been overlooked by the company, was that a greeting card is reacted to not so much as a physical object, but as a symbol of the sender's attitude towards the addressee. The more trouble the sender apparently took in selecting it, and the more it seems to be specifically designed to please the recipient, the more it is appreciated. We say, in a way, how considerate of the sender to have taken so much time and to remember so many details about our personal interests. In the American culture, most of us suffer from embarrassment when we have to express our emotions. The greeting card serves as a printed substitute, but even there we are inclined to reject as "corny" any emotional expression which is too open and obvious. We often go to the other extreme of disguising our true feelings with humor and sarcasm. This is the explanation for the success in the last few years of greeting cards which seem to make fun of most sentiments. We seem to think it more pardonable to send a good friend who is ill a card which teases him than one which expresses in an open fashion our wishes. In other words, communication is taking place not on a verbal level, but by going back to the symbolic emotional meaning of the message.

2. THE DIALOGUE OF COMMUNICATION

Western languages are full of expressions which assume that when we communicate, one person or group does all the influencing and the other is the passive recipient of the message. Teachers and advertising and propaganda specialists often ask themselves if their message gets across. There are elaborate testing methods, rating services, etc., to find out which one of various commercials or messages was the better one. In a study on anti-Semitism for the New York Mayor's Committee on Intergroup Relations, it was our job to find out what the best way to combat the painting of swastikas on synagogues would be. Dramatizing the acts of vandalism to show how dangerous they could potentially be seemed to be the right way to impress the public.

Our study showed, however, that too many people reacted to the events themselves by various forms of escapism. They said either that these acts of vandalism were simply perpetrated by young pranksters, or they exaggerated their significance to such an extent that they felt nothing would be done about them. Portraying the events themselves in a dramatized version on TV, for example, would only increase the desire to escape the conclusions, the necessity to act. The concept behind this first wrong communication was one where the listener was seen as a passive recipient of the message. Communication, however, is a two-way street, a dialogue. Seeing this, our goal was not to dramatize the event, but to cut off the desire to escape. We dramatized instead the escapism. We showed either an individual who stated that these vandalistic acts did not mean anything, or a person who exaggerated their importance. We illustrated the fact that both were escaping. What was needed was to take the response of the listener into consideration and to control it. We showed that to run away from these issues was natural and we indicated how the answer could be found by individual and group action.

3. COMMUNICATION IS A TWO-WAY STREET

We often say in everyday language, and unfortunately also in quite a number of scientific studies, "Let's find out what this particular stimulus did to people." It is almost as if we thought that by opening up the skull we could measure the depth of the grooves created by the stimuli. We erroneously think that if we could only measure accurately how deep an impression one message makes compared with that of another one, we would have an accurate measurement of its effectiveness.

Communication is a dynamic process of vocabulary that describes effects, comprehension, reading, listening. It should be cleansed of all connotations that assume a passive recipient. The concept of a passive subject whose retentions, or engrams, are being measured is about as nonsensical as to talk about a brother without visualizing a second person whose brother a brother is. The problem in communication posed by a client may vary. It may range from a church asking us what message, what sermons it should preach in order to attract more people, to an advertiser asking what type of TV commercials he should utilize to sell his products. Which ones of the many hundreds of messages received by the viewers, listeners, and readers will penetrate their minds, and which ones are shed without leaving the slightest impact?

We have been asked these questions many times. They are always asked with an expectation of getting as an answer a panacea. Are cartoons better than straight selling? Should I show my product on TV or only tell about it? Are people more impressed by women than men? Is a long sermon better than a short one? When we bend our psychological ear, however, to the people themselves we discover that what is of interest to the communicator, the advertiser, the message transmitter—his categories, classifications, and divisions—disappears almost completely in the mind of the respondent. As happens elsewhere in life, so with regard to communications of whatever form—the consumer measures the commercial, the sermon, the book, not by whether it is a cartoon or a serious message, but by what it does for him. The respondent is continuously seeking the satisfaction of needs—physical and emotional. This is the basic law of behavior governing most human activities. This concept is also basic when we seek to determine the effectiveness of various aspects of communication. They are then effective, and effective every time, when they succeed in satisfying some need that the respondent may have. This postulation ignores such superficial distinctions as cartoons versus straight selling commercials, movies versus books. Rather, it emphasizes the very simple but most important mechanism—the satisfaction of needs. If a message affords some degree of satisfaction the listener will absorb it, integrate it into his own life experience. He will be sold by it and the commercial will be effective. But if it fails to satisfy some of the consumers, it is quickly eliminated from the individual's conscious perception and never acquires meaningfulness. It fails to communicate, and thus to sell.

4. THE VERBAL ILLUSION

Primitive cultures know and use non-verbal forms of human strategy without blushing. We, as logical people, insist on verbal communication, logical appeals. Our true communications, however, are not too far removed from primitive symbolism. Flags, uniforms, the way we build our houses, how we dress, and what we use and buy in everyday products are all part of a second language, a language universally spoken, hardly taught.

There is much evidence to show that it is the non-verbal, implied communication that is much more often the effective one than the pure logical verbal form of communication.

In a recent court case, an old problem of differentiating between verbal and implied communication became an important issue. The Federal Trade Commission has as its purpose, of course, to protect the public from misleading claims. Such control, however, of communication within the form of advertising or press reports necessitates a clear-cut understanding of how communication really takes place. In an advertisement for an airline, for example, a complex airplane engine was shown. The verbal statement was made that the ingenuity of this engine and its qualities could serve as a proof for the safety of these particular planes. Our tests, however, showed that what people did react to, the real communication that was taking place, was on an implied level. People looked at the picture of the engine and were induced to develop a chain of associations in the exact opposite direction from the one desired. They simply felt their attention drawn to all the many intricate parts, nuts, and bolts of the engine with a resulting feeling that it was a rather hazardous thing to rely upon. Only a few of these nuts and bolts had to go wrong to make the engine stop and cause the plane to crash.

Relying on the verbal communication level, this approach seemed to be a perfectly correct one. In view, however, of the implied communication, it is very obvious that the advertisement could not have been constructed in a more dangerous fashion.

Too often strategy in human communications is based on the verbal significance of a message rather than on its implied one. I have found many advertising messages or propaganda attempts in the political field ineffective because no attention has been paid to the meaning behind the message. In studies during political campaigns, we found, for example, that the modern sophisticated public very frequently paid much more attention to the gestures, the hidden smile, the facial expressions of the candidates when turned away from the camera on television, than they did to the verbal meaning and content of his speech. Often too it was the tone of delivery and all the complexities of non-verbal symbolic communications which took place between the audience and the candidates which determined their acceptability. There are a number of rules that can be applied in determining and anticipating the implied level of communication.

5. MENTAL SET

When we read an advertisement or see it shown either in movies or on television, and also in human contact, there are a number of signals that we react to right from the beginning of the communicative process. In a study we did, analyzing the reactions to a motion picture, *The Showoff*, we found that the fact that Red Skelton was playing the main role served as a symbol for the interpretation of the total program in a humorous fashion. Instead of recognizing this fact, however, the show itself started with a series of very realistic documentary shots of streets in Philadelphia which confused the public and prevented them from applying the proper set of reaction patterns. When, furthermore, during the show, a number of realistic scenes of an unpleasant nature occurred, such as the loss of a job, these scenes by Red Skelton, because of the confused mental sets and signals, were reacted to in an unpleasant fashion rather than in a humorous one, as had been intended.

In other words, we have learned in life to apply a set of different psychological filters to the messages and communication events that we encounter. An interesting psychological experiment, for instance, was the following: two identical messages were shown to two comparable groups of people; in one case with the signature of John L. Lewis, the other one with the signature of Fulton Lewis, Jr. Two dynamically opposed results were produced. Thus, what people reacted to was the signature and not the content of the message.

Listening to short-wave broadcasts, for instance, shows that the recognition of the originator of the propaganda broadcasts determines to a large extent the reaction to the message. It is almost as if a switch was turned, when you discover in the middle of a broadcast that it originates from Moscow rather than from Washington. Anybody who has ever listened to such broadcasts and was in doubt in the beginning of the program who was making the statements and then suddenly discovered who it was, will have noticed this snapping-in, this sudden functioning of the mental set.

Another illustration of how powerful the implied meaning of words, the non-verbal communication, can be was demonstrated by an interesting experiment. Two doctors carried out a study showing how a good drug can be made better if the physician shows enthusiasm when he gives it. The study was a contribution to the "placebo" phenomenon. The usual placebo is a blank pill given when an active pill is unnecessary or might do harm. Twenty patients who had stomach problems because of anxiety were given careful personal attention on each visit. When the drug was administered, the patients were given strong assurance of benefit. Ninety per cent of the patients showed marked improvement, but when the physicians gave the drug abruptly, it indicated they had little time to spend with the patient and the improvement rate dropped to 70 per cent. Even the blank pill given with warmth achieved an improvement rate of 30 per cent.

Even such things as symmetry can take on symbolic meaning. Hermann Weyl devoted a whole book, entitled *Symmetry*, to the subject. He pointed out such interesting facts as: "People shake right hands. Sinister is the Latin word for left, and heraldry still speaks of the left side of the shield as its sinister side. But sinister is, at the same time, that which is evil, and in common English, only this figurative meaning of the Latin word survives."

6. MOODS

Another aspect of non-verbal communication that is often overlooked is that reactions to a message can vary strongly, depending on the mood in which a person finds himself. The following anecdote illustrates the importance of mood. A salesman was instructed by his sales manager to canvass a particular area in a city. He was given instructions to knock on doors of all those homes that had a two-car garage, a well-cared-for lawn. He was supposed to do that at a particular given time and use a set series of sales approaches. After a few days he returned to his office and he had to report that he could not produce any sales. The sales manager checked whether he had followed all his instructions. The salesman affirmed that he had actually done so. "Was there anything else that occurred?" finally asked the sales manager in desperation. The salesman said, "Yes, but that could not have had anything to do with my success or failure as a salesman, it was not in the list of things you had told me to watch out for." "What was that?" asked the sales manager.

A tragic accident had occurred in this block only the day before. It is obvious that the mood created by this accident must have had a major influence on the sales situation in this neighborhood. Yet this apparently unimportant psychological factor had been completely overlooked in the sales instructions. When doing media studies, the mistake is often made of thinking of the reader of *The Saturday*

Evening Post, or *Time* or *Look* magazines as a physical and psychological identity. In reality most people of the magazine-reading type read anywhere from three to seven magazines. There is, therefore, no such animal as a *Look* reader or *Time* reader. What does exist, however, is a *Time* mood, a *Look* mood, a *Post* mood. It is this mood that the reader finds himself in when opening *Time* magazine or the *Post.* It is, at the same time, this mood that the space buyer really buys. Of course, the same kind of reasoning applies to other media such as television and radio. Mood is, therefore, another important aspect in the communicative process that has often more significance than the verbal content of the message being communicated.

De Gaulle recently erected a statue in the form of a V, twenty feet high, and, at the same time, he used the same V to symbolize the Fifth Republic. This is an example how we, even in this day and age, still use the same primitive symbolisms people used thousands of years ago.

Philip Wylie in his book, *The Innocent Ambassadors,* describes very many cities and areas he encountered during his trip around the world by their odor. Their odor represents a symbol as primitive and old as mankind itself but still operative even in this twentieth century.

7. THINGS AND SYMBOLS

Even the object, action, or thing-in-itself, which is a non-symbol-thing, can come to acquire other meanings and associations and thus symbolize other ideas and concepts. In the business and advertising world the automobile is a good example. An automobile is first of all its supposedly concrete self: a machine for transportation. However, an automobile is almost never *merely* that to any human being. To some it is prestige; to some it is a symbol of prosperity; to some it is a part of one's woman-hunting equipment; to some it is travel, or family togetherness, or vacation fun, or a symbol of luxury; and to others it may represent an occupational work horse. To a savage who has never seen a car it is a living thing, magic, a spirit, an omen. To the factory worker in Detroit a car is (in addition to the things it is to other Americans) also a symbol of his toil, his living, his working week, his pride and skill.

We see from the above that anything can come to represent almost anything else. There is probably nothing intrinsic, inherent, or absolute in any symbol. Symbols available for non-verbal commercial communications can be described by three main categories: connotative, interpretive, and intentional symbols.

In a research program for a large Chicago food market, we found that the role of the butcher, despite prepackaged meat, still had not lost its symbolic significance. The butcher in many ways still represents Esau, the hunter, the man who handles red, bloody meat. The American housewife in most instances feels inferior as far as her meat knowledge is concerned. It is, therefore, the butcher who can act and must act as an adviser. He is the hunter similar to the warrior in our fur example, quoted before, who can hand out good or bad cuts of meat, who can be honest or cheat. Putting emphasis on the honesty of the butcher, introducing special ways of cutting meat which would protect the housewife, and using the meat department as a strong asset of their supermarket proved to be very successful recommendations.

8. CONNOTATIVE SYMBOLS

By a connotative symbol we mean the representation of a recognizable object which has both a manifest and a latent meaning. The number of signs or objects which represent a cluster of meanings beyond their intrinsic objective meanings is, of course, limitless.

For example, the anchor tattoo of the Marlboro man represents for the viewer "masculinity," "strength," "ruggedness," "intensity of pleasure," associated with sailors. It is hoped, of course, that these attributes will be transferred to the product. Research indicates that under favorable circumstances these symbols do, in fact, aid in defining the product for the respondent.

In a recent ad test we found that the presence of a glass of champagne, a pocketbook, and theater tickets, accompanied by a big city in the background, literally told the respondent that the product advertised was a very expensive, luxurious product to be used for special occasions. It is obvious in this case that the objects within the ad defined the respondent's understanding and perception of the product. The reader can surely draw on his own experience to elaborate this idea.

An automobile manufacturer used a middle-priced car in a setting where the connotative symbols suggested great wealth and upper-class status (i.e., wedding scene, butlers, people dressed in tuxedos, etc.). Respondents were intensely offended by the ad—they were frankly hostile. Here is a typical reaction:

> Are they kidding? What do they think they're selling, a Cadillac? They'd like to make you believe millionaires buy that car. It's a lot of bunk if you ask me.

The advertiser's attempt to upgrade the status of this automobile through the use of high-status cues failed because the status definition of this automobile in the public mind was at complete odds with the intended message. On the other hand, this same automobile placed in a setting of use suggesting ordinary folks, vacations, and driving pleasure was completely and positively accepted by the respondents.

9. INTERPRETIVE SYMBOLS

By interpretive symbols we refer to those symbols which stimulate emotional elaborations within the respondent and invite interpretation. In this area we group the reaction patterns to such non-verbal stimuli as a) color; b) form; c) human expression or situation (empathic projection). We are particularly concerned with the deeper feelings which these stimuli excite.

Color. Perhaps the most phylogenetically primitive emotional reaction can be induced by color. This dimension precedes developmentally all the other basic areas. Color rapidly induces an emotional tone.

A simple blotch of intense red, for example, will readily induce associations in respondents with "heat," "fire," "blood," "loudness," etc. Combinations of black and red overlapping in an unsystematic order readily evoke "anxiety" and "depressive" reactions.

A simple field of light blue with elements of white invariably stimulates associations with "sky," "soft," "quietness," "awe."

Colors will frequently induce feelings of movement, i.e., a black circle will often move toward the person while the same circle in pink will often recede.

Basic human motivations are most readily communicated and stimulated by the effective use of color.

Form. An interesting symbolic relationship exists between color and form. Although form usually accompanies color in communication, it may be viewed as being inversely related to color.

Color represents *free emotional expression,* the specific direction of the emotional reaction being determined by the surrounding symbolic field and the specific color. Color is impulsive and suggestive of emotional indulgence. Form, on the other hand, generally suggests the relative degree of control and organization.

Hence, a scribble may represent confusion or, if it is well-patterned, may suggest control and organization.

If the reader can visualize the steel framework of a building that is being erected and compare this to the form patterns of a surrealistic painting, he can easily appreciate the symbolic significance of formal elements in the communication process.

In order to illustrate the function of form and color, we conducted an experiment using logotypes common in commercial communication.

Because the logotype appears to the human eye as an over-all image, it also portrays secondary connotations about the company and product, beyond the intentional meaning of the word. Ingenious designers can subtly vary the lettering styles to suggest different traits—smartness, strength, integrity, femininity, tradition, dignity, modernity, etc.

The logotype can even suggest the form and function of a product. Well-designed initials take on symbolic associations, so that they register in our minds as split-second images of the company name rather than as abbreviations.

Our basic hypotheses in this brief experiment were:

a) There is a logotype which is most appropriate to a particular concept.

b) It is possible to determine a concept image by association techniques.

c) There is a relationship between verbal images and graphic forms.

In order to test these hypotheses the following techniques were used.

Word Associations. A standard word association test was administered prior to any other test. The concept being tested was "lamb." This word was imbedded in the following list: water—hat—dog—lamb. The respondent was asked to give his associations to the words. Usually two additional probes were used for each word. This was done in order to induce an association set; i.e., water—R1 drink—R2 thirst—R3 cool.

Card Selection. Five cards were made up consisting of the word "lamb," marked A–E. The type varied and each card had a different color background. The respondent was asked to pick the card which went best with the word. After the selection was made the respondent was queried regarding the thoughts that passed through his mind when the selection was made.

Matching Ideas. All the cards were spread on the table in random order. A group of five sentences was read to the respondent. After one general reading, the sentences were read one at a time. The respondent was asked to match each card with the sentence. This was then followed by a brief non-directive probe trying to get at the factors that influenced choice.

Summary of Results: Fifty Subjects. Word Association: The following concepts emerged most frequently in association to the word "lamb."

1. Wool	40%
2. Warmth	70%
3. Soft	60%
4. Light	20%
5. Food	10%

Total is above 100 per cent because more than one association was given to each word.

Card Selection (Most Appropriate Test)

A	0%
B	0%
C	0%

Card Selection (Most Appropriate Test)

D	60%
E	40%

Reasons Influencing Choice

Soft	40%
Gentle	40%
Restful	10%
Fluffy	10%

Second Choice (Word and Concept—Matching)

1. Name of a restaurant
2. A little female lamb
3. A sign at a meat counter
4. An "old lamb"
5. Title of a story about lambs for a children's book

Statement #1—B 100% of the cases
Statement #2—D 80% of the cases......E 20% of the cases
Statement #3—C 60% of the cases......A 40% of the cases
Statement #4—A 60% of the cases......D 20% E 20% of the cases
Statement #5—E 60% of the cases......C 40% of the cases

The results clearly indicate a relationship between form, color, and associated concepts. The word "lamb" is associated with softness and warmth. These are feminine concepts which graphically are expressed in pastel colors and free-flowing, rounded type. If the type is sharp and solid, even though it may be on a pastel background it is likely not to be associated with the major images for the word.

Both color and form must be consistently related to the image of the concept being communicated. The consistency of the results even for our small sample suggests that the relationship between the image, graphic elements, and color tends to be shared culturally and is not individually determined.

Previous learnings are an important influencing factor. Card B clearly illustrates that Old English type is strongly identified with tradition, most likely with objective non-animated ideas. Choices of Cards D and E relate very clearly to the associations with the idea of "lamb." In instances where color was appropriate but type not, the respondent tended to hesitate and be confused as to what choice to make; however, he invariably responded to the type.

Aside from the degree of relative organization, form patterns suggest moods. Quick jagged lines, for example, can easily suggest aggression and excitement. Free-flowing elongated lines suggest femininity.

Formal elements when properly combined with color intensify the projection of the message.

Empathic Projection. Another dimension of importance in the area of interpretive symbols is human expressions and interpersonal situations. In using these elements we communicate the more complex emotions such as love, respect, anxiety, pride, and countless other meanings related to our human situation.

In this area we can develop thematic configurations which tell a whole story and do not simply represent a number of isolated ideas or feelings. A good example of an empathic projection is a well-known trade-mark which has succeeded in becoming thoroughly identified with the company it represents: Aunt Jemima. This "jolly mammy" is not only linked with the product, but is psychologically appropriate.

The associations to Aunt Jemima are consistently in keeping with the ideas of good eating and cooking. She suggests abundance, pleasure, and happiness. Coupled with these feelings she has a traditional quality associated with serving food in the grand manner.

When a person (historical, mythical, or real) is used as a symbol, the symbol usually takes on a functional role in relation to the company. For example, Father Knickerbocker is generally seen as a mythical salesman for the beer. Betty Crocker, on the other hand, is the guiding light who oversees the manufacturing of the product.

According to our data, Aunt Jemima is felt to be the "originator" of the recipe.

Oh, I'd say she made the recipe up a long time ago. Maybe her boss liked it so much he figured he could put it in a box and sell it.

My guess would be that she's the original cook who made the pancakes. I don't think she owns the company or has anything to do with it now.

10. INTENTIONAL SYMBOLS

Intentional symbols are those elements used for manifest description. They are the obvious surface symbols; for instance, a wing standing for the notion of flight. We in this work are less concerned with intentional symbols because they are the rational, syntactic meanings attached to the symbol which are consciously and conventionally accepted by everyone. Since intentional symbols are more abstract and agreed upon, they reach the highest and most conscious levels of man's psyche. Unlike interpretive and connotative symbols, intentional symbols generally do not evoke strong emotional reactions on this level.

Intentional symbols, however, invariably function on deeper levels of the psyche as well; hence, even an abstract word or self-explanatory picture also functions as an interpretive and connotative symbol.

The power of intentional symbolic communication is also illustrated in the controversy raging during a typical hot New York summer. It concerned how the weather bureau's statements were being given to the public. For a while the term "discomfort index" was used. This aroused the indignation of many New Yorkers. They felt admitting that New York was uncomfortable in summer was similar to Florida's admitting to rain. The discomfort index is composed of heat and humidity. The general recommendation finally accepted was to switch over to a more positive term of "comfort index."

IRRATIONALITY IN THE SERVICE OF LEGITIMATE GOALS

In education, all too often the important job of removal of resistance and emotional encouragement is overlooked. Socially desirable goals are naïvely pursued by straight presentation of facts and arguments, while promoters of less desirable goals pursue a more realistic approach by effectively playing on emotions.

I realize that social scientists are inclined to consider only an appeal to *reason* as worthy of being used in real education. What I am advocating, however, is that we use our knowledge of the emotional mechanism in the *service of reason*, in order to prepare and facilitate its acceptance by those who cannot be made to listen to reason in any other way.

In one of our studies, we had an opportunity to advise our client, a large book club, on how to remove emotional resistance. The club was concerned about the large number of members that dropped their memberships. Our analysis showed that many members unconsciously felt ashamed of not being able to keep in step with the incoming books. To the subscriber, every new book became an additional token of his own inability to stick to his reading schedule, and his membership developed into a symbol of guilt feeling and frustration. Seemingly, his only way out was cancellation of his membership. We advised the club to redirect its advertising policy from praising the value of its books, to reassuring the reader about his reading habits. Reading, it was suggested to the reader, was not to be considered a "job" or a "duty," but rather an exciting and happy opportunity. A single page read in a restful mood could do more for a person than hastily reading a voluminous book. Thus, the book club tried to change books waiting on the shelves from a menace into a hope and to make members feel better about themselves.

How such an appeal to irrationality, to emotions we are usually unaware of, was utilized for socially unquestionable purposes is illustrated by the following examples.

It was our assignment to find out how New York landlords could be persuaded to accept Negroes as tenants. Direct questioning permitted these landlords, interviewed in our study, to use a number of excuses and rationalizations. "It is not our fault," they said, "it is the fault of the other tenants. They do not want Negroes." When we interviewed the tenants in turn, they tried to put the blame on the landlords.

Accepting the fact of the possibility of irrational aspects in the landlords' motivations, in other words, motivations that they themselves might not have been aware of, we found this: asking these landlords to voluntarily accept Negroes in their apartment buildings was equivalent to asking a soldier to volunteer for an extremely dangerous duty. It was much easier for him to be a hero when the choice was between being killed by the enemy or being executed for cowardice by his own officers. The landlord indirectly attempted to tell us something very similar. "Enforce the law," they said, "I can hide behind the law, be a hero, if the real choice is one between showing tolerance or being thrown in jail."

The real applied psychology, then, in this case was not to concern ourselves with the fears, the resistances, and the logical argument of the landlord, but to figure out a strategic device which would bring about a change of attitude and action. This advice is being put into practice now by the Mayor's committee on intergroup relations by applying the law in the most stringent fashion.

When Dr. Ralph Bunche's son was recently refused membership in the New York Tennis Club, the full application of existing laws brought about the resignation of the president of this club and a radical change in their attitude towards minorities.

Emotions operate of course also in non-commercial fields; e.g., charity. In interviewing people about what is involved psychologically in giving, of what emotions are mobilized when somebody is asked to give money, we find this: When we give, we play God. We feel very "uppity." We're very arrogant. In one way or another, instead of feeling humility and being grateful for being given a chance to pay back our debt to humanity, the true factor that is involved is, "I am capable of giving money." That's only one side of the coin. There's a much more serious one, an unfortunate side: That by *not* giving money, I can play God just as well. "I could give to you; you keep on begging me, keep on asking me—I just won't."

THE NEW HORIZON

When we have introduced this kind of analysis, I think an entirely different kind of horizon starts opening up. We find that every time we ask someone to give money, we're really caught in a competitive situation. We have to depict, describe, portray to him the giving as being *more* pleasant, *more* satisfying than the *not* giving. In other words, you have an invisible competitor every time you introduce a payroll deduction plan or whatever technical form of giving you are concerned with.

As psychologists we are often confronted with a difficult problem of communication. Some of the things we know sound silly when they are presented in a cold, unsympathetic surrounding. A physician may explain to you that the headache you complain about comes from the infection between two of your toes. You're inclined to say, "What an idiot. I have a pain up here, and he starts treating me down there." It might take this physician quite some time to explain this to you. Fortunately, our schools have helped a lot, and he doesn't have quite as difficult a job any longer as a psychologist still has, but he can describe the connection between an infection, white blood cells, and the circulatory system. If the doctor takes a little bit of time to explain what he's driving at we say, "All right, I didn't realize it. It's interesting."

That happens quite frequently in the medical field. It also happens quite frequently when we are dealing with problems of the human mind. Unfortunately, there we are a little bit more arrogant, because we say to ourselves, "What does he know about my mind. He can't possibly understand me more than I can understand myself."

Giving and not giving is somehow related to attitudes that originate in our childhood days. We found in our studies that in some peculiar way it has something to do with the relationship between children and parents. A child can give or not give in some spheres where parents are interested, and in giving or not giving at his will the child maintains power over the parent. Toilet training, for instance, is such a phenomenon and so is the brushing of teeth. What is really involved in asking someone to give is that you are asking the giver to repeat childhood attitudes. The child may not think it in words, but he is thinking, "If I give in to Mommy, if I give up my power—if Mommy can't control me at her will—if toilet training is written off and I am now trained and clean—then I've lost one very nice instrument of my power. Mommy can't do anything to me any more."

When we're dealing with motivations, and dealing with the motivations of giving, we have to penetrate to the unconscious. We have to concern ourselves with what resistance exists. If this is true, and this is my point number one, then when I am giving blood and also when I am giving money, there is some secret fear of giving away something in an irretrievable fashion. Therefore, there has to be developed a whole series of public relations measures reassuring the person that this is not the case.

For instance, in the case of giving blood, you can come to see that you are *lending* the blood; you're not giving. You may want to consider such a similar change of terminology in Community Chest and United Fund work. We found that, for instance, showing a crippled child or a needy child or a needy family has a very peculiar effect emotionally on the individual. There is a subconscious feeling that "the moment I give to this needy family I am somehow assuming responsibility in an irretrievable fashion. In a way, I'm almost becoming needy myself. The moment I do *not* give, I'm not just a villain; I also gain something very definite from it. I have nothing to do with it. I'm not responsible for their difficulties and problems in my community. The moment I get myself involved, somehow I have been made responsible by the organization. Rather than having this happen, it's much simpler and cheaper for me not to respond, not to give, not to co-operate!"

So one should not show pictures of needy people or needy families. It is much easier to show a group of fine, upstanding people in the community, to show how wonderful they feel because of giving. It is much more correct psychologically, because identification with the positive aspect of giving is a much more rewarding one than identification with the negative aspect of giving.

In the field of voting, we found for instance: "Isn't it a shame that only 48 per cent of our voters participate in national elections? So, why don't you vote? It is your duty as an American citizen. Don't sell your birthright" and so forth.

Now, here is the peculiar thing that happens in this unpredictable human mind of ours when reading such an announcement. "Oh," you think, "the majority of people in this country don't vote! Well, I always like to join the majority. Apparently only the suckers vote. So, why should I join the suckers. Thanks a lot for the advice. I'm not going to vote."

"Everybody has switched to Calvert" is a better advertising line than "Isn't it a shame that you haven't discovered the wonderful Calvert whisky yet." Therefore: "Everybody is voting—see you at the polls. We're all going to vote this year," was the translation of this kind of analysis. A public announcement about the lack of interest of the public in United Fund or Community Chest, or how little public spirit the American people had, or anything of that sort that has the slightest resemblance to this kind of complaint has the exact opposite effect from the one intended.

THE FEAR OF EMOTION

A great many people do not give because they are afraid of seeing themselves as soft-hearted. Why? There seems to be a complete contradiction between what we are learning in church and school and in all the nice stories about the kindness of humanity. It's true, and yet it isn't true, if we approach the problem in a very brutal and sober fashion.

In our competitive world, literally from the first year in kindergarten, we're being trained to be competitive as often as we're trained to be co-operative. "What are your grades?" "How come you went down five points?" All of us have made that mistake with our children. Instead of saying, "Oh, you've been getting along with all your friends in school very nicely," we are much readier to challenge and complain. On Sunday we listen to the principle of co-operation; on Monday in the office we are being forced to compete. This arouses a lot of emotional conflicts.

We are gradually trained to be very worried about our own emotionality. We are becoming on the one hand more sophisticated; on the other hand we are ashamed to say, "I love you." If you watch some of the current movies you find this beautifully expressed. In a movie that is twenty years old you might find the couple on their wedding night saying to each other, "At last we're alone, darling." In the movie of today you're much more likely to find the couple saying to each other, "Gee, I didn't know you wore garters." We are ashamed and embarrassed of calling an emotion by its true name. That is very directly and very specifically connected with emotional appeals of giving. We're being asked to change from the everyday life experience to a very unrealistic kind of thing which then in turn becomes a very exceptional thing. It becomes a Sunday kind of giving, rather than a normal, everyday human experience.

In one of our studies, we actually tested one kind of letter against another kind. One letter appealed to the emotions, the sensitivity of people; the other one said, "Look, this letter asks you for money, and you better darned well give us the dough. No matter what excuses." There is another example in connection with registration of voters in which we actually went out and said, "You know where the place is for registration. Here's the address. You do have the time, because all you're doing anyway is watching television between six and eight. The weather is going to be nice, and even if it isn't, you don't even have to get out in the rain. If you still use an excuse not to register, you're just a louse!" This kind of approach has much greater effect. It's the kind of language we're accustomed to. This is the kind of language our boss uses when he bawls us out—and he gets action.

THE FEAR OF EMBARRASSMENT

In a study we did for airlines the question came up, "Why won't some people fly?" There were all kinds of very nice explanations, including the one, "I don't want to die young" or something of that sort. However, using a deeper approach we found something new. We asked people to close their eyes and then we said, "Well, so you are afraid of dying. So close your eyes and tell me what comes to your mind." We would expect that a man would tell us about the crash and his funeral and maybe the insurance policy, and how his wife would find out what the insurance policy is. Instead of that, men did think of their wives, but in a completely different way. They said, "You know, there's something funny. I can just see my wife receiving the news. She loves me and all that, I know. But I could just hear her grumbling, 'The darned fool, why did he have to get himself killed in an airplane crash? Why didn't he take a train?

He would still be alive and be able to provide for the family.' " The fear of post-humous embarrassment!

We found something else. Most of us don't know exactly how to behave in an airplane. We know what to do in a train. We know that we can say hello to the neighbor and we take our hats and coats off, but what do you do in a plane? If you've never been in one, you don't know how to behave. We found also the following silly little things. Some people (and it was a large enough number of people) worried about the toilet.

In the same way, in giving, we found that quite a number of people are embarrassed. They don't know how much to give. They don't know whether to give anonymously, how large to sign their name, or whether to feel elated or to feel shy about it; whether to boast about it or to hide the fact. They do not know the very simple principles of giving gracefully.

THE GIVING RELATIONSHIP

In giving, there is some peculiar kind of relationship that is parallel to the child-parent relationship. The child is withholding the secret, while not giving in to the attempts at training on the part of mother or father. This child-parent relationship is repeated when you're being asked to give. In a way, psychologically, you always give only either to mother or to father, possibly to an uncle. You *never* give readily or, as readily, from the psychological viewpoint, to an anonymous person or to an anonymous entity. If that's so, then United Funds and Community Chests are not all capitalizing upon this psychological phenomenon.

It might be well to have a community mother or father symbol, or an uncle symbol. Somebody that I'm giving to, some *real* individual, and it could be a real person rather than an anonymous organization. If giving is a replica of a parent-child relationship, let's take advantage of it.

INDECISION IS POWER

If you make a decision, you give away power. There's something very closely resembling this in the problem of giving. "As long as I haven't given to you, you'll keep on wooing me. You'll keep on being nice to me. You're going to send me another letter, and another representative will pay attention to me. The moment I have given you money, I am gone and forgotten. Nobody cares about me any longer. All I get is a tiny little plastic thing and I never hear from you again till next year. Why give up this very desirable state?"

In the process of asking someone to give, you have, in a different form, a very powerful competitive force at work. "As long as I don't give, I am in the saddle. I'll keep him guessing.

"You are a wonderful guy, a customer to be wooed until you sign the purchase order or receive the merchandise. Then they forget you."

This is a mistake made by many advertisers or salesmen. It can be remedied by devising a whole series of techniques for paying attention to customers after they have made a purchase, or to donors after they have given. Many research studies show that there are more people reading ads after they have bought the product than before.

GIVING BUYS POWER

Giving does involve emotion. People can be made to give if we do not approach them in a dreaming, hopeful kind of fashion, but realistically look upon them as normal human beings.

Much of our modern unhappiness comes from our aspiration to be rational. Even most Western religions suffer from this defect. Zen Buddhism appeals to many people because it talks about enjoying each day, accepting life and oneself in its tangible reality rather than living in the future.

7 ■ THE WHOLISTIC APPROACH

Many communication efforts have collapsed, many advertising campaigns have failed, because too much time and effort were spent on details. The eyes were not lifted to see the frame of reference within which the specific problem lay anchored. When the brain was utilized in a bifocal fashion, understanding the far and the near, proper interpretation and thus proper action was achieved.

"GESTALT" VERSUS ATOMISTIC APPROACH

Attempting to find an answer to a practical human strategy problem without consideration of the total framework often leads to a very basic shortsightedness. In a famous experiment with chimpanzees conducted by Wolfgang Köhler, bananas were placed outside a monkey cage just far enough so that the monkeys could not reach them with outstretched arms. There were, however, a number of sticks placed inside the cage. If two of these sticks were put together and used as tools, it was very easy to get the bananas into the cage. The experiment showed that very few of these monkeys had enough intelligence to tear their eyes away from the immediate goal of the bananas to turn around in their cage and discover the possibility of putting the two sticks together.

Many of our approaches to the problems of how to motivate people show a similar lack of intelligence. Many advertisers, public leaders, people in charge of bringing about a certain goal, too often feel that it is sufficient to take this goal, put an exclamation point behind it, and use it as an admonition. As parents we still suffer from this illusion. "Be sure to be home on time," we tell our youngsters. "Why can't you work harder? You will fail if you don't make a real effort. Why aren't you interested in more important things than dances and parties?"

The mistake we make is to consider each one of these problems as existing in isolation. Before tackling a problem, it is imperative to ask first some basic and very fundamental questions. We are attempting to determine the frames of reference of our problems. We see, in other words, the particular product or question of service that we are investigating in the center of a series of concentric circles. The largest one of these usually deals with the over-all goals

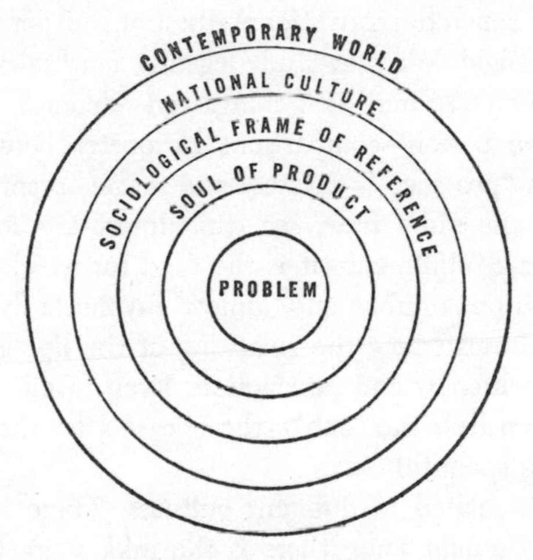

—the philosophy surrounding our contemporary world. The next one of these concentric circles deals with the national cultural peculiarities that we are dealing with and their development and trends. A third circle, closer to our real problem, is the role the product or problem plays in interpersonal relationship, its sociological frame of reference, as it were. The next concentric circle that we deal with is the personal and emotional meaning of the product, its soul, its function in the relationship between object and subject. Only in the last one, in the center of all these circles, is the product or problem itself that we have been asked to investigate.

Suppose our problem is how to represent soup in the general market. Long before we concern ourselves with the specific problems of the company that has invited us to represent its soup, we attempt to understand the real meaning of soup, the frame of reference within which soup exists in our culture. Attempting to get the answer within our largest frame of reference, our largest concentric circle, we find that soup, while it is food, is at the same time more than a food. It is a potent magic that satisfies not only the hunger of the body, but has something to do with the yearnings of the soul. People speak of soup as a product of some mysterious alchemy, a symbol of love which satisfies mysterious gnawings. Soup, particularly in its hot form—the brew, the potion—seems to have existed almost as long as the first signs of civilization of mankind. In an attempt to answer the concrete motivational questions of our client, we have to go first far afield. We may study legends, fairy tales, far-off history of the human race to find such things and references as the witches' brew, the love potion—comparisons in poetry between soup and fog. The term "pea soup"—mystery and magic—seem to go together with fog. At the same time, we can almost say soup is orgastic. Eating soup is a fulfillment—it is the food for which people express their appreciation audibly and almost involuntarily. There are a number of cultures where the smacking of the lips is considered to be a sign of politeness and satisfaction. Even in our more inhibited cultures, we can hear the "aah"—the release after the first warming, strength-giving spoonful.

Soup is also related to different cultures. There is French soup, Italian soup, German soup; there is the milk soup, the bread soup of the Austrian farmer, the beer soup of the German. People for hundreds of years have learned to judge a restaurant by the quality of the soup it serves.

Soup has the power to satisfy. It is a product of kitchen magic. Herbs have always been associated with more than earthly power, and since so many herbs go into a good soup, it partakes of the transcendent properties of legendary potions. It is the brew of the good fairy, of mother's mystic skill. When you have eaten this soup, it does magic things for you. It protects and heals and gives strength —it gives courage and the feeling of belonging.

Our first step in attacking a motivational problem is to set up hypotheses and concepts. These concepts are not idle speculation. They are the results of accumulated experience by the social sciences and by our own group. What we're doing is to establish frames of reference, the concentric circles within which our problem finds anchorage. We are practicing cultural anthropology more than anything else. One of the new thinking processes that we feel is necessary not only to solve motivational problems in a meaningful and intelligent sense, but also to solve many of the problems that confront us in our modern life is to forget about narrow-minded atomistic, naïve approaches, and to first spend considerable time in understanding the phenomenon that we are dealing with, to see a problem within its *Gestalt*, within its field. To establish the vectors that it relates to is one of the first tasks of motivational thinking. Long before we go out and interview people, observe them, experiment with them, we attempt to determine the various levels of obstruction and frames of reference our problem belongs to.

Lifting our sights from the technological aspects of soup and getting into these broader, at first nebulous-sounding, spheres, we found that there were half a dozen adjectives and nouns which continuously occurred in statements about soups and whose frequency set the emotional tone of the interview. For instance, we asked people what words they associated when we mentioned the word soup. About 98 per cent thought of the word "mother"; 41 per cent "family"; 32 per cent "warmth." We found further that soup runs the gamut of emotions. Soup evokes extreme emotions, whether they are positive or negative, whether a person is in a state of dejection or exhilaration.

THE WHOLISTIC APPROACH

The single elements of an ad or commercial are not what determine its effectiveness; it is rather the total, over-all integration of its elements. Modern research techniques must take these configurational factors into consideration.

In attempting to form an answer to a practical problem of human strategy and motivations, the following error is frequently made: the manufacturer of a detergent, for example, has not succeeded in making a major inroad into the market. He comes to us and wants to find out what appeals he has left out in selling and advertising his detergent. Should he tell the public that his detergent produces less sneezing, makes the wash whiter, and is more economical than competitive products? Similarly, the manufacturer of an air conditioner asks us what additional aspects about his product should be told to the public and in what form.

In reality, none of these approaches is successful, not because the products themselves are not good, but because wrong communication techniques have been tried and erroneous assumptions have been made. The real problem that we were faced with was this: most people accepted the desirability of the improved air conditioner or detergent, but weren't capable of establishing a relationship between themselves and this product. In several ways they said, "Yes, I agree. These products are excellent and better than the ones I've had up to now, but they do not apply to my case, I do not need them."

What had been attempted was something comparable to asking an individual wearing dark glasses which of the various colors applied to a wall in his room he prefers. If, after a while, he does not seem to react much differently when a red color is put on the wall than when a green or a blue one or a yellow one is applied, it becomes obvious that the problem may not lie with the colors that are being applied, but with the individual.

The new kind of thinking that we recommend to solve the problem is to look at the consumer, the individual, the recipient of the message in the total framework of his culture, and to figure out techniques by which he can be induced to remove his dark glasses.

TIME BINDING

Semanticists talk about the basic human ability to see things related timewise that may have happened over long stretches of history. Never has this ability been more necessary than now. Yet it is a basic conflict of our era that we are still in the stage of children who want quick solutions. Just as a boy solves his controversy with his opponent by "shooting him dead" we, too, as citizens or as a nation think we can cut through the Gordian knots of history by dramatic quick solutions. History forces us to learn patience, to wait, to find laborious, undramatic solutions. Understanding this conflict may permit us to bring our attitudes more in line with the requirements of modern life.

FLIGHT OR FIGHT

Many of the human motivations in buying and in almost all other aspects of behavior can only be understood when we take the broadest framework into consideration. Nowhere did this become clearer than in a study conducted by us for a large cemetery. Their problem was to find out why people wanted to be buried in one cemetery rather than in another, the role of the undertaker, the relationship between a mortuary and the actual cemetery—should they be separated or together in one locality? When we started to read our interviews we found a very interesting thing: both the cemetery and the mortuary are symbols of a deep-seated conflict. Specifically, two attitudes are present in the face of death, and it is these two attitudes which compose the basic conflict. These can be summarized as Flight and Fight. Flight is characterized by an inability to face death. The person actually tends to deny the existence of death. This denial is most dramatically expressed by the fact that when we asked people to talk about death, they talked about life.

> We are here for a purpose and it is the will of God that we live by His Bible. I don't really know but I do feel that if I live as I am expected to, I will be judged as well as anyone . . . We are expected to live by the Commandments and think as Christians.

Such phrases as "I, too, will probably die some day," "His death was so unnecessary," also demonstrate this need to flee from every reminder of death.

The Fight attitude, on the other hand, is characterized by mature acceptance of death. The person, in a sense, looks death in the eye, accepts the realities of the situation, and is able to make a realistic adjustment to an actual death in the family.

> As far as I am concerned it is something that you have to face. There is no sense running away. It is not that I am preoccupied with death; I am not. However, I do realize that it will come some day. I try to make my life as meaningful as possible. I try to spend my time well. I think that this is the only sensible approach.

One of our most searching and important findings is that very few people have a clear-cut Flight attitude with no overtones of

Fight. Very few people have a clear-cut Fight attitude with no overtones of Flight. In the majority of the population, these two attitudes live side by side in everlasting conflict and combat.

The people who deny the existence of death and are afraid to look it in the face nonetheless have a deep and underlying need to face it maturely. In a way, they realize that they are "kidding themselves" through the denial attitude. They know perfectly well that under the smooth surface death exists and that they themselves will die some day. They seek and hope for a way to face the fact. They yearn for the strength and ability to have a mature attitude.

The people who accept the existence of death and face it squarely nonetheless have usually not completely conquered elements of fear. They hope to forget, to push the fact out of their minds; they indulge in fantasies which deny the existence of death. Deep down, they dislike these symptoms in themselves because they represent an immature approach to death.

THE CLUES TO THE FLIGHT RESPONSE

The attitude revealed most clearly in the interviews was people's need to flee from death. We found a number of overt statements of this desire. It is reflected in attitudes toward the mortuary, toward the cemetery, and toward death. It pervades every aspect of the picture.

"I want to lead a good life." As we mentioned, we found that people, when asked to talk about death, talked about life. Over and over again in the interviews we found this reluctance, this inability to discuss death. People told us of their aspirations and their hopes, they told us of their family and their jobs. Only under pressure would they tell us what death means to them. The statement of a middle-aged housewife illustrates this point well:

> Well, my father died when I was very young. It meant that we all had to change our plans, rearrange our lives, so to speak. It meant that I couldn't go to college. From then on I started to think of the things that I could still do. And I must say I have had a very good life.

"I don't think of death." We found this statement frequently. The respondents told us that they rarely, if ever, think about death and that they certainly don't discuss it. Most expressed a considerable amount of annoyance that the interview forced them to think about and to discuss this topic which they had so long ignored.

Upon closer analysis of their comments we discovered that this problem went even deeper, that people *cannot* think of death. This represents one of the clearest indications of the Flight need.

I don't think most people think about death. I don't think about it anyway. What is going to happen is going to happen. There is not any use thinking about it when there is nothing you can do about it.

The reason I don't think about death is because I don't feel that I am close to it.

Why should I think about it? Only maudlin people do. I have a life to lead and I don't have the time to give to such a subject.

"I can't look at the body." A large number of the respondents stated that they could not look at the body, that it is frightening and disturbing. They mentioned that they couldn't understand why other people looked. The whole experience is seen as terrifying and unnecessary.

We tried to find out why people have this reaction. The whole subject is surrounded with a great amount of anxiety. Looking at the body is threatening, as it shakes people's belief in their own immortality. It is graphic proof that life does stop; they, too, will die some day.

My second cousin died in July 1951. I would not see him, I refused to look at him.

I couldn't even look when they took him out of the room. My whole system was low at the time.

I just couldn't look. I was too scared. The whole thing was so scary. Anyhow, I wanted to remember him as he was alive.

The emphasis which people place on the embalming of the body, the work of the cosmetician, etc., is irrational and emotional in nature. Numerous respondents discussed the way the deceased looked after embalming. Many praised the embalmer because he had made the deceased appear so lifelike, so natural. Here, then, in another fashion, we find the desire to deny death.

They called me and when I saw my mother in the Slumber Room, she looked natural and everything was just right.

And the body must look natural. Yes, if there is anything they must do, it is make it look natural. They should wave the hair and paint the lips and put rouge on the cheeks—everything that they can do to make it appear that the person is just sleeping.

I guess that I will probably die some day.

It came as such a surprise. I didn't think she was going to die.

A small but significant number of people in our sample tend to use their belief in immortality as a bulwark against death. These people seem to have an even greater amount of anxiety about death than most of our respondents. Their belief in life after death helps them in their Flight.

Sure, I believe in a hereafter. I don't know what it's like, but I can imagine—no, I guess I can't imagine. There's a heaven and a hell. It's pretty nice in heaven and pretty bad in hell. The body has nothing to do with it. The soul goes either to heaven or to hell, depending on what kind of a person he was on earth. The body goes to dust, where it came from.

Well, let me see what I think it really means, the spirit. What it means to one may mean another way to another person, but I feel there is an everlasting life. I don't think there is any definite place for a spirit. You can't point and say the spirit goes there. I cannot say what direction it goes. I do believe there is a universal life but I cannot say that the spirit goes here or there. I can only say it goes home. It goes where it belongs. I don't think that death means the end. I think it means a step into something else. I don't think there is any death, what we commonly mean by death.

THE CLUES TO THE FIGHT RESPONSE

Buried underneath people's desire to flee from death is a need to find some mature manner of coping with death. In almost all the people we interviewed we found this desire for mature acceptance underlying the Flight response. The clues to the Fight response are, on the whole, far more subtle than the clues to the Flight response. As a rule the individual is far less aware of this desire to face death. However, in little clues such as tone of voice, gestures, etc., and in certain overt statements this Fight response is revealed.

"I am not really running away." Pervading all the respondents' discussions of their need to flee from death was an underlying anxiety and unrest. This is the most important clue to the Fight response. Not one of the respondents feels completely comfortable, completely free of the fear of death. We find that this anxiety is expressed in a number of ways.

The respondents have an intense need to repeat themselves, to offer long, extended explanations about their disregard of death. Frequently, in these explanations they implore the aid of the interviewers: "Don't you agree with me, am I not correct?" Such overemphasis is a direct indication that the individual is not satisfied; in fact, he is actually trying to convince himself.

I just don't talk about it. I don't see why I should. Why should I? It is a long way away. At least I hope it is. Well, I mean you never know, but I just have that feeling. I just know it isn't near. After all, I am young. You see what I mean, don't you?

Perhaps the most frequent index to the Fight response is the recurrent contradictions we find in the interviews. Whereas the respondent will tell us at the beginning of an interview that the deceased is really not dead, a few minutes later he will say he really must go on living even if his friend has died. These contradictions which run throughout the interviews are a clear indication of the basic conflict which the individual faces.

My aunt died last year. I was very close to her. She brought me up. My aunt *is* a wonderful woman. She is always near me when I need help.

In daily experiences when death comes up, we find people joking about it. Such comments as "Drop dead," and "You look as if you are dead," clearly indicate the humor surrounding the problem.

We know from psychology that humor is frequently used to cover up anxiety and disturbance. When people are unable to handle a situation, when they are tense and nervous, they tend to find relief through jokes. We find in the interviews a high incidence of this conversion of anxiety into humorous relief. Here, again, then, we find evidence that the Flight response is not need-fulfilling, that people are yearning for a better solution.

I don't know how I'd feel if a close person died, whether I'd want the eyes used for the eye bank, the ears for ear banks, the bones for bone banks.

What do I feel about death? (Respondent laughs nervously.) Sometimes I think it is a marvelous solution. Every time my wife screams at me for not fixing the toaster, I tell her "What are you going to do when I die?" She is scared to death of being a widow so she shuts up fast. Boy, I think it's a howl.

Thus, we see that the Flight response never really furnishes the necessary answer to the individual's problems. The conflict between the reality of death and the need to flee is always present.

Many of the interviewees mentioned that they could not believe in life after death. They said so in an almost regretful fashion, for death to them is necessarily more of a reality. These people, however, tend to be more accepting of death, more capable of dealing with it.

I don't believe in life after death. I think that the person is gone. There is no hereafter. It doesn't prevent my thinking however of being a good man while I am here. It doesn't mean that a man should be a pig just because there is nothing when you are gone. No, there is no spirit, not in my mind.

I don't believe in reincarnation exactly, but it's something like that. I think we go into a kind of state of animation in which all of the wants and desires and needs that we felt on earth are not fulfilled. I mean they are fulfilled. Maybe we don't have the same desires after we're dead.

I don't think there is a life after death. I believe that some people are more alive with live people than others because their special qualities live on in people's memory. More people remember them far more than others due to their personality.

"I wish I knew what to do." Probably the most overt statement of the Fight response is people's bewilderment and loss when faced with the problem of death. They don't know what to do, they don't know which way to turn. The Flight response is not need-fulfilling; it proves inadequate at time of crisis. The bewilderment, the loss, the pain, all engender the need to discover a new form of response.

After the first shock of the surprise, as far as I remember it, I kept walking around in a circle repeating, O My, O My, O My. My main reaction was the horror of telling Leon [son] and how to spare him the grief and what was awful for me was my helplessness of preventing him from having this grief. I candidly did not have much concern about myself. I don't know what people do in mourning.

All of these clues led us to the belief that people have an underlying need to face death. As we stated, there is little explicit evidence of this desire. It is expressed in a far more subtle fashion than the Flight response. However, careful scrutiny of our interviews has shown us that the Fight need does exist and that it exists side by side with the need to flee. Moreover, we find the Fight need a clear and ever-present call for help.

This wholistic approach permitted us to find concrete answers for the cemetery company. We could tell them that the man picking up the body should never refer to it as such, but ask where is Mr. Smith. The funeral director should not refer to the deceased in the past tense; the family has not gotten accustomed to this, etc.

But the final fears and hopes of man also help to understand apparently far-removed practical problems.

THE WHOLISTIC APPROACH IN SOLVING INDUSTRIAL PROBLEMS

In trying to find answers to questions posed by industrial companies, we had to reach more for an understanding of basic human goals.

A large company for whom we did a study described its problem as follows: "We make ten different products. How can we get purchasing agents or engineers to buy more than one or two of our products? Why don't they buy all of them? They do need them in their particular enterprise." The company had tried to promote, very elaborately and very much in detail, the advantages of each of their products. Steel brake shoes and boilers and pumps were some of their merchandise. On the assumption that they were dealing with very rational individuals, they gave the engineers and purchasing agents all the many engineering details of these products. If they could convince them that their particular steel plates or their particular boilers were sturdier or consisted of better alloys, they might be induced to buy.

Well, it didn't work. We were interested in finding out first what an engineer sees in his job. What is it that induces him to become an engineer? We discovered that when we permitted him to talk about his life goals first, he would open up much more rapidly and we would discover a lot of interesting factors. There are various types of engineers: those who consider themselves very systematic, those who consider themselves adventurous, others who consider themselves creative, and still others who just love to play the role of Goliath, who just have to work with enormous things. There are others again who are craftsmen. Like the German craftsmen, they are psychologically compulsive, insisting on minute detail and minute accuracy. They prefer only those jobs that permit them to express the compulsion to work on minute details.

We found we could get the engineer to feel a relationship to the products of the other nine divisions of this large company if we could prove to him that we understood him. In other words, the ad, instead of talking about a boiler, for example, could ask, "What kind of engineer are you? Do you like to do the following things? Well, we do too."

The ad might emphasize the importance of minute details in all the company's other divisions. It would indicate to the engineer that the company was speaking the same language in all ten divisions, the engineer's kind of language, despite the physical dimensions of the product, whether a brake shoe, a boiler, or a pump. In connection with inducing purchasing agents to decide between using glass or tin for the packaging of their product, we gained more insight into the engineer's motivations. The glass company had carefully prepared exact data on the advantages of glass, and the tin company on the advantages of their product. We found that while the engineer or the purchasing agent pretended he was being impressed by these engineering data, the depth interview uncovered his true underlying motivation: He either liked glass or he didn't like it, and the same went for tin. If he didn't like glass, he'd give you a number of rash arguments against the use of it—each one of them defeating the rational argument that the company had presented in defense of glass.

The motivational approach to industrial advertising was not so much to collect more data on the advantages of using glass for this particular packaging problem as to sell the engineer on glass and to make him love it.

Here as elsewhere we find a complete parallel between the psychology of the engineer and the purchasing agent and the consumer. You may remember, for instance, what happened in the detergent field when one manufacturer developed the concept that no rinsing is needed. In many of our surveys, we found that most of the housewives continued to rinse anyway. They just didn't think it was proper to wash clothes without rinsing afterward, no matter how many impressive engineering data the detergent industry provided. As often as they told the housewife, "You don't have to rinse or soak. This is a different product, this is a detergent," the housewife would reply, "Yes, I know, but what's wrong if it makes me feel better to rinse anyway?" This reaction was so common that at one point the detergent industry simply had to give up and tell the housewife, "Go ahead and rinse if it makes you feel better." It is only after many years that the "no rinsing" claim is finally being accepted.

I would like to cite another illustration of consumer reaction. Several years ago it was discovered that the housewife likes cake mixes and piecrust mixes, etc. because they permit her to retain an interesting kind of illusion—the illusion of doing it herself without actually having to go through all the trouble of preparing the cake. She would have been even more enthusiastic, more intrigued, and more influenced if the cake-mix industry had given her permission to add fresh eggs to the mix. In other words, she needed a rational excuse for her self-indulgence. It was as if the air-conditioning industry had come up with an advertising appeal that stated, "Now you can open your windows with our modern air conditioners. You can enjoy fresh air at the same time." The housewife had strong misgivings about using the mix. This is typical of what the average housewife said: "Yes, I'm using a cake mix; it saves me a lot of trouble but I really shouldn't." The industry recognized this feeling of guilt and said, "All right, if you feel that bad about it, add your own eggs." Now the housewife felt very happy because she could use the cake mix and still express her individuality.

SEXUAL CHARACTERISTICS OF MACHINERY

In one study, we discovered that tractors and steam shovels take on sexual characteristics when filtered through the engineer's emotions. One recalls such terms as "male" and "female" applied to nuts and bolts. Most engineers and technicians refer to engines by female names. "She is a beauty, isn't she?" says the driver of a steam shovel, irrationally revealing that he is not interested only in the engineering features. We also found that power in an engineering product can create a different kind of irrational reaction: one of fear. An ad that says, "Our 2D4, or our steam shovel, or our caterpillar tractor can lift two tons of these boulders" will frighten both the reader and the potential driver. The latter is confronted by an enormous beast, a sub-human monster, and he's really scared. This is not psychological myth-making but a conclusion drawn from a considerable amount of insight into the motivations and attitudes of a driver or steam-shovel operator. But if you have the steam-shovel driver in your ad it should say "Come on and sit down next to me. How would you like to lift two tons of rock? All you have to do is lift this little lever," and you have changed the relationship between the machine's power and the driver's own power in a very radical and exciting fashion.

An enormous job that looms ahead in the whole industrial field has to deal with this acceptance and integration of size and power. The average German, before and during the war and even now, refers to "my" or "our Krupp works." I have not met many Americans who say "our General Motors." That applies not only to General Motors, but to every industry. The intriguing, vital aspect of it is the necessity of inducing the individual consumer (whether he be an engineer or a purchasing agent or a housewife) to participate in the strength and growth of large companies. As long as that has not been achieved, the individual is much more likely to be frightened by strength than if he considered it his own.

We have conducted a number of surveys, in the shelter field, one for the red cedar shingle industry, another for a lock company. We interviewed architects, builders, contractors. Again, we found very rational individuals, people who study tables, people who are experts, people on whom you want to rely when you build your home, your factory, etc. We found that they are just as emotional as anyone else.

BASIC MOTIVATIONS FOR BUILDING A HOME

In a study on the use of red-cedar shingles and in the one we conducted for the Qwik-Set Lock Company, we were interested in the basic motivations for building a home. Interestingly enough, most people when building a home are guided by the desire to be rational about it. They study architectural books, they make plans, they discuss in great detail how they can save money, how they can build a beautiful house that will not require much upkeep. We found that most of us, including the architect and the contractor, are influenced by the completely erroneous assumption that most of our houses are built for eternity. You only build a house once, you might as well put the best possible materials into your home. Our studies showed that the average length of time that we live in a home is somewhere between ten and fifteen years. If this factor had been recognized right at the beginning, when the individual was contemplating building, a completely different choice of materials and of architectural forms would have had to be introduced. This kind of information proved very valuable to the contracting and shelter industry because, having convinced their customers that they are going to occupy their house not for the next hundred years, but only for a relatively limited time, they can more easily sell the customer on the idea of beauty and emotion in building.

The architect or the builder very often found himself in this kind of conflict. When considering the recommendation of red-cedar shingles and shakes, he was supposed to be rational in his choice of materials. He was asked by his customers, "What is the most practical way of building a house, what's the most economical way?" His answer should have been, if he were honest, "A steel-reinforced poured concrete box is the most practical, the most economical, the most durable house that you can possibly have." Yet he was forced to introduce right from the start irrational elements such as beauty, and so forth.

We found the whole industry had made the mistake of believing in this so-called rationality of the architect. When we asked the builder or architect what guiding principles he followed in recommending materials, he usually answered, "Efficiency, economy, durability, low upkeep, etc." and the red cedar people proceeded to advertise accordingly. They claimed that their shingles and shakes were very efficient, very economical, etc. Unfortunately, they really are not. Red-cedar shingles and shakes are not the most economical, nor are many other materials the most economical. They are, however, very beautiful. They are very likable. They have a very definite emotional quality about them. What the red cedar shingle industry had done was to rely on superficial answers and to proceed to advertise accordingly, and by doing so they invited very unfavorable comparisons.

Their new approach represents a complete change. It emphasizes the product's beauty. It discontinues the former emphasis on efficiency, durability, and economy. It is not directed at the consumer but at the builder and contractor. It gives the customers "moral permission" to be emotional about the things they want in their homes.

This wholistic approach can also be applied to the political field. Less attention is being paid to the political views of a candidate than to his total philosophy, his personality, and the degree of identification that the voter can achieve with him. He reacts to the candidate's melody in the *Gestalt* sense, rather than to the individual notes.

During the elections of 1948, we conducted a number of experiments in our laboratory. Instead of asking people which candidate they would vote for, we showed them photographs of the three candidates and asked them to listen to records of their voices. Then their emotional reactions to each one of the three candidates—Dewey, Truman, and Wallace—were determined by depth interviewing. These experiments showed that Truman stood out, and that he represented the underdog; he had made many mistakes but people considered him only human in his erring. As some people said, "I can understand how he must feel. It is almost as if I had been called upon to be President myself."

Women in particular stated that they felt a motherly feeling toward him, wanted to protect him and give him a chance to make good. The general feeling of warmth and sympathy, though not necessarily admiration, was in complete contrast to those attitudes the people expressed toward Dewey, whom they considered to be distant. The emotional factors may very well have been the ones that determined the election in favor of Truman. These feelings, however, are of such a nature that they would not easily be brought up to the surface. Deep probing was necessary in order to get at the real emotional factors deciding people's actions.

When scientists go out and try to predict people's behavior in elections, or any actions, such as buying, they rely upon the *status quo* for making predictions for future developments. This is very dangerous, because human nature is basically dynamic. Therefore, politicians, businessmen, or advertisers who have learned to go beneath the surface, who accept the fact that human beings are basically irrational, and understand the basic needs and desires of people, will have a better chance to succeed. What Truman did, either by instinct or by sound psychological advice, was to discount the overwhelming statistical facts, the rational data given him, and seek out those deeper appeals of a broader emotional nature which lay hidden from the eyes of the professional pollsters. He built his campaign on the dynamic nature of the human personality rather than on static facts. Thus, he won.

In some interviews which we conducted, we found that the following interesting psychological process took place in people's minds. As one New York business girl put it, "At first, I was firmly convinced that I would vote for Dewey, and this was the answer I would have given any public-opinion interviewer. In the last two or three weeks, however, a peculiar series of thoughts and feelings took place in my mind. Apparently I did not want to admit them to myself, but now in our discussion, it seems to become more and more clear. I read all the reports about how the Dewey election was completely assured and how the pollsters had stopped asking any more people because they felt Dewey's election was in the bag. Not a single newspaper seemed to have any doubts about the outcome of the November 2 election. It slowly crept up on me that I was being discounted. I, an individual voter with a mind of my own! It seemed that all the pollsters considered themselves so much smarter than I, and they just took my vote for granted. I think I voted as much against the pollsters in the end as I voted against Dewey."

Many other examples can be given. In various studies which we have done in the field of proprietary drugs, we found the following: The success of these remedies depends to a very large extent on their psychosomatic effects; i.e., more on our belief that the remedy will work than on the physiological powers which it intrinsically has. What the human mind asks for when it is supposed to accept the effectiveness of a remedy is some tangible and immediate proof. It is peculiar that this proof often has little to do with the effect. The example that best fits in here is that of the so successfully used appeals of Alka-Seltzer ads. "Listen to the fizz" is a promise that can be checked upon almost immediately. You drop it in the water and sure enough, it does fizz. Few people ever questioned what the fizzing actually had to do with the intended effect of Alka-Seltzer.

In some research which we did for a stomach remedy, we found that when we suggested to people that they take the bottle and watch how the remedy coated the inside of it, we used exactly such an irrational appeal to create the conviction of the eventual efficacy of the remedy. It so happened in this case that the coating of the bottle could be in some logical way tied in with the coating of the stomach walls, which would thus prevent the acids from affecting them and produce a curative result.

TWO ■ STRATEGY IN A CONFLICT ERA

INTRODUCTION

When my son started his studies at the university, he came home with the complaint that the course in humanities which he was taking left him confused. He was reading extensively from Calvin and Luther to Plato and Thucydides. Yet what he was missing was the link between what went on in the world around him and the content of his erudite exercises in reading. What was labeled "contemporary civilization" had little to do with the contemporary world. Many of us are similarly confused. Yet I think it is possible to provide a key to the world around us. We have reached a stage where many of the thousand-year-old conflicts of humanity have finally reached a critical point. We have made progress at least to the extent that the conflicts have become visible and that more and more people are becoming aware of the necessity to find a solution. I am convinced that the techniques of the strategy of desire, the techniques of persuasion, are at our disposal to find solutions to these conflicts.

A. N. Whitehead states in his *American Essays in Social Philosophy:*

> Civilization is the victory of persuasion over force. Civilization is the maintenance of social order, by its own inherent persuasiveness as embodying the nobler alternative. Civilization also involves more than a mere knowledge or imitation of the best of the past; it involves freshness and novelty.

Throughout this book I have tried to demonstrate how such freshness can be achieved by new and better forms of thinking, by rejection of preconceived notions by the application of motivational thinking. Many of the examples given came from the commercial field, but it is in the larger issues of contemporary life where freshness of thinking really comes into its own. I see several such major conflicts which face us today. They apply equally to the immediate problems of the advertiser and businessman as to those of the more farsighted social philosopher. They can serve as a guide and key to understanding many of the events which pour in on us day by day.

Many of these conflicts have become obvious only now because of basic changes in our technological developments necessary to our fight for survival. These issues of our conflict era will be discussed in our following chapters.

Resolution of these conflicts can be brought about by education of mankind, by persuading it gradually and, often, against resistance. Eventually, however, infantile solutions will be replaced in favor of more mature and rewarding ones. How long it might take to reach these goals we do not know. Bit by bit we shall reach, through the continuous adventure of life and realization by the human individual of his utmost potentialities, the final goal: the evolution and birth of Man.

8 ■ THE PSYCHO-ECONOMIC AGE

There are so many continuing crises that we have become crisis-immune. We have decided that it is safer to live in capsules of individual isolation. We shrug our shoulders and try to get the most out of life. While on the one hand atomic energy and electronic developments make us more and more the masters of our environment, we become at the same time convinced that we have little influence as individuals over the economic and political developments of our time. We have been caught in one of the major conflicts of modern times: to know whether we are the masters or the slaves of our destiny.

Millions of Americans own stocks. To decide whether to sell or to retain stocks is only one of the minor forms of gambling we are forced to do in our modern world. Decisions on jobs, on our children's choice of a career, on whether or not to buy a house in a given neighborhood—all these require the wisdom of a Solomon and the ability to safely predict the future. Even the professional economist or historian has a hard time telling us what the future economic development of a given period is going to be.

There is scarcely an issue of a newspaper or magazine today that does not have one or more references to recession, inflation, or economic cycles. In explanation, one sees frequent references to "overstocked inventories," to the "erratic behavior of the stock market," to "consumer indebtedness," to runaway inflation, or oversupply of capital. These explanations of current situations have one thing in common: they make economic phenomena the supreme arbiter of man's destiny.

Such theories have a familiar ring. Where else does one hear that the relationship between supply and demand, the movement of merchandise and the functioning of various economic mechanisms have their own innate laws and developments? That prosperity, recession, depression are all predictable stages in the economic crises inherent in the capitalist economy? Where else except in the dialectic materialism of Marxism? In fact, according to Marx, our very lives, our achievements, and our failures, are really the result of materialistic developments.

It is disturbing to note that Americans, with their heritage of individual incentive and self-determination, have become fatalists who sit and wait for mysterious economic forces to determine their failure. Meanwhile, in the Soviet Union, where Marxist philosophy allegedly rules the nation, incentive and initiative are the chief weapons employed to change the course of human events. The Russians have five- and eight-year plans, they set themselves economic goals, they proclaim themselves masters of their destiny. They know what the future holds in store for them, because it is they who will determine their own future.

On the other hand, we in America accept the superstitious belief that magic forces control our lives, and we pray that our medicine men will assuage the threatening powers of evil forces and malevolent spirits.

If we wish to deal with economic and historical forces, we must begin by rejecting the fatalism we have absorbed from Marxist philosophy. We must accept the fact that crises and recessions, like prosperity, are man-made and that, to a large extent, they are the reflection of a people's psychology and of its outlook on life. There is nothing mysterious and there is nothing inevitable about the future. It is ours to mold.

Modern life, particularly in a democratic society, entails the necessity of making intelligent decisions. We must decide whether to remain in the same job or to change jobs, whether to buy a house or take out a mortgage, or whether to vote for one candidate or another. In all these and in other cases, intelligent decisions can only be made within the largest possible framework—the future of the nation and of the world. Whether I buy stock or real estate or take another job all depend on whether we are going to have prosperity or depression, war or peace. At the same time, the state of the nation and of the world depends to a very great degree on how each individual exerts his own personal influence. But if modern democracy is based on the ability of its citizens to make intelligent decisions, then it is one of the basic dilemmas of modern democracy that so many of us still reject our own power and importance in changing the destiny of the world.

Among the declarations of faith in the future is the act of buying. Each time we go out and buy a new car or decide to purchase a new suit, a pair of shoes, a house, we base our decision on a philosophy of life, a *Weltanschauung*. Buying is more than a commercial function. It deserves scientific study without moral judgment. If, for example, I believe that the world is heading for collapse or that the nation is on the verge of a long, drawn-out depression, I will buy less or I will buy differently than if I have a more optimistic philosophy. When I buy more or less expensive food, when I buy cheaper or more expensive cigarettes, when I curtail the quantity of my purchases, I am, in effect, underwriting a life philosophy with my buying act.

If we were to rely exclusively on the fulfillment of immediate and necessary needs, our economy would literally collapse overnight. For our economy is one of psychological surplus, in both consumption and production. Fifty per cent of the people in this country and in many others could get along without cars, and 80 per cent without television sets, movies, liquor, cigarettes, or candy. The real defenders of a positive outlook on life, the real salesmen of prosperity, and therefore of democracy, are the individuals who defend the right to buy a new car, a new home, a new radio.

When I argue with a car salesman that I must postpone the purchase of a new car because I fear a depression, or inflation, it is up to him to sell me not only the new car but, even before that, *to sell me a positive philosophy of life*. He must sell me the idea that things are going to be good, not bad. More than that, it is up to him, and to me, to make things good rather than bad, to prove that we are not living in a world controlled by dialectical materialism, but in a world built on individual initiative.

When the President of the United States says it is up to the individual buyer to assure continued prosperity, or control inflation, he is on sound psychological ground. But he does not indicate exactly how this kind of positive attitude can be created. It is precisely here that I feel that we, the experts in communication, can make our contribution by applying the techniques of the social sciences. We cannot content ourselves with making demands and statements about what people ought to do. Rather, it is our job to make concrete recommendations which will assure the development of the positive attitude on which prosperity is based.

BUYING IS AN EXPRESSION OF CREATIVENESS

Most people like to shop. When we ask them, however, why they bought a product, the answer implies a need. A much more important aspect of buying is that it gives a person the chance to be creative. In other words, every time we go out and shop for something, we are really trying to express our own creativeness in as easy a form as possible. Our products have become more and more reliable from a technological viewpoint; a GE refrigerator is not very different from a Frigidaire, as long as I pay about the same amount of money. What I do buy, then, is the personality, the image, the size of the product and brand: what it can do for me psychologically and not just technologically.

I think this factor is a very important one and should not be too easily overlooked; every time we go out, we do so really to prove to ourselves that we have the power to express our innermost desires by the selection of a specific type of merchandise. It is important for the advertiser to be aware of this, and to leave a wide enough margin in the various ways he offers his merchandise for the customer to derive the feeling that it is, after all, his own cleverness, imagination and creativeness that makes him choose and decide the way he does.

$3,000 FOR ONE-HALF HOUR OF FUN

It sounds fantastically expensive, and yet there are millions of people who do exactly that. They spend large amounts of money for a few minutes of fun. Don't laugh at them. Most likely you have done the same thing. You may have bought a car recently. Sure, the old one was not safe any longer, or it looked bad. Are you sure, however, that this was the real reason for your purchase? Didn't you buy it finally from the dealer who promised you delivery this Saturday?

Was not the real reason the fact that you could drive it over the weekend, this weekend, right away?

Most car salesmen know that immediate delivery, and weekend delivery in particular, gets them the sale many times. The first few moments of the weekend, right after the car had been delivered, when you started it and drove around the block or down the street, were moments more pleasant and full of satisfaction than any others. Never again will the same pleasure be duplicated. You bought your car for the intense enjoyment of those ten minutes. In a study which we did for a large car manufacturer, we found that most people enjoyed a thrill and satisfaction with their very first car, right after its acquisition, no matter how old a jalopy, which was never equaled again.

When an executive buys a dictating machine, his eagerness to learn all about it, to try it out, to hear his own voice, has no bounds during the first half-hour after it has been delivered to him. Another example is your television, black-and-white or color. Did you not attempt to reach home earlier the day you knew it was to be installed? Did you ever again feel that same high-pitched thrill that you did those first few minutes on the first evening when the picture flashed on the screen right in your own home?

Most people react the same way in this respect. The modern communicator can learn much from this fact of human nature. The utilitarian and economic technical aspects of his product are far less important as motivations than those first few minutes of intense enjoyment. They have such an irresistible attraction that we feel we have to have that new fountain pen, or that new golf set right away. We can't stand another day without it. There is hardly a product which does not promise such moments of intense gratification to be dramatized and used as buying motivations.

It is not surprising that these first minutes of enjoyment are so strong. There is a deeper significance. Every new acquisition represents an enrichment of our personality. What we experience so vividly is the process of integration and incorporation of a new pleasure, a new wisdom, in our stockpile of accumulated knowledge which spells the meaning of life for us. What takes place in a few minutes when the new purchase is unwrapped and put to use for the first time, has psychological consequences which last for the rest of our lives.

One of the reasons why people like gadgets so much is anchored precisely in this desire for creativeness.

The advertiser too often makes the mistake of wanting to get the credit for himself even at the expense of his commercial success. That he wants this compliment of having manufactured a clever piece of merchandise is only further proof of the powerful attraction of such a feeling of creativeness. However, if he does so without permitting his customers to feel like the discoverer, he very definitely harms his sales.

In a study which we did for a large insurance company, we found that exactly this kind of mistake had been made. They had been running a series of newspaper ads in which the benefits of life insurance as an American institution were constantly dramatized. When we tested the reactions of people to this form of advertising, we found that it aroused resentment. Of course, they expressed this resentment by directing it against life insurance companies, but actually it was an expression of these feelings: "Do they think they are the only smart ones? If I have to succeed in life, make a go of it, that's my benefit. That is my merit. I did it. It is I who selected the life insurance plan and incorporated it into my over-all foresightedness and life management. Therefore, it is I who should get the credit for acquiring security and an income after sixty-five" and so forth.

This life insurance company had used the wrong psychological approach because of their own desire to reap the compliments for the ingenuity of their merchandise. Instead, later on, they followed our advice—to permit the reader of the advertisement and purchaser of life insurance to be proud of his own ingenuity and discovery.

Wherever a communicator, whatever his message, approaches his task in the same fashion, being too obviously proud of his own skills and the message he offers, without giving the recipient credit for the choice, he is making a vital mistake.

In a study we did for the Chrysler Corporation, we found that whenever a car was displayed in the showroom in such a fashion that the prospective buyer could see himself in a large mirror while sitting in the car, sales were much easier. In other words, what impressed the buyer was not only the quality of the car but the dramatic realization of what the car would do for the buyer, and how smart his choice would prove to be from his own viewpoint.

This is particularly true in the field of fashion. Who does not know those moments of anxiety when, after having shopped for either a dress or a hat, or in the case of a man, for as unimportant a product as a tie, one had to expose one's choice to the criticism of the family? "You certainly do have good taste." "Where did you find this?" "Isn't this darling!" "My, how cute!" All these types of reactions are really nothing more than expressions of admiration, and compliments on the creativeness of the buyer.

THE MOMENT THAT SELLS

Buying does not consist of a single step. Instead, it is a continuous drama. Similarly, taking possession of a product also represents a drama. Among the many acts of buying a car and finally owning it, which is the most important one? Is it the second when the family settles down in the car and you go on your first long ride? Is it the moment the car is put in the garage? Is it the time you first give your car a good wash? Or is it when you take possession of it by filling the glove compartment with your personal belongings?

When writing a communication, whether on safety or on products, or when preparing a television commercial, it is very important that the most pregnant moment be chosen in illustrating the action and the drama of possession. The moment that convinces and sells is not necessarily the one that shows the product or the problem at its peak performance, or in the most dramatic sequence. It is much more frequently the one that is closer to the human heart. In buying tools, for example, or even books, it is not necessarily the use of the tool or the reading of the book that presents the most exciting aspect. Placing the book on its preassigned space on the shelf, hanging the tool next to the others in your workshop, often represent more exciting psychological moments. It is not the accident illustration that "sells" safety, but the safe return. Unwrapping and uncrating a new dishwasher or washing machine can often be more exciting than the white glamor of the machine installed in the kitchen.

In some of our own studies, we found that it isn't the finished cake that is the most dramatic moment in the baking process, but the few seconds during which the cake is being pulled out of the oven. Did it come out all right? is the question that is answered at that time.

This problem of selecting the right moment to tell the story and invite identification and rehearsal of the purchase is a problem that is not new. In a famous discussion by Theodore Lessing, the German poet and art critic, entitled *Laokoon,* he deals with the question faced by a Greek sculptor of which moment to choose in the battle between a serpent and a Laocoon and his sons. Should he picture the second when the serpent is about to attack, and the father and sons are stricken with horror? Should he choose the moment when they are battling with the snake? Or should he choose the moment when the struggle is over and they have fallen prey to the monster?

The writer, the propagandist and persuader, the art director, often are faced with a similar problem. Here are several rules that psychologists can provide on how to choose the moment that sells:

1. *The moment chosen must permit projection into the future.* The listener must be capable of visualizing what will happen during the next few minutes or hours. The family seated in a car about to go on a trip leaves a chain of associations in the reader's mind, permitting him to visualize to a certain extent the experiences of this family in the new car.

2. *Insight into the past.* The family could also be shown having come home from a long, exhausting, but wonderful trip in the new car, getting out of the car, the kids bringing their treasures into the house, such as minerals, flowers, etc. Again the reader would be capable of seeing into the past as to what has happened before.

3. *Sudden recognition must be provided.* A "Gee, that's true" kind of feeling must take place. Many of *The Saturday Evening Post* covers do exactly this. When, in a scene, parents are shown admiring the landscape and the view from a skyline drive, but the kids instead are studying comics without paying attention to the beautiful scenery, the reader gets an immediate "aha" experience. "Yes, this has happened to me, too. I've never expressed it as sharply, but I remember, I can recognize myself."

4. *There must be a hidden message.* A photographer could go out

and take a picture of Sutton Place South in New York City, an elegant neighborhood. This could be a simple realistic portrait of the buildings and the people living there. The same photographer, however, could go out and show a very elegant lady with a tiny Mexican dog walking in front of the buildings. The same caption—Sutton Place South—would suddenly take on an entirely different meaning or, better, the right kind of meaning: utter elegance. This message would be understood by the reader. A photograph or an ad with a real message would have been achieved, the moment that sells would have been chosen.

We know that interest in ourselves overshadows almost everything we do, and yet, one advertiser who consulted us had not been alert enough to take this into consideration. Our advice to him, once we had proved this, was to pay special attention to the psychology of the housewife when she enters the store, and to acknowledge officially that housewives are individuals. A practical translation of this analysis is not as difficult as it may seem at first. One ad, for example, simply said, "What mood are you in today, Mrs. Brown?" We then went on to describe the various moods housewives usually and normally feel. Some days they feel like splurging, and other days they have inferiority feelings about their homemaking abilities. They feel that they have been spending too much money and have not been careful enough in their buying. On still other days they feel that shopping is a nuisance; it is very unrewarding as an activity. Our approach resulted in attracting more shoppers. They felt that they were being treated as individuals.

The drugstore of the future, the restaurant of the future, will be, in my opinion, places where the individuality and personality of the consumer will be taken more and more into consideration. Service and personal attention rather than marvels of technical gadgetry will become all-important.

Buying can also be a form of escapism. It gives us the illusion that we can control our destiny. People often go out and buy something to get rid of a frustration. Particularly when things seem to close in on you and you feel there is very little you can do, going out and spending money gives you the belief that you are not completely helpless. When buying insurance, for example, we have found that people often feel that they are less likely to die or less likely to have an accident when they carry coverage.

We have done many studies on liquor. It is a product that is consumed to help people solve many conflicts. Interestingly enough, we found that even when you are drunk, you do not really run away from your difficulties; you often begin to face them for the first time. It is then that you confide in the bartender and tell him about your resolution to quit your job or ask for a raise. The simple explanation for drinking is that it is a form of escapism. Yet we face our problems, rather than escape them, when we are drunk. Some individuals only then have enough courage to think of decisive steps to solve them.

Other forms of escapism, such as watching TV or going to the movies, often have a similar motivation. They are really attempts to solve our problems, to change from fatalists and gamblers to people who plan and find solutions. We are looking for lessons in living all around us. Even a TV comedian provides answers to our problems of living. When he makes fun of taxpaying, exaggerates the fights of a married couple, as Jackie Gleason did, for example, he makes it easier for us to face our own marital problems.

Many of our daily activities can, therefore, be understood as manifestations of this conflict between actively deciding on the proper procedure or letting things take their course.

We can look around ourselves and understand advertising and its effectiveness as proof that people would rather be influenced than to make up their minds by themselves. Consumers Union and government-controlled brand-grading and listing of ingredients are attempts to provide the public with the facts on which intelligent buying decisions could be based. But what happens? We study all the technological data which tell us that Brand X is the best one, but we don't like the color or the salesman is not friendly enough and our logical resolutions are gone with the wind and we buy exactly the brand that Consumers Union advised us against. It seems that the more facts we are given about cigarettes and lung cancer, the more we smoke.

It is much easier for most of us, when we buy something that we really should not have bought, to blame the salesman or advertising and, in the last few years, motivational research, than to admit that it was our own stupidity or vanity which persuaded us and seduced us.

When the quiz scandals became a national topic, few people admitted that it was their own gullibility and their own support of these programs that made them possible and successful. They searched instead for scapegoats in the contestants, the producers, and in TV networks.

The realization that we ourselves are the forgers of the swords which serve us as weapons in our life, that we are the masters of our own destiny individually and nationally, is one of the most difficult to accept. Possibly the present historical struggle between free enterprise and communism is but another variation of the same conflict. Communism gives you the illusion of relieving you of individual responsibility. Everything is planned, you do not have to gamble and speculate as in the Western world. You do not have to worry about inflation or depressions. When I was in India not too long ago and discussed with some Hindu friends the possibility of asking all the people living in a given block in Bombay, for example, to clean up this area, to put all the holy cows in a corral and to create a self-help organization, I was laughed at. The only thing that would achieve this, I was told, is communism. These people have to be forced to do this. You will never succeed in getting them to do anything voluntarily, they are born fatalists.

To convince and persuade people to become the controllers of their own lives, to manage themselves and their country from the bottom up, is possibly another important job for the new field of applied and goal-directed persuasion and motivational techniques.

KEEPING UP WITH THE INNER JONESES

In various researches we carried out in Australia we discovered that this country was rapidly upgrading its standards. Roll-your-own cigarettes, harsh tobaccos, and rougher "out back" forms of living were rapidly being replaced by more refined forms of living in many fields.

In the United States we found repeatedly that while Americans did not mind at all being publicly accused of BO, halitosis, and similar unpleasant afflictions twenty years ago, they had become so refined in the "acculturation" process that such advertising scares had to be replaced by more refined and subtle hints at these conditions in order to be still effective. Lifebuoy soap changed its odor and its color.

Carrying this analysis of the acculturation process still further, we have made an interesting observation. There is a definite trend in this country to worry less about the impression left on friends, the "outer Joneses" and the groups of your peers, than on whether or not we are living according to our genuine standards, the standards of our inner Joneses. Happiness is beginning to be more discussed than success. It may be the result of an affluent society, but it is a fact nevertheless.

It is much less common for a man to be proud of the fact that he works twelve hours daily than to mention the achievement of getting away from his work every so often for complete relaxation. Not too long ago, *Life* magazine ran an article on people who had retired at an early age, anywhere from forty-five to fifty, and loved it. Such an article might not have been possible twenty years ago. We would have considered such early retirement improper and almost immoral.

Suburbia probably has been the first area to adapt to inconspicuous consumption at least in a certain number of living patterns. Few men or women there, for example, dress up particularly when visiting over a weekend. Leisure clothes are the rule. The older the hat or the pants, the prouder the man.

Unusual hobbies and trophies from foreign lands are displayed, the more different and the less easily duplicated the better.

Baking bread at home, sewing our own clothes have become more important than ever. A pattern company for which we studied the problems of the psychology of sewing was advised by us to concentrate particularly on the younger generation. Contrary to the logical and historical expectation, it was the young girls who represented the most important market for sewing patterns.

Swimming pools, as we saw in a study for the Esther Williams Company, are now much less a status symbol than a way of discovering a new life for the family, changing daily habits in a radical fashion.

Conflicts and changes in what we call the "expressive status power" of various products take place continuously. Such a change occurred recently as far as cars are concerned. While they represented for a long time definite status symbols, these have gradually shifted over to such things as swimming pools, homes, lawns, hi-fi, which in turn are losing their own status value. Each new development, invention, and discovery changes the natural and potential sum of human wealth and makes necessary a rearrangement of the relationship between the groups and the individuals within that particular environment. Every time new ideas in mechanical things are introduced and accepted, someone has to invent or change custom, habits, laws, codes, and conditions by which the group has lived before the new invention arrived. Social status symbols and values of classes can, therefore, be considered to be continuously changing—in contrast with what Vance Packard states in his book *The Status Seekers.*

I feel there is evidence that the middle class in this country is taking over and engulfing all other classes. Within this middle class, however, a wide range of possibilities of expressing oneself does exist. The changing values and expressive powers of products stem more from such factors as the age of a product and psychological reasons. Our taste and values change. We are discovering more and more what we could call the tenets and directives of the inner Joneses. We are much less inclined to copy other people.

THE NEW MIDDLE CLASS AS BUYERS

Since the beginning of World War II, the bulk of purchasing power in the United States has shifted to the middle class. Because of a complex variety of factors, economic and social, the upper class and the lower class alike have become severely restricted in size and, in the case of the lower class, in purchasing power. The public for almost all ideas and products must, therefore, be defined within the limits of the present middle class.

Since the war, and especially during the past five years, the middle class has undergone two very important changes:

1. Its actual and proportionate size has increased tremendously.
2. This increase has derived from what were formerly the upper and the lower classes. More and more, the middle-class income bracket, limited formerly to white collar, professional, and managerial

workers, is being extended to include craftsmen, skilled and even unskilled laborers, technicians, etc.

We find that the individuals comprising this large new middle-class group come from families which, prior to the war, were generally economically deprived. In addition to economic deprivation, these families were not instilled with those traditions which are symbolized by such products as sterling silver, furs, good furniture.

In a study conducted by us for the Silversmith Guild, this change in class status was found to relate to the symbol of sterling in the following way:

1. Of those respondents who now own sterling silver, almost 90 per cent were middle-class members *prior* to the war; i.e., they are members of that middle-class group which we categorize as "permanent."
2. Ignorance of sterling is found, almost without exception, only among respondents new to the middle class, the recent middle class.

The symbolic value of sterling silver is not part of the heritage of the recent middle class. Respondents were asked to rate five products used in setting a table in terms of their importance to today's housewife; i.e., they were asked to choose one of the following statements as being most appropriate to the item under consideration:

1. "She probably wouldn't want it under any circumstances."
2. "It wouldn't matter much to her one way or another."
3. "She'd consider it very important to have in the home."

These statements may be assumed to represent negative, neutral, and positive attitudes respectively. Four of the five items were traditional symbols of status, the fifth (stainless steel) was included, first, to conceal this intent of measuring traditional symbols by the inclusion of a uniquely modern one and, secondly, for comparison with sterling flatware.

THE NEW MIDDLE CLASS LEARNS MIDDLE-CLASS VALUES

Recent middle-class members acquire values, attitudes, and behavior appropriate to their new class membership.

We find that there is occurring an increasing dependence upon ways other than the traditional ways of acquiring such values and attitudes. In projective tests, we asked respondents to check any of seven ways in which they were guided in buying household articles, with the following results:

DIFFERENCES BETWEEN PERMANENT AND RECENT MIDDLE-CLASS MEMBERS IN CERTAIN DETERMINANTS OF PURCHASING

	PERMANENT MIDDLE-CLASS MEMBERS	RECENT MIDDLE-CLASS MEMBERS
Advice of relatives	82%	36%
Sees in friends' homes	78	28
Interior decorators, professional advice	64	38
Magazine articles	62	67
Women's pages in newspapers	52	84
Radio and TV programs	40	91
Newspaper advertisements	38	65

(Totals exceed 100% because multiple answers were permitted.)

An analysis of this data reveals a highly significant difference between the two groups. Whereas the permanent member of the middle class depends largely upon personal relationships in order to decide upon household goods that would be appropriate to her class membership, the recent member of the middle class turns to impersonal sources. Young wives and even older women who were reared on a lower social stratum learn their etiquette, dinner recipes, clothes, conduct and, especially, the products that are to symbolize their class membership, from radio and TV programs, women's pages in newspapers, magazine articles, and newspaper advertisements, rather than from relatives, friends, or professional advisers.

Thus, the recent middle-class member does not, and indeed cannot, depend upon the primary channel for the communication of traditional values, the instructions of parents, relatives, and friends, for acquiring the knowledge necessary to her new role.

The new middle-class member must learn whole new sets of complex values, attitudes, and behavior, and because her sources of information are often in disagreement among themselves, she is frequently insecure regarding the "right" thing, the "right" symbol, the "right" manner of behavior.

THE NEW MIDDLE CLASS CHANGES MIDDLE-CLASS VALUES

While it is true that the new middle class must study new values and absorb them, it is also true that, to some extent, where the recent and the permanent middle-class members come into contact and intermingle, traditional middle-class values may be modified.

We find, in this as in other studies, that some of these changes occur in terms of homemaking. *Traditional* symbols of status and prestige are being replaced by *modern* symbols of status and prestige.

A DOMINANT CHARACTERISTIC OF TODAY'S MIDDLE CLASS

The single characteristic that may be said to dominate today's middle class, whether permanent or recent, is prosperity, both as an objective reality and a subjective experience. People not only are more prosperous, they feel more prosperous.

It is again a psychological truism that *economic status* has little meaning for most individuals unless it can be translated into outward, concrete, *prestige status*. Thus, prosperity must be symbolized by the purchase of concrete articles that will say to the beholder, "Look, I am making money, I am prosperous, I have gained prestige."

In a study for a woman's magazine we found that these changes in prestige values and the conflicts involved are dramatized even more strongly by the role of the modern woman. The contemporary woman, as a representative of this middle class and as a buyer, is very different from her ancestors, both as an individual and as a consumer. Way back, as we know, woman's place was exclusively in the kitchen, in the home. She had to work very hard and live up to very exacting standards. If she didn't work like a fiend, she acquired a bad conscience and possibly a bad reputation. All that tended to make her feel guilty.

In the twenties and the thirties, the career woman emerged, wanting independence, fascinated by outside interests, and considering household chores as an inferior task in life.

Today's woman is a balanced type; she is a happy compromise between the two extremes. Once again she's interested in her home and is willing to do household work. At the same time, her horizon is considerably enlarged. She is interested in social action, in education, even in politics. This balanced type of woman is today's shopper. She is the person with whom manufacturers, retailers, and ad writers are dealing.

A knowledge of her psychology and a recognition of her motivations are extremely important to the status conflict of today. The findings of hundreds of our research studies show that the main motivations of today's balanced type of women may be summed up in the following four categories:

1. *Creativeness.* The modern woman, as it was stated, is returning to her home but in a new, more sophisticated status. She wants to cook and take care of her family, but, at the same time, she also joins clubs, reads books and magazines, and possibly holds down a job if she has to; at any rate, more likely than not, she's capable of holding down one.

This change expresses itself in very many ways as far as the woman's motivations as a consumer are concerned. She may spend less time in the kitchen and she may buy canned food, but *she makes up for it by greater creativeness.* She "doctors up" the ready-made food, she adds to it original ingredients, on occasions she tries to surprise her husband and her children with new combinations, new taste experiences. This desire for creativeness is not restricted to the kitchen. In home furnishings and decorations, and in many other areas, she similarly is interested in experimenting, in trying out new kinds of materials, in putting articles to unconventional use. In short, she doesn't work at drudgery in the kitchen or around the house any longer. She wants to put her new talents to good use around the home, she wants to feel that she is employing all those facilities which would be called to play in an outside career.

This is a very important point for people dealing with her. They must satisfy the woman's need for creativity and safeguard her pride in her achievements. The women don't want the manufacturer to say: "We are producing the world's most wonderful cake mixes. Try and see what delicious cakes you get." What the woman wants to hear is this: "You are a wonderful cook. Our cake mix will permit you to use your wonderful talent without drudgery. You are the one who does a remarkable job. We only furnish the tools."

This kind of approach awakens an enthusiastic reception; it also answers a basic need for creativeness.

2. *The Morality of Affluence.* The old-fashioned puritanical mortality condemned the housewife to constant hard work. She had to do everything herself, otherwise she was open to the charge of being lazy and not being a satisfactory homemaker and housewife.

The modern woman is still partly caught in this conflict, but she is emerging from it very rapidly. After an initial hesitation, she has accepted canned food, instant coffee, frozen foods, etc., and she saves herself from guilt feelings by the following line of reasoning, which is partly rationalization but partly quite sincere: "I am using frozen foods because they permit me to save valuable time which I must have available in order to fulfill my other functions as a mother and wife."

An important practical application of this motivation is that the advertiser must never tell the consumer that he is replacing her as a housewife, by labor-saving devices. Rather, he ought to tell her that he is liberating her from drudgery so that she can use her time in other equally important, equally moral activities.

3. *Partnership.* A third motivation which is emerging is the feeling on the part of the modern housewife that she is becoming much more of a partner in the whole family operation. The traditional division of labor between the two sexes has changed. Men are deeply interested in freezers and other household appliances. They are also more frequent shoppers in the supermarkets. Women, on the other hand, learn to tinker around the house, or, as we found in one of our gasoline studies, are increasingly the family drivers and are in contact with filling stations and mechanics. They also buy two thirds of the men's shirts.

All this is reflected in the very layout of the modern American home. The boudoir has disappeared, a fact which has an important bearing, for instance, on the sales of cosmetics. The housewife, the modern woman, doesn't have a room of her own any longer. To some extent, the husband still insists on his den, but even that isn't too strongly defended. *The walls are going down in the homes.* These are unified living concepts.

This whole changing concept of the relationship between the sexes has tremendously important consequences in every sphere of life. I remember a picture which offered an interesting example and illustration of this change in attitude. It was *The African Queen*, with Katharine Hepburn. In this film, Humphrey Bogart gets tired of fixing a broken propeller shaft and Katharine Hepburn says, "I'll go down and fix it." He looks at her and answers, "You can't." She asks, "Why not?" He replies, "Because you are a woman." She says, "What does that mean? You are tired, aren't you? All you need is a screwdriver and a wrench and I know how to handle them." He sort of hesitates, then looks at her, "Well, I guess so, I don't know, I just always thought women are not suppose to fix propeller shafts." With this, she goes down and fixes it.

Now this scene is a symbol of a whole new kind of concept. But where does this new concept come from? It is a result of our whole national evolution during the past three or four decades. It is a result of the wars, of depressions, inflation, and insecurities and crises and what not. You don't feel safe, you don't want to marry a sweet little creature who is just cute and helpless. You want a woman who can chip in, who can take a job, who can drive a car or who can drive a truck, if need be—who can be a partner. To this challenge the American woman has answered with great alacrity, great enthusiasm, great positiveness.

All our studies show that subconsciously the modern woman also transfers these desires for partnership to buying situations. She considers herself grown-up and mature; she wants to be told the truth. She knows an advertising slogan when she sees one. She wants to know the reason behind the manufacturer's moves. Why does he lower the prices; why is he putting out a new kind of product? You could put it this way: she is much less readily fooled, or if you want to be cynical, she has to be fooled in a different way. But from now on she will insist on being taken into confidence, on becoming the psychological partner of the firm, the brand, the manufacturer with whom she is willing to do business.

4. *Happiness and fun.* Another motivation of today's woman is

her conviction that life is here to be enjoyed. She is happiness-conscious and fun-conscious and I think that this fact has great influence on her economic attitudes. With all her realism and conscientiousness, she believes that she and her family are entitled to little extras, little luxuries, unexpected little pleasures.

There is an over-all feeling that life is too short and why postpone so many purchases? The typical young housewife is much less concerned now than she used to be with preserving every dollar. Instead of saving money, often she wants to save happiness—a very surprising, very interesting, and on the whole very healthy psychological development.

When she has a choice between the cheaper cut of meat and the more expensive cut, for instance, I believe that if she can afford it, she will buy the costlier one, provided she is certain that her family will get a kick out of the unexpected steak. Or she may say, "Have we had enough fun this year? Perhaps not quite. So let's have a vacation. It may cost us a thousand dollars, but if we have it, the vacation may be a safer investment than shares because nobody will be able to take it away from us; while the thousand dollars in shares may be lost through some combination of events we don't even understand."

I would say that she has a feeling that it is not right to do without certain things, that it is much more right to have things. And if the husband cannot provide them she may go out and get a part-time job herself or work at home for these extra luxuries.

In the promotion and advertising of many items, nothing is more important than to encourage this tendency to greater inner freedom and to give moral permission to enjoy life through the use of an item, whether it is good food, a speedboat, a hi-fi set, or a sports jacket.

We are being confronted by more and more such status conflicts. As time progresses I am confident we shall be more concerned with whether or not life has given us our share of inner satisfaction rather than simply the shallow trimmings of symbols of success.

9 ■ THE VISIONS BEFORE US

Several years ago we studied soap operas. The assignment was to find out why twenty million women at that time listened day in and day out to such continued stories as "Ma Perkins," "Joyce Jordan, M.D.," "Big Sister," etc. on the radio and on TV. One of the hypotheses was that women who listen to the stories must be different from women who do not. This was not the case. What we did discover, however, was that soap operas are not very much different from fairy tales, or, for that matter, from Shakespearean dramas or modern Broadway shows. Almost all forms of communication represent interpretations of real life. They act as a lens through which the reader or listener can see life as it really is. One of the conflicts of modern times is to look for a simple and clear interpretation of life through such a lens. When listeners were asked why they liked daytime serials, they said, "They are so true to life." Interestingly enough, the same criterion was used by women who were not interested in the serials. They say they do not like daytime serials because they are *not* true to life. We can assume, therefore, that this "true to life" quality in a story is of great importance.

What do people mean when they use this expression? Some listeners mean that these stories remind them of their own lives. Others who use this phrase may react like the naïve art critic, who likes a painting because he can almost reach out for the orange painted there. All these different meanings of "trueness to life" have, however, one common denominator. They all refer to the relationship between the life seen through the lens of literature, or art in whatever form, and real life.

Whenever we perceive literary matter, whether in the form of a movie, a book, or even personal verbal narration, we do so within the framework of a larger field of perception. This field varies with each different set of reactions. When we listen to a mystery story it is a different set of reactions from those we use when listening to a "true to life" story. Just as we apply different sets of criteria to a photograph and to a painting, our "psychological grammar" differs for a detective story and for a sophisticated psychological novel.

For instance, to apply the psychological grammar of "trueness to life" to a surrealist painting is usually a sign of misunderstanding of the artist's attempt. A layman who says that the watches shown in one of Dali's paintings are not well painted because watches do not look like that in real life merely makes himself ridiculous. This observer has applied the wrong psychological grammar to the painting.

In listening to literary content also, the subject tries first to determine the appropriate field in which his perception should take place. This field then enables him to apply the correct set of criteria.

There are many factors which can serve as signals or signposts to the observer in telling him what field to select. All of us to a great extent live our lives by the grace of literature. When we get married, for instance, we cannot help being reminded of some movie scene, or of some specific novel in which a detailed description of a marriage ceremony with its accompanying feelings has been given. Even if a person has never had any contact with literature in the common sense, he still will have heard neighbors and friends tell stories of their own lives. His parents may have described their own wedding to him. In other words, it seems as though the relationship between a tale and actual reality is of extreme psychological importance. Any form of reality probably has its counterpart—its literary portrayal on a lesser level of reality. We cannot act properly if we do not come as close as possible to real reality. Newspapers, TV, novels, dramas, all are portrayals of reality. We are afraid, however, to see things the way they really are.

Levels of reality, and the dynamic mechanism operating between two or more such levels, constitute the problem. There are certain basic differences between literary portrayal of life and actual occurrences which will have certain inevitable effects upon the modern citizen. Real life is not an entirely different level of reality from literary or other depiction of life situations. The difference is rather one of degree. In our normal everyday life, there are certain episodes which have a high degree of reality and others which are rather vague. We may have walked through a certain street many hundreds of times, but somehow never noticed it. Then one day we return from a long trip; we are more attentive than usual. It is only then that this street takes on reality of a higher degree for us. It is then that we really "experience" this street for the first time.

In his normal everyday life, the citizen probably lives on a relatively low level of reality. Or rather, the horizon of his reality is quite limited. Literature, in any form, through headline, dramatization, or accentuation, makes the individual aware of certain elements in his real world. Thus it widens his horizon of reality. Our communication forms put the accents on the relatively flat world of the citizen and make his field of life a structured relief.

At the same time, however, seeing the world on a different level of reality has several other effects. There is a direct relationship between the level of reality and the degree of difficulties we encounter in trying to reach our goals. Usually, the lesser the degree of reality, the easier it is to reach these goals. Dreaming takes place in a field of lesser reality; so do fantasy and illusion. Therefore we often find that goals which we cannot reach in reality can be reached easily enough in our dreams or our fantasies. The greater the blockage in the field of reality, the more we are inclined to strive toward a goal on a lesser level of reality. Fiction, no matter how true to life, is always on a lesser level of reality. Our interpreted world is easier to understand than a world in the "raw."

Our educational system should train us to see reality in as real a form as possible, at a time when we are not yet ready for it. But instead we are often forced into "good literature." Many people consider any form of complex literature an assignment, an unpleasant task, and have developed a sort of inferiority complex with regard to good literature. They consider it too complicated and too time-consuming for them. They reach, therefore, for anything that promises them the same type of satisfaction, but in an easier and more palatable form, and provides them with a more simplified view of the world.

What, then, is this psychological function of literature which the more primitive stories and presentations fulfill? It might help us to go back for a few moments to the historical origin of drama and stories. Whenever primitive people were in trouble, they invented games and ceremonials wherein their problems were dramatized in such a way that the desired solution was integrated into the general plot. The idea was to influence the gods, to show them how the mortal wanted to have his problems solved. It was like saying to the superhuman forces: "See? This is how I want you to arrange my destiny and my fate." Even now, peasants in the Balkan countries, for example, when they want rain, suggest to God in rituals and religious ceremonies the pouring down of rain. The original purpose of any fictional portrayal of life was to influence the powers that be to conform to our wishes. One explanation for the frequent "happy endings" in fiction can be found in this fact.

While the clear outlines of this original function of the drama have been largely blurred and covered up by the immense number of technical and literary improvements which have been added to the drama over the centuries, there is still enough left of this original purpose of fiction to permit us to draw the conclusion that, even now, much low-level literature fulfills the purpose of influencing the gods.

In an esthetic sense, such literature may be very poor. But we are not concerned here with esthetic evaluations as such. By referring even to daytime serials, or to who-done-its, or to Westerns, we do so because they serve the need which is served by any form of literature. This need stems from the factor of trueness to life. This trueness to life is so important that in itself it almost covers the whole field of the psychological role of literature. People want true-to-life stories. In other words, man has a psychological need of hearing about his own life, of finding it interpreted, explained, and analyzed. Different people have different means of fulfilling this same need. They read novels, they go to the theater. But they too want true-to-life stories; they want interpretation of life. A radio or TV drama is also an imitation of life, for a purpose; a true-to-life story with an intended effect. This effect is often not consciously intended by the script writer. At the same time, it is not directly evident to the listener, nor can it be attributed to any specific plot. It is more often a cumulative effect, created by all the media containing fictional material to which the listener is exposed during the course of his life.

All fiction of a true-to-life nature, and probably even other forms of it, help people to solve problems, just as literature of any form was originally intended to indicate the desired solutions of problems to the gods. In other words, it boils down to the fact that much communication is listened to as lessons in psychology. Very few people have ever received systematic training in psychology. We have rarely been taught in school, or elsewhere, how to live, how to get along with other people, how to educate children, how to solve marital problems, how to combat our own inertia, and how to meet other difficulties. At best, we have received a few such lessons in church, from parents or friends, or from books on popular psychology. The great mass of people has had to rely upon the opinions of parents, grandparents, etc., for solutions to such problems.

Literature fulfills the very important function of giving lessons in everyday psychology. They are actually the only types of psychological lessons with which the average person comes in contact. Here he learns how to behave in difficult situations, how to face crises, etc.

This importance entails definite responsibilities. If we could prove, for instance, that the TV stories were lessons in medicine, we would be most careful to see that these lessons were correct. The same concern should be shown when psychological lessons are being taught. Are they correct?

We must first determine what we mean by the term "correct." Despite many different psychological schools, there is pretty general agreement that to create insight on the part of the subject or patient into his own problems is desirable and correct. Any psychological lesson, in the correct sense, will intend therefore to achieve a satisfactory degree of independent thinking in the student. We should be trained not to accept stereotyped explanations of human behavior, but rather to consider the varied and manifold nature of each individual.

While the individual lessons about life and the world taught in modern communications are not necessarily wrong with regard to specific advice given therein, we must state that, unfortunately, they do not fulfill the requirement we have just established for correct psychological lessons. Most problems are solved in a relatively simple and stereotyped moralistic fashion, without taking individuality or the richness of actual life into consideration. Such a method of teaching is the more dangerous because it finds ready acceptance in the listener. Stereotyped, clear-cut solutions are always easier to understand than more complicated and subtler interpretations of difficulties. Stock responses are not too far removed from prejudice and narrowmindedness. Ready-made attitudes are always more convenient to accept and to apply.

It may sound exaggerated, but right here may lie one of the crucial problems of democracy. If daytime serials, TV fairy tales, and tabloid newspapers present stories with tremendous mass appeal, they tend to perpetuate mental laziness, stereotyped reactions, and stock responses. In a time of crisis like ours this is a disservice to democracy. Because it is not too far a step from the acceptance of stock responses of a moral nature, as they are offered in these media, to the equally blind acceptance of Fascist or Communist ideology.

A criterion for the positive or negative for the effect of communication, the lenses through which life is seen should be judged, therefore, by whether or not the average person has, by looking through them, been better enabled to cope with his life difficulties.

It would be utterly wrong, I feel, simply to reject these forms of literature. Why do people watch them? Because they fulfill a psychological need. If we want to replace them with what we all agree to be "better" material, we have to satisfy the same needs on a higher level. We can't tell a hungry man not to eat, but we can change his diet.

THE MONSTER INSIDE US

What are these needs that are satisfied? We conducted a study of horror shows and found the following: Horror films horrify and fascinate us because they show us forces out of control. What is horrifying is that the uncontrollable monster is, in many aspects, really ourselves. What is fascinating is that we would not really mind being a little bit out of control every once in a while, if only just to redress the balance.

Central to all horror films today is the unmotivated lethal impulse of some kind of monster and the total inability of these monsters to control it, as well as the almost total inability of society to control the monsters. Yet beneath the surface of these horror films there are cross currents which show us that the behavior of these creatures is really quite well motivated and that they are anything but powerless to control themselves. What's more, society itself is not as powerless as it seems.

Actually, these films are really concerned with the origins, the forces, the uses of power, and the evil and guilt which are a consequence of its use: the power of the creator—*Frankenstein*; the power of omnipotence—*The Invisible Man*; the power of brutishness —*King Kong*; the power of knowledge—*Dr. Jekyll and Mr. Hyde*; the power of resurrection—*Dracula.*

As for the motives of these creatures, they are living in worlds they never made, or at least worlds they could not possibly have anticipated. They are living through a somewhat exaggerated but nevertheless recognizably human predicament. Frankenstein's monster is the creature of a man who has played God. King Kong is a monster wrested from his preternatural world to become an exhibition in the world of men. Both Jekyll and the Invisible Man are men of science who unwittingly step on the toes of their creator. Dracula would rather be dead than undead. Their motives are their grudges against the forces which have turned them into monsters. The inability of society to act quickly to control these creatures is really a consequence of society's own guilt. And this guilt is a result of four factors:

1. A feeling of sharing the responsibility for the creation of these creatures.

2. An expression of a failure to act on the recognition of the essential humanity of these creatures.

3. The feeling that "there, but for the grace of God, go I."

4. Society's recognition of the monster in itself—"How like myself that monster really is."

A horror film embodies forces which are essentially ambivalent.

First of all, there is the monster upon whom a cosmic trick has been played. He is an essentially gregarious creature who is forced by the circumstance of his brutishness, ugliness, and other handicaps, to become a solitary creature. He is unloved by others and kills God's own creatures as a way of getting back at his true creator—whatever human hand has intervened. Even more agonizing is the fact that he has been made practically invulnerable. It takes a long time to kill this monster, and he feels that, too. But the invulnerability of God's other creatures is in their superior numbers. The monster can never kill all of us. What makes the creature ambivalent is his uncertainty about where the real evil resides. Is it he who is evil? Or is it his creator? At the end, perceiving his own monstrosity in the faces of his victims, he is taken in by their perceptions. He becomes the cause of his own undoing.

The other two ambivalent forces are society as it is represented in the film, and the audience watching the film. The film's society is a victim of both the monster without and the monster within. So it is with the audience watching the film. In the form of the monster, they have the vicarious and powerful expression of their own grudges against the powers that be; in the form of the monster's eventual punishment they have the vicarious and powerful expression of their own disapproval for their own impulses.

Today, in the age of the Sputnik, man turns to science for solutions he once found in spiritual experiences. In horror films, he finds a combination of scientific and mystical appeals: they provide a scientific aura, without offering the testing, the experimentation, and the proof which are the core elements of science.

It is perhaps unnecessary to point out that the audiences for horror films are as intelligent as those for any other form of entertainment. And so they will prefer good horror shows to poor ones. People in general will not turn off a horror show because it is a horror show, but because it bores them. If it is clever, they will watch it and come back for more.

Serving as a link between single members of their audiences and the outside world, mass communications have developed a particularly effective technique to present their material. To most people, especially to the majority who do not possess the power of mental organization and a complete system of references, the world as it surrounds them and confronts them is somewhat confusing and disturbing. There are no simple and clear-cut political and economic developments, there are no naïve dichotomies of good and bad people. Every single problem, when answered more thoroughly and truthfully, is loaded with "ifs." The very first people to use mass media—the storytellers—realized that they had to structure and simplify meanings of events in order to perform their functions. They introduced fairies and devised heroes and villains for the sake of young and older children; and the modern mass media—radio, film, television, newspapers, and magazines—found it wise to follow suit.

Every form of mass communications deals with this problem of structurization in its own peculiar way. The newspaper starts its short cuts to reality by means of its headlines, which are but structural scaffolds, while its columns are cubbyholes into which the rich but chaotic variety of life is neatly stacked.

All media are, therefore, biased in one form or another. They distort, they condense, they accentuate and emphasize. In doing so, they make life digestible, understandable, and interpretable. The real difference among various forms of literature and art does not lie in their content per se, but in the taste level, the level of abstraction and style which is used to get the message across. Fairy tales have good and bad people—villains and fairies and princes and princesses—just as a Shakespearean drama or a Broadway show does. The difference lies in the obviousness of the solutions, the flatness and primitiveness of the portrayal of the characters, the lack of depth in their motivations.

Viewing a painting, or reading a novel, or listening to a TV show, really consists, in a psychological sense, of a re-creation on the part of the audience of the original creative and artistic process necessary to interpret, condense, and digest the real world. The onlooker sees and follows in the same path as the artist who interpreted reality. There is almost a temporal element involved. The longer this participation with the artist can take place, the more enjoyable, the more pleasing the art is. If there is no interpretation, or the interpretation is understood in a split second, something like a psychological short circuit takes place. You are robbed of your pleasure. It is almost as if your companion at the movies kept nudging you all the time and explaining what was going to happen next. The pleasure in communication lies in participation. If this participation is short circuited, the pleasure disappears.

On the other hand, it is also possible to make interpretations so complicated and abstract that pleasure fails and communication becomes impossible.

The ability to go along with the artist at the level of abstraction and interpretation on which communication takes place best depends on the cultural background of the audience. It is this that is the true measurement of what psychologically could be called taste. The artist searches for the essence, the soul of the scene, the object, the motivation, the personality and character that he is portraying. In absolute music, in symphonies, the composer removes his acoustic portrayal almost completely from "realistic" sound. He comes much closer, however, to the essence of the message that he is trying to communicate. Simple music is more obvious. It portrays the sound of real life. Some people need this crutch of reality. They end up, however, without any new understanding or insight into the essence that the artist wanted to create.

Almost all media, therefore, on different taste and culture levels, are lessons in living, whether in dramatic form, in psychological textbooks, or through paintings or magazines. They represent attempts to cut through the confusing chaos of everyday life and get closer to the essence of living. Understanding this essence should contribute to understanding oneself and the art of living. Many practical problems have their answer in an understanding of this real process of communication. When a Committee on Intergroup Relations approaches us and wants to know how they can get policemen to like Puerto Ricans, one of the real answers and a very basic one is that this can only be brought about if we can get a policeman to understand the essence, the soul, of a Puerto Rican and vice versa.

THE NEED FOR STRUCTURE

It is no accident that many mass media use strong black and white structurization. This desire for order even at the expense of truth is a basic human characteristic.

When we studied a plastic wrapping, we found that housewives were disturbed by the sloppy way it sealed in food. It was shown how meat, for example, could be kept fresh; no odor would escape or enter, etc., because of the quality of the wrapping. While everybody believed these claims, the disorderliness and lack of neatness of the package which resulted was so disturbing to the need for structure that the technological superiority of the product failed to attract customers. Later on neat, orderly packages were made and resulted in much greater receptivity.

Even from the beginning of kindergarten days we are taught in our lives to ritualize, to squeeze the unorganized day into strict rules. Clock time itself represents such ritualization. Almost to the end of our days we stay caught in this ritualization. One of the most interesting remarks made by Samoan leaders to me was that their brief visits within Western civilization were made particularly difficult by the existence of clocks. Time to them was unstructured. Western man is afraid of unstructured time.

Structure provides most men with a feeling of security. In many of our studies we found that particularly emotionally loaded situations have been ritualized by folklore, religion, and tribal customs. Such situations are marriage and death; almost every tribe, no matter how primitive, has developed a rigid control of these events. In the study we did for the Forest Lawn Cemetery we found that attempts to eliminate rituals during funerals aroused a lot of resistance. Rituals in many ways represent escape mechanisms. If things develop automatically, one does not have to worry about them. They take place without the involvement of the individual.

WHY WE LIKE WESTERNS

Westerns on TV represent an interesting aspect of ritualization of one phase of American life and history. They are basically morality plays, where everything is clearly structured into good and bad people. What are their appeals? We were asked to study them. Here are our conclusions:

Last year my fifteen-year-old nephew visited us for two months. It was his first trip from France to the United States. He hadn't been here more than twenty-four hours when he discovered American Westerns on TV. Had we permitted it, he would have sat in front of the TV set for six or seven hours a day watching one Western after another, despite the fact that he spoke hardly any English. At the end of his first week here, his rapt and enthusiastic addiction to Westerns remained untarnished, and I finally became accustomed to being greeted by a casual "*Bon soir,* boss" or "*Comment ça va,* podner" when I entered the house in the evening.

This is by way of pointing out the universal appeals of Westerns which cross age and economic and even language differences. By analyzing some of these appeals, we will have a clearer insight into our own motivations in watching, and secretly enjoying, Westerns. We may even let ourselves go and enjoy this form of entertainment without feeling guilty once we realize that Westerns are not really beneath us.

First of all, Westerns are an American Odyssey, an epic which never dies. Their characters are larger than life, as is always true of epic heroes. The Western is a typical folklore, a popular art. It is always formalized; its characters are always the same.

A second appeal which Westerns hold for all Americans is that they provide a common basis of identification with this country. Vast numbers of Americans are first, second, third-generation citizens. They have no real roots in this country compared to people who have lived in a European village for a thousand years. In their search for American roots, they adopt the West because the struggle for the West allows them an emotional identification with the past.

Westerns, moreover, incorporate certain moral values which are understood in all cultures. Superficially, they are all gunplay and noise. But the horse pounding across the prairie dust is carrying a hero who eternally fights "the slings and arrows of outrageous fortune." Heroism has an element of purity about it which is uplifting. A sophisticated world laughs at the knight in shining armor riding on a white horse. Nevertheless, something deep within it responds to pure heroism.

WESTERNS ARE MORALITY PLAYS

One might almost compare the Western with the morality plays of many lands. In the morality play, pure virtue is extolled and some of this virtue rubs off on an audience waiting to be reminded that these are the only worth-while and eternal moral values. The response to a morality play is something close to a religious experience, and the response to a Western embodies many of these qualities in a more remote and indirect way.

Because life today is inordinately complex, people feel a sense of frustration and hopelessness when they consider the problems of their world. The atomic age promises both plenty and destruction beyond comprehension. And nowhere, it seems, does the individual share in the shaping of the future. In contrast to atomic weapons and world war, the Western offers man-to-man fighting with guns or even with fists. Watching a Western, a man can identify himself with the hero. He can forget, for a moment, the frustrations of a complicated society as he watches problems settled in a way that is just and understandable.

For women, Westerns have still another appeal. Everywhere else in the world, at the time our West was being shaped, women were living in Victorian subjugation. They were completely under the thumbs of their husbands or fathers. They were mild, weak, and passive. Western women, on the other hand, are hardy and physically enduring and they are actively fighting on the side of right. In Westerns, women make the decisions and share in the building of a good society. Here are the roots for woman's independent and and responsible position in our nation today.

It is a human characteristic to seek orderliness—a reliable plan, a method of doing things. The housewife sets her house in order according to her own system of planning meals, cleaning, and activities. A businessman sets his desk in order or maps out a production or a sales plan. Yet life is never as orderly as we would like it to be. "The best laid schemes o' mice an' men gang aft a-gley."

In Westerns, however, quite the opposite is true. The good people are rewarded and the bad people are punished. There are no loose ends left as our Western hero rides off into the sunset. Watching a Western drama gives the viewer a feeling of protection and orderliness. It is very much like a good chess game or a solution of a mathematical equation. And the orderly completion of a Western gives the viewer a feeling of security that life itself cannot offer.

The mood and the setting of a Western provide us with many characteristics of the "good" life. There is an unsophisticated intimacy about the Western. It makes us feel closer to the earth, closer to life. The Western is simple, direct. It is realistic in that it lacks the veneer of a more polished art. Because it is divorced from the urbanity and the sophistication of other types of entertainment, it necessarily holds its own niche in the entertainment world. Intellectualized critical standards do not apply to the Western. In fact, its appeal is this very simplicity of plot and character which allows us to identify with an earlier and more primitive life—a life that was more real and somehow better than life today.

RITUALISTIC TRAPPINGS OF WESTERNS

Even the typical paraphernalia of a Western—the cowboy hats and boots, the guns and horses, and such activities as fast riding, hard drinking, and pure romance—hold more than a superficial appeal for today's TV viewer. They offer a ritualistic framework within which certain deviations are allowable.

Both children and adults perform little rituals every day. They brush their teeth or their hair at certain specified times and for a certain number of strokes in a given direction. These rituals are far from unpleasant ordeals. They are reassuring links in the activities of a day which may well bring unforeseen events, problems, frustrations.

In the same way, the ritual of a Western links it to all other Westerns in a manner that is pleasing because it is always the same. It is familiar and friendly. It is this way because it always was this way. To change it would be to destroy its accepted form.

Just because the Western exists within a formalized framework, however, there is no reason to assume that it is a static art form. While all the psychological appeals outlined here are necessary attributes of the successful Western, they need not be used in their simplest forms. And in fact they are not. The Western today is an evolving art form and a new name that implies the direction in which it is changing. The adult Western is coming into its own. It is a Western with more bona fide historic details. It is Wyatt Earp; it is based on the realism of the West. The hero has more depth than the

Western hero used to have. He is faced with real conflicts; he has decisions to make. He is less and less the stereotyped cowboy.

As Western characters show their motivations, they reach a larger and more loyal audience, which finds satisfaction in all the appeals a Western has to offer, but can identify more closely with real people than with stereotypes.

THE CONFLICT BETWEEN STRUCTURE AND CHAOS

In studies done for various airlines we found that it was not so much bad weather itself that was experienced in a negative way when it caused the delay in flight, it was instead the apparent helplessness of the airlines to cope with the situation. It produced in people a feeling of anxiety. It gave them the impression that the airline was insecure, had no proper anchorage in the system of controlled events of everyday life. Possibly many fears directed against socialism or Communism are not so much based on the rejection of an economic system as on the fear of having to give up one's present structure and substitute absolute, almost lawless, freedom.

On the other hand, the police state, in addition to its political basis, may have a psychological origin. During revolutions, which precede the police state, all structures are destroyed. Therefore a new, even more rigid structure has to be substituted. Young nations, because they change so many things in their transition from colonies to free countries, are in need of basic and strong structures. We found this in Samoa. The Samoans could not give up their feudal organization overnight; they needed the strength of their tradition as a basis in the new era of their independence. The conflict between nationalism and internationalism, growing at the same time, again may have its basis in the dilemma between freedom and structure. To have strict boundaries around one racial or national group provides people with a feeling of security. To give up these boundaries means to give up rigid structurization, to give up security.

Travel represents one of the means of coping with this conflict. A discovery of the difference and the basic alikeness of peoples all over the world through traveling is important in adopting new physical and psychological boundaries. Adaptation to change represents a very important task of the modern citizen in the modern world.

Many new nations have sprung up. The ability to live with them necessitates the learning of a new psychological and geographical map. At the same time, even such countries as the United States have to learn to reappraise their role in the world. I contend that we fight more against the necessity of relearning the new structures than against the actual result of the re-structurization.

PREJUDICE IS INSECURITY

In dealing with the problem of prejudice, we often make the mistake of throwing fact after fact at the prejudiced groups, expecting somehow that by logic they suddenly will change their mind and start liking Negroes, Jews, or Italians. In reality, we are dealing with something quite different. A prejudiced person, and everybody is prejudiced in one form or another, has evolved a comfortable adjustment to the world in which he lives. He has grouped people together, put them in cubbyholes, organized a chaotic world in such a way that it takes on meaning at least to him and to his group. The educator, the reformer, is in the true sense of the word a troublemaker. He is a destroyer. He destroys the comfortable way of security. He is asking this balanced and adjusted person, maladjusted only in the eyes of the reformer, to give up his structure and substitute for it a different structure and even, for some time to come, chaos and lack of structure. Instead of knowing for sure that dark people are bad and white people are good, he is now confronted with the necessity of accepting that there are good white people and bad white people and good black people and bad black people. Instead of having a neatly organized black-and-white world, he ends up with a gray world.

To ask a person to become tolerant is really to ask him to give up his rigid structure and to substitute for it a frightening reorganization, to abandon his reference system. On a still deeper level, there is a need for psychological separation. We are afraid that we really are not different from the rejected minority groups. Part of racial intolerance may come from the fact that the Negro is alike in most ways to the white person. Nazis hated Jews because Jews, German Jews, were almost even more German than the Germans themselves. Mothers-in-law are disliked because they show the same features, the same characteristics as one's wife but at a later age and in an exaggerated fashion. It may be that white people often dislike Negroes because they are in a sense their in-laws. An attempt is made to demonstrate dramatically and frantically that there is a difference. We're not alike, say the southern segregationists or the *apartheid* defenders in South Africa.

Most media can be organized according to the degree of black and whiteness or grayness with which their lenses operate in dissecting and interpreting the world. They can further be organized according to the degree of obviousness or abstraction. Both these categories are related. Such publications as the *Daily Mirror* and the *Daily News* use a much more obvious and a much more sharply differentiated black-and-white technique to organize the chaos of the world, than does the New York *Times* or a Broadway show. Which one of these forms represents a better way of communication? This is a very difficult question to ask. The need to organize the world is a universal one. We simply cannot understand reality in all its ramifications, its grayness, and its confusion. When we first, as children, attempt to understand the folklore of almost all cultures, either in the form of religious myths, fairy tales, or legends, this provides us with an overobvious black-and-white organization. Order is brought into chaos. The fact that this sort of literature persists in the form of Westerns and detective stories and is really the basic pattern of very many if not most Hollywood productions would seem to indicate that this level of communication is still necessary. At the same time, however, there is a very clear beginning of a change. Movies that are only ten to fifteen years old are often greeted with laughter when shown today. The reason is that many of the stereotypes, exaggerated and overobvious solutions of problems, and the overacting are not acceptable any longer to the modern public, which has learned to accept subtleties and more human grayness. Such concepts as inferiority feelings, insecurity, and many others have become almost standard vocabulary of every modern individual in attempting to understand the true reasons, the true motivations of his contemporaries.

It is my belief that the same principle of structurization and simplification which has proved so successful in communication in general should be applied by the modern social scientist in his efforts to spread socially significant messages and to combat the fear of reality. He has the equipment to do so in a meaningful and planned way—by preserving the essential aspects of the issue and indicating the principles used in its simplified presentation. Thus he can prevent the public from structurizing and oversimplifying the issues in their own often socially dangerous way. This they always tend to do in defense against the mass of unstructured and confusing reports and data which threaten to overwhelm them and make them feel insecure. Whoever makes the world more simple and understandable for them will make them feel good. But it is necessary to do this for the purpose of true understanding and not to simply provide a false feeling of security. Structurization is a prerequisite for the removal of the basic resistance the vast majority of people feel against learning things that are complex and involved. The desirable therapeutic and educational aim of any lesson in psychology, such as we have claimed literature in the deepest sense to be, is to teach people flexible responses. Stock responses, as they are taught now, make people unable to develop an appropriate response in a new situation. Instead, they are inclined to look in their inventory of responses for the adequate, or what to them seems adequate, stereotyped reaction. Although it may seem farfetched, there is still a grave danger that such stock responses will lead to a uniformity in emotional life and human relations, which must appear undesirable in a democracy.

It should be the aim of any good fictional lesson in psychology to train people to become aware of the emotional and cultural forces with which they are interacting. The more insight the individual acquires, the more he will be able to accept or resist such forces, the more independent a thinker and voter he will become, the less he will be afraid of reality.

10 ■ THE FEAR OF CHANGE

Within a short period of two weeks I visited Florence in Italy and São Paulo in Brazil. Here are two dramatically opposed expressions of life. One is an almost medieval city; the other is one where there is hardly a building more than thirty years old.

Which is the more desirable form for man's striving for happiness? Many hours of discussions are being wasted in trying to solve this conflict. A professor of Greek history challenged me on a TV program not long ago for advocating change. Many people feel that the world was much better fifty years ago. Increases in heart disease and cancer are being blamed on the faster pace of living.

Many of the dramatic headlines and laments which we read in the newspapers and magazines are rendered less tragic if we can understand them as reactions of mankind to change. It has been pointed out by political leaders that reforms over which pitched battles were fought not long ago are now so generally accepted that no one gives them a second thought. Awareness of change and evolution is all around us and yet we are afraid of it. To understand this is to understand another one of the human conflicts and motivations. It is a key to mankind's progress towards a goal.

The fear of change is often hidden and rationalized. People waste valuable energy to hold on rather than to progress. Many companies and trade associations have called us in to defend them against the inroads being made by new technological development. This was the case with the record industry when radio came into being. It is now the case with radio due to the advent of television. People making home movies thought their last day had come when television entered every American home. In all instances, they had to learn the hard way that the real job was one of reorientation and rediscovery. The lack of dynamic thinking has often caused destruction and produced fears. Whole industries often lag behind because they fail to realize the public they serve is changing radically. In a broader sense the adaptation of the dynamic principle means saying yes to all aspects of contemporary life rather than continuously dreaming of the good old life which, upon closer examination, usually proves not to have been so good at all.

In a study for a large company selling vacuum cleaners, the problem was how to attract salesmen. They had become accustomed to higher incomes and more comfortable lives. They refused therefore to sell from house to house as they did before. The manager unhappily tried to induce these salesmen to continue to work under the old conditions. When they balked he talked about the good old days. He hoped that a new depression would solve his problems and that it would make the salesmen hungry enough again to want to knock on doors. Our study showed that the only solution was to change over to retail selling, to price the vacuum cleaners in such a way that the salesmen could afford cars and sell their products in an atmosphere of dignity. A chain drugstore company in Los Angeles was told by us that their bargain-basement atmosphere was being rejected by people, who still wanted bargains but in an aura of luxury.

Such changes take place continuously. Restaurants of the future are probably going to be more personal and smaller rather than electronic marvels. Modern supermarkets will return to a compromise between the grocery-store and the push-button forms of merchandising.

A large Brazilian company commissioned us to find out what could be done to speed up the acceptance of sanitary napkins. Brazilian women felt that their old methods were good enough and that sanitary napkins were an unnecessary luxury. In the light of this, we found that to stress the softness, comfort, and whiteness of these products was exactly the wrong thing to do. We suggested instead, with success, that these women be first sold on the idea of their right to be self-indulgent, and at the same time that the napkins be made in a less luxurious fashion. There was greater security in the admittedly less perfect form. It was not as radical a change as the first product.

Many of our actions are motivated by a conflict between security and change, which often spells insecurity. In the many surveys which the author has conducted to find out why people vote, give blood, buy cars, soap, chewing gum, records, coffee, or whatever other commodity may be involved, there was only one need, and a most important one, which was uppermost in people's motivations. The specifications of this over-all need varied each time and took on more or less vacillating forms dependent upon the circumstances. The common denominator, however, was always the same one: security.

With all our fancy disguises of mannerisms and "savoir faire," we are still occupied with the main tasks of creatures living on this earth: to keep on living in security as long and as comfortably as possible. Even the idealist with blue eyes still follows the same principle. He desires to acquire the feeling of intellectual security which comes from having clear goals and pursuing a set objective. Reaching it despite obstacles gives him the proof of his spiritual stamina and strength, a prowess more important in our advanced civilization than purely muscular fist-making.

At some point, every living human being is concerned with the question: What is the best way of life? This is only another way of asking: How can I best acquire security? The answer seems to be this: We can never succeed in living intelligently if we apply the wrong techniques of living to our life. In other words, if we live according to principles which are contradictory to the innermost laws of human nature, we fail. But are there such laws? Absolutely. There are clearly distinguishable characteristics which are true only of human beings and of no other form of life. These unique qualities can best be described by two factors: the ability to look ahead in time, to overcome the fear of change, to plan for the future; and second, the ability to have a wider horizon than animals have.

As a child grows up he learns to consider more than the immediate world which he can see. Bit by bit he will widen the angle of his mental lens until as a grown-up he will let the whole world be the limit of his visual and mental field. Similarly, the time span which the child covers with his intellectual searchlight is at first not more than the immediate moment he lives. Further back and further ahead the search swings, until future and past become, in their full extent, the time perspective of the mature man.

Were we to educate our children in such a way that they would be handicapped in this growth of horizon and time perspective, which is as important as their physical growth, we would teach them the wrong techniques of living. We could not talk ourselves out of our guilt with vague philosophies. We cannot claim that no one really knows what is the right way of living. In the case of a maturing child, it can be stated as clearly as in a scientific law. A correct way of living for a child is to develop all those detailed abilities which permit him to grow in the two dimensions of horizon and time span.

The human race grows too. The individual repeats the development of the centuries within the physical boundaries of his birth and his death. Each man is an infinitesimal link in the steady growth of our whole culture. If you in your own life never reach the full height of your own species, you have failed to that extent to count in the human development.

Many people stop maturing at the age at which they have reached physical completion. They have resigned themselves to not going beyond the scope of the animal in its development. In doing so, they have contradicted the basic law of human nature. They have neglected the factors which make man different, able to look ahead and to look further than any other living being. They are using the wrong technique of living.

Wrong forms of living come from the inhuman, the animal residue within ourselves—from the childhood of humanity repeated in each individual childhood. We are still afflicted with the dark forces, the invisible enemies, within ourselves. The more we learn to expand our knowledge, to look ahead to the farthest dim future which we can intelligently conceive and to the widest edge of the human horizon which our imagination will permit, the more we will feel at home on this earth and the more secure we will feel.

The difficulty that makes this simple formula somewhat more intricate lies in the discrepancy between an animal type of security and true human form of security. As we have pointed out, what characterizes the human being is that he is capable of thinking ahead and of covering a wider horizon. Korzybski, the great semanticist, calls it the "time binding quality" of humans. Psychoanalysts might refer to it as the reality principle, the ability to forego momentary pleasures in favor of later ones. Many humans are plagued, however, by searching for security in a form in which it does not exist; they hold on to the present, not permitting it to change. Yet it does change. Thus the struggle is one between protection from change, which is impossible, and the acceptance of a dynamic form of security, which is the only correct one.

This concept of dynamic security to be acquired by swimming along with the stream, by constantly growing rather than holding on, would seem at first to be far removed from human strategy, from advertising, selling, voting, and other practical problems. Yet it is not. It is its very essence.

The specialist in human strategy, whether he is a politician, educator, or advertiser, is caught in this very dilemma. He is a merchant of security. He has no other choice, no matter what his product, his intentions, and his purpose. But he can exert his influence to encourage acceptance of change.

When we are faced with rapid change in one area of our lives we tend to cling ever more strongly to something unchanging and traditional in other areas. As a result there are certain fields in which the public demands the traditional and rejects the new.

Bourbon must be seen as a product of the old-fashioned Kentucky process, scotch as a product emanating from centuries of Scottish conservatism, beer and ale as products perfected by the old German braumeister. Products such as these which have tried to sell themselves on the basis of modern chemistry, of spick-and-span dehumanized plants, have destroyed the desired sense of the traditional and have had small success.

What to do? How can the really new product be successfully sold in a field where the public demands tradition? How, in other words, can the producer utilize the asset of newness in such a field?

We have found that the dilemma posed here, and in any number of other products as well, *can* be overcome in this fashion:

1. Show the *product* as new but its *function* as traditional. Do not

assert that the new product breaks with traditional values, but on the contrary, that it fulfills its traditional functions better than any of its predecessors. For a liquor, this would mean showing the new product actually at work fulfilling its traditional role—creating warmth and conviviality, providing good hospitality, cementing old friendships, and creating new ones—doing these traditional things *better* because of its unique new qualities.

2. Show the new product in intimate continuity with the past—not as a break with the past. Indicate that all of the old art and science, skill, and labor of love that created the traditional product *had to lead* inevitably to the new product; show the new product as the culmination of all the old dreams, the perfecting of the skills developed by men who were thoroughly steeped in all the old traditions of the ancient processes. Indicate that the new product was created by men who, like all the masters, have continued to strive to add an additional touch of perfection—again in order that the traditional functions might be better fulfilled. These rules apply to many other "intimate" products besides liquor—to bread, cheese, cake in the food fields; to shoes in the apparel field, to armchairs and beds in the furniture field, and so on down the line.

In many studies, for example, we found that many Americans are afraid of big corporations. Size has become inevitable in a modern world of economic concentration. The individual, however, still lives in a small circle, he still is a provincial. He enjoys smallness, at the same time benefiting from the size of big corporations and from a large country. One of the jobs to be performed is to train the average citizen to accept growth of his country and its economy as *his* growth rather than as a strange and frightening event.

THE SPIRAL OF TIME

In many discussions, even among intelligent people, talk will turn to the good old times. There is in this a good deal of what I call "platform thinking." We think of goals as definite elements and marks on a time scale. Probably one of the basic frustrations of human life is to want to hold on to time. Seen from the observation tower of the present, the past at least seems to be full of things that did not change. Looking back they seem desirable. While we actually lived in the past, the change was just as rapid as it is in the present. This, however, we have forgotten.

This nostalgia is so strong that many products can be sold more successfully, as we have found, if the promise is made that they are homemade and old-fashioned. In a bread study we saw that the aroma of fresh home-baked bread is still remembered and represents a powerful appeal. Grandma's ice cream, old-fashioned cheesecake and real homemade Vermont cheese, all these indicate how much reliance we still put on the "real" things, the "old" things.

In trying to find out why men don't buy new shoes more often, we discovered that the real reason was not financial. Most men hated new shoes. They become attached to their old shoes. Of fifty shoe closets which we examined, we found forty-five to contain one or more pairs of old shoes. The advertising campaign stressed, therefore, this love for the old shoe, actually showing the battered-looking, faithful servants in the ad. The promise made was that the new shoes would be almost as comfortable as the old ones and would soon become dear friends.

In a study of office safes, we saw that even sober businessmen would develop an attachment to their not-so-safe old safes. Instead of stressing soberly the inadequacy of the old safe and speaking of a safe roundup in a replacement drive, we promised that the old safe would be comfortably retired, its valuable parts used. The new safe was introduced not as the usurper but as the son, the successor of the old one, keeping pace with the progress of the business.

Hegel and Marx used to talk about the development of world history in the form of a spiral. Thesis, antithesis, and synthesis, according to them, characterized the steps of this spiral development. What is needed is to consider the possibility that this political and material spiral development is accompanied and paralleled by a superimposed psychological spiral. Ortega y Gasset, the Spanish philosopher, stated that each nationalistic state puts pressure on the walls with which it surrounds itself and pushes them higher and higher. When they have reached a certain height, they collapse and out of two states a new one, a solidified and larger state, is created.

Modern means of transportation have made traveling much easier. It seems, however, as these physical boundaries and distances have been reduced, the desire for separation and limitation of one's horizon have increased. We are dealing here with a conflict created by one aspect of technological development. It is dramatic to observe in cities like Marrakech the sharp differentiation between the European section and the Mohammedan section. Buses, cars, even bicycles have reduced the physical distance, yet the walls around the Medina, the Arab quarter, still exist, at least as a symbol. Similarly, many American and European homes have man-high fences, as if these fences would really provide security. In the United States in many areas these fences between neighbors have disappeared. In Samoa the fences around individual huts have been abandoned, but villages are banded together under the leadership of a *matai*, a chief, thus acquiring their security by living in security groups. American juvenile groups often circumscribe a certain area, making it their own, and fight viciously against any intruders, although physically no boundaries exist. With each development of transportation, attempts are being made to barricade and consolidate existing boundaries. The antithesis of physical communication is created; only when the pressure becomes too great is a synthesis produced, such as a common market or a United Europe. On a trip around the world you can find dozens of examples of each phase of this spiral development. Adjustment to physical distance, its reduction by psychological means, is slowly taking place. In some areas in Europe, passports are not even stamped any longer at the borders. In others, usually in very young, often insecure nations, extreme efforts are being made to demonstrate to you that you are entering foreign territory.

PROGRESS INSTEAD OF PERFECTION

We wanted to find out what it was that made people buy one brand of gasoline rather than another. In most cases, we were told in convincing terms that the individual car driver had gone to quite a lot of trouble in testing one brand of gasoline over another and then had finally arrived at the conclusion that Esso, or Mobilgas, or Texaco, or whatever might be the case, was the one that gave him more mileage, better pickup, etc. So far, so good. But the situation, however, became much more complicated when we attempted to really check on these statements. In almost 40 per cent of the cases the statements simply were not true. While the buyer was convinced that this brand was the best buy, in his actual trips to the filling station he might neglect altogether to buy this brand. What he had done instead was to try to impress us, and even more important, to try to impress himself, that he was a planning and systematic person who was really arranging his actions in an efficient manner.

The truth of the matter was something entirely different. We found out that many times the gasoline bought was not the one that the buyer thought was the best one as far as quality was concerned, but rather the one that happened to be sold at the gas station whose owner Mr. Buyer knew. If he felt that the gasoline station attendant or owner was a nice man, that is the person he would go to, and more often than not he would not even remember what brand of gasoline was sold there.

Another factor involved was that whenever the gas station was located in a place that made it difficult for the driver to pull up, he soon would find excuses for not frequenting that gas station. Rarely, however, would he admit that he did not like to be shown up as an inefficient and unskilled driver.

When people went on long trips, we found the following situation: Most people, when they ran low on gas during the journey, would discover a station selling their preferred gas, but because of a lag between their decision to buy gas and actually stopping, would often end up two or three stations later, disregarding the brand sold there. Yet even they would tell us, in our interviewing procedure, that they definitely planned ahead and had fixed opinions as to what brands of gasoline to buy and which not to buy.

We all want to appear as if we planned our lives very carefully. We try to keep up this illusion at all costs. In most cases, however, we will find that there was pitifully little planning involved in selecting the kind of job we are holding down at the moment, or in picking out the kind of profession or occupation that we happened to have. There is even less planning, of course, in the selection of our marital partners. The truth of the matter is that in the majority of cases, we are exposed to quite incidental developments. Often a very slight incident is sufficient to change the whole future course of our lives. Had I not, for example, been asked by one of the leading advertising agencies to look into the psychology of soap because they had need of a new slogan, I might never have hit upon the idea of applying modern psychology to advertising and sales problems. Sometimes an accidental meeting with a person whom one has not seen in years may be the beginning of a whole series of fateful events. Yet we hate to admit this. We persist in keeping up the illusion that the events of our lives are properly planned and thought through in most cases.

Fear of change, one of the conflicts of our era, can be remedied by doing everything possible to help the individual keep up this illusion of planning. Prepare people for constant changes and teach them to plan ahead.

Few people buy their tires ahead of time. We are always unpleasantly surprised to discover that we "suddenly" need new tires. Many customers shy away from buying new suits because they might have to wait for a day or two before the necessary alterations could be made. When we consequently advised a store to make it a practice to make all alterations within two or three hours, sales took a decided upswing.

Most people employed in the retail sales field know that to display merchandise uppermost on a shelf will push the merchandise almost automatically. The specific brand or quality of the product will be of far lesser importance in comparison to the accidental factor of its position.

In a general psychological sense, the illusion of planning has also a detrimental effect. It has worked as a counteragent against our ability for spontaneity. When we observe children, we find that most of them, at least to an age of eight or nine, still have their spontaneity. They will make decisions without great deliberation. They will want to enjoy the present moment, will refuse to plan far ahead. As we grow older, we are more hesitant to make decisions. It does not mean that we really deliberate more intelligently and arrive at more systematic conclusions. What really happens is that we postpone decisions and then often make our choice much later on just as unsystematically as we would have made it had we given in to the first impulse.

It is a good salesman, therefore, who is capable of influencing the consumer to give in to an innate desire for spontaneity and who has persuasive power enough to give the consumer the moral permission to enjoy himself and satisfy his momentary preference.

The choice the strategist has is one between selling momentary satisfactions or types of long-range security. What is more desirable and more profitable and successful will depend upon the type of offer. However, inasmuch as the businessman lives by grace of the never-ending growth of the individual and his constantly renewed desires, it will be to his interest to join forces with the modern educator who, too, feels that simply holding to established possessions and behavior patterns is wrong and dangerous, particularly if this is done out of fear. A practical application of this principle was found in an analysis of insurance buying.

SECURITY FOR SALE

In our modern world even security has been merchandised. While, as we have stated, most products represent security, it is possible to buy security in an unadulterated form as life insurance.

We have found that in most cases buying a life policy hinges on an emotional state which we can call the inner readiness of the customer. Inner readiness is a state of mind in which a man has finally overcome his resentment at, and his resistance to, setting aside part of his cash income for regular and unending premium payments because he sincerely feels that he is receiving deep and ample emotional compensations for his "sacrifice."

In view of this psychological situation, we find that the most effective advertising, promotion, and sales presentation in this field are the ones which

a) help develop inner readiness by nurturing and building up the motivations on which it is based;

b) create a direct emotional tie between these inner forces and the image of a specific company.

Agents in the field and executives in the home offices are, of course, aware of the obvious major motivations which cause men to consider taking out a policy, such as fear of leaving wife and children unprovided for. The fact is, however, that true inner readiness is often generated by much less obvious and more subtle, even if equally potent, psychological factors. Taking out life insurance often stands as a symbol of a man's entrance into adulthood. At the time of marrying and planning a family, a young man is confronted with new duties and responsibilities which at the same time flatter and frighten him, make him feel both proud and anxious. He will now be free to enjoy the pleasures, satisfactions, and privileges of adulthood, to procreate, participate, and create a little world of his own. The gratifications of adulthood provide a number of convincing and sincere, emotion-packed appeals. And when the young adult is faced with the obligation to pay an admission price to adulthood, in this instance in the form of insurance premiums, reference to his psychological satisfaction furnishes realistic new answers to the question so crucial to life insurance: "What can I get out of it NOW?"

Much has been written about "momism," the tendency of many American men to remain dependent upon their domineering mothers. In this state of dependency the childhood pattern remains intact, the emotional subservience persists, and the mother continues to guide, direct, suggest or make decisions on behalf of the son. In these circumstances the latter is unable to cut the umbilical cord, "grows up" late, or doesn't grow up at all.

However, during the past decade or so, and at least partly under the influence of modern psychiatry and psychoanalysis, there has been a growing will to develop genuine masculinity and to enhance emotional health and maturity by a greater independence from one's parents.

Life insurance can represent a tool in this movement of liberation from overdependence by marking a man as standing on his own feet, as being a provider and a protector instead of being the protected one. It can symbolize an act of "creative rebellion," a declaration of independence. A man who is about to marry or has just gotten married and who makes his fiancée or bride his beneficiary, announces that he is not a passive member of a family any longer, but the active male who has finally struck out on his own.

Closely connected with this gratification, yet different from it, is the role of life insurance as a symbol of adult love. Essentially, a child's love is self-centered. He wants to receive, he seeks for proofs that he is being loved. He has a tendency to identify the family with himself, rather than himself with the family. (Here are the roots of emotional dangers for an only child: he does become an emotional center, the focus of all emotions. In contrast, where there are a great number of children, circumstances force each of them to think and feel in terms of the entire family.)

The very act of giving, in buying life insurance, cuts through the childhood pattern of love. The policy holder proves the maturity of his love by giving. By the same token, he also thinks in terms of larger units: his wife, his family. He identifies himself with them even beyond death. The reward he receives for this adult love is purely emotional: his relationships grow fuller, ampler, warmer—he feels like a "richer" person.

By permitting the man to experience this growth, this greater depth of feeling, life insurance becomes a touchstone of emotional maturity and adult love.

The amount of money a man has decided to invest in the happiness of his wife and family reflects, on a deeper level, the amount of sexual power he is capable of mustering and investing in making her happy. This is easily understood when one realizes that money and power are to a large extent identified in our culture, and that a man's "power" is in itself an ambiguous term implying position as well as potency. The man who can answer the question of his potency with a large figure feels deep down almost as though he were boasting of his sexual achievements which, of course, decency and custom forbid him to publicize.

American psychotherapists have found that a great many men, even in their younger years, worry and feel insecure about their sexual potency. Since almost all of these worries are for psychological reasons, life insurance can become a reassuring symbol of masculine power and sexual ability.

When he sets out in life, a young man has many a mountain to climb, many an obstacle to overcome before he is able to show conclusive results or boast about a completed task. He has to prove himself in his job and make his way determinedly toward an adequate position; he has to take out a mortgage and pay slowly for his house over many years; he has to accumulate furniture, appliances, household objects. His life is a series of beginnings, of partial accomplishments. Success is as yet veiled in the uncertainties of the future.

In contrast, a life insurance policy is a completed task. Should the young man die tomorrow, his family will automatically have the security he had dreamed about. In a very real sense, this first completed task of the young man is his first success. Here is more than hope, more than excellent potentiality: here is a positive achievement. The policy is a symbol of the young man's first success.

In many religions, indeed in many whole societies, entering into adulthood is marked by important ceremonies. These ceremonies may signify either that a person is biologically adult, or that he has become a full-fledged citizen of the community, or both.

There is great psychological wisdom behind these solemn occasions: they correspond to an inner need for reveling in the knowledge that one is a grown-up, responsible individual in his own right and no longer a "mere kid." In our modern American society there are no similar institutionalized solemnities. The psychological need for them still exists, but it is only partially satisfied by such occasions as graduation ceremonies. The young man who has an inner desire to prove that he is now an adult American may refer to the fact that he votes, or that he has done military service, that he holds a steady job. Beyond that, an important, almost ceremonial moment proving that he has been integrated into his society as a member with full rights may be the moment when he signs his first life insurance policy.

Young men are anxious to be accepted as equals but they also want to be appreciated, to be judged "worthy." In view of the nature of our society, they find gratification and reassurance not only in participation in social activities and in forming friendships but also in competitive endeavors where they can prove their worth.

To a considerable extent, worth is measured by the amount of money a man makes or puts aside, by the things he is able to afford. At the beginning of their careers, most young people are not in a position to boast of noteworthy financial achievements. They may, however, carry insurance as a proof of their capacity to earn money in excess of their daily needs, of their ability to afford a highly valued service.

The question "How much do you carry?" probes this aspect of a man's striving to prove his mettle. It becomes a vehicle and an easily readable measure of his competitive achievements.

The small child lives for the moment, the immature person lives within the limitations of his own life. The man who has taken roots possesses a wider time perspective: he has succeeded in stepping out of his own individual time span, as it were, and views himself and his life from a longer vista. He sees his life not only as purposeful in itself, but also as a bridge between his parents' and his children's generations.

For the healthy and mature man, this consideration, instead of being a source of disenchantment, despair, or cynicism, is an inspiration. He will feel that it is his duty, even his mission, to fill his place as well as he can, to serve and advance the process during his lifetime and prepare those who will carry the torch after him.

Taking out life insurance is one expression of such care and anticipation. Seen in this context, it reflects man's experience of himself and his existence on the highest level. It can give him the feeling of having taken deep roots in the process of life itself. It can help him to reassure himself about the meaning of his evanescent place in the scheme of things.

Before a man may feel that he has matured, he needs a perspective not only on life but also on death. Here, however, the trend in our national culture is of no great help to the individual. While religions and civilizations under strong philosophical influences constantly scrutinize and prepare the individual for death, according to most psychologists and other social scientists we in America have a tendency to run away from death instead of accepting it maturely. Occasionally we almost deny death, and glamorize and beautify our dead as if they had never departed. We thereby deny the tragic element in all life, the very one which lends a deeper dimension to living.

The American attitude toward death poses a particular problem to life insurance advertising. One way of solving it is, no doubt, the emphasis on insurance for *living*, which in recent years has considerably stimulated and enriched insurance thinking.

Nonetheless, the thought of death cannot be completely excluded from the thinking of the young man who takes out a policy. Probably for the first time in his life it is pointed out to him that not only others die, but that his turn too will come one day. And try as he will not to let this thought penetrate his subconscious mind and take root there, he must make his peace with the idea of non-existence. The way, we find, he often accomplishes this necessary adjustment is to tell himself that he will remain pure and moral even beyond the grave. He will not feel post-humous guilt because he will prepare for death by being thoughtful during his lifetime.

SECURITY A SIGN OF SOCIAL MATURITY

I was asked recently when to start training people to accept change, to adjust themselves correctly to life. The answer is, as early as kindergarten. We conducted a study for the Equitable Life Assurance Society, stimulated by Mr. Leslie Shope, promotion director for the company, which shows that even in high school we have not succeeded as yet in teaching the truly adjusted dynamic security necessary for modern life. The study's purpose was to measure the degree of social maturity of American youth. Maturity has been defined in a variety of ways by many authorities in the fields of personality theory, education, human relations, etc. None of these definitions, however, has an absolute value. In the last analysis, maturity is a cultural concept which can only be applied within the limits and context of a given cultural matrix.

In our definition, maturity is the adjustment to the realities and difficulties of living. It is performance based upon an objective and realistic appraisal of facts rather than upon the influence of irrational impulses, habits, wishful thinking, and superstitions. These criteria, however, are too strict for practical application. Psychologists have long been aware of the fact that people's actions are only too often motivated by irrational impulses and magic. If we attempted to determine practically who is mature and who is not, we could be confronted with the impossibility of finding a single individual who would fit our description of maturity. We must be content, therefore, with a measurement of what degree of maturity can be found in one given population section as compared to another. Similarly, the degree of maturity of one individual will be determined by comparing his adjustment to the adjustment of others; that is, to the average (mean) level of maturity. In our social maturity test, we tried to measure the individual's or the group's deviation from the average adjustment of our population sample as measured by performance on the same test. The test was standardized on the basis of the performance of a representative sample of the American student population between the ages of fourteen and thirty. The test was based on the conviction that mature attitudes must coincide with adjustment to the difficulties of reality and living. These adjustments depend to a great extent on the degree and type of thinking of the individual. Maturity is the ability to cope with realities in an adequate and successful fashion, rather than to be guided by magic, irrational influences, or wishful or infantile thinking. These psychological adjustments must be measured through the patterns of action and the attitudes of thought of the individual. The function, therefore, of each unit of our test is to measure the maturity of the psychological adjustments and the actual and potential actions and thoughts of the examinees. The frame of reference which guided us in setting up the test is based on our cultural pattern. There are certain aspects of our life which are as basic and accepted as final characteristics of reality. Four of these we feel are primary:

1) life is constantly changing;

2) life is multi-varied, not a singular or one-sided phenomenon;

3) the parent-child relationship and dependency is predominant in the development of the individual and is repeated in many forms throughout life;

4) life has a meaningful structure based on relations and order.

We tried to translate each of these four major aspects of reality into test situations; one of them is shown below. The more readily each one of these aspects is recognized by the individual, the more readily he can adjust himself to them, the more mature we consider him. With this in view, we organized a test under four major sections:

a) Dynamicism

b) Authority needs
c) Self-motivation
d) Insight

By dynamicism, we understand the subject's readiness and ability to accept the ever-changing nature of life or to resist it. We attempted to measure the individual's ability to change in his cultural surroundings. Authority needs imply the degree of dependence or independence an individual shows. Self-motivation attempts to reveal the individual's readiness to stand up for his own rights in the face of infringements by authority figures and outside forces and his tendency to meet conflict situations by self-reliance or by calling on authoritative parental forces. Insight represents the degree of understanding of one's motives. The technical details of our social adjustment test were the following:

The test on self-motivation and authority needs overlap to some extent, and they have been used in our scores jointly. The original test was comprised of 16 sub-tests which contained 100 items in all. In its original form, the test was administered to two small groups in Portland, Maine. The first of these groups, called the Leader Group, was comprised of young people selected for their leadership position in schools and community organizations. The second group, called the Problem Group, was comprised of emotionally maladjusted children. This first step permitted the screening of some test items which failed to discriminate significantly between the performance of the two groups. We were then ready to proceed to the next step. The test in its revised form was submitted to the 2,000 students between the ages of 14 and 30 in 12 schools. Tabulation of the responses of these 2,000 subjects enabled us to eliminate from the tests those items which appeared to be controversial, confusing or difficult to understand. Only sub-tests were finally retained of the original 16 comprising 40 individual items. We were then ready to proceed with the next step; that of standardizing the tests so that they could be put to practical use. A sample of 500 individuals between the ages of 14 and 30 was selected for this purpose. The test was weighted for scoring purpose on the basis of the performance of this group.

Three evaluation scales were developed to take care of the influence of age and educational background upon test performance. One of the tests used was the following:

Here is what we found after analyzing all of them: The specific purpose of this test was to measure the subject's readiness to accept the changing nature of life or to resist it. These tests which measured ability to accept change were scored correctly only by about 30 per cent of the adolescent population tested. A detailed analysis of the responses shows an even more distressing result. We normally assume that youth is radical. We found, however, very little evidence for the proverbial rebellious nature of young people in this country. Most of the young people showed an almost resigned attitude. Take, for example, the statement of eighteen-year-old Allan. He is a very alert young fellow with a hand in everything that goes on in school. He is now looking forward to an active and successful college career. He feels "the only influence I can have in any election is to express my thought to intelligent people of voting age and let them weigh my ideas with others and take what I say for what it is worth. There is no sense in my being interested in politics and worrying about what changes are going to take place in this country. What will happen will happen." We found that many of these youngsters develop feelings of impotence because of a sense of insufficiency. The task for making intelligent decisions based on belief and conviction seems too complicated. When issues are not clearly presented, youth cannot master the facts.

Our lives are steps of constantly increasing and better forms of adjustment to the difficulties of the world in which we live. As animals or small children we are handicapped all around. We can't see further than our noses. Anything that comes to threaten us from beyond that horizon is ignored and can harm us because of our shortsightedness. The wider our horizon becomes, the further we can look with the powerful field glasses of our technical acquisition, the safer we become. We are able to recognize immediately any potential danger for miles and miles around. To learn to use mental and psychological field glasses instead of relying on our eyes would, therefore, seem to be a smarter way of living, because it provides us with the means of adjusting ourselves better to the exigencies of living.

How can we learn the correct techniques of living? By growing up more thoroughly than we have done heretofore. By widening our horizon and time perspective much, much further than we have so far.

Too quickly we freeze our lives into accustomed patterns of thinking and behavior. We do so because in the animal corner of our brains it seems to us the safer and more secure form of adjustment to life. If it is true, however, that life moves on and progresses, this form of adjustment cannot possibly be correct.

Particularly in our present atomic age, acceleration is taking place at an unforeseen speed. We must learn to think in entirely new forms of mental grammar. Our whole scientific progress, which is a form of better adjustment and a better way of life, was only made possible by the acceptance of new rules in our thinking and concepts about the material world. We had to learn that there were no elements and no substance in the old, accustomed sense of our school chemistry. Instead, we found ourselves confronted with electromagnetic forces, with movements of electrons and protons. The solid, conservative world had to be replaced by a world in constant movement where one element can be changed into another. If we do not adjust ourselves to these new sets of circumstances, we are going to stay behind. Our way of life is going to become a wrong one again. And that at a time when we have hardly caught up with the technical progress and the changes in the world prior to this development.

A correct way of life, then, is constant adaptation to the world, a development and growing up without end. This may seem frightening, with an element of restlessness and constant struggle in it. This is not so. If it is true that life is a stream constantly flowing and progressing, would it be wise to hold on to an overhanging branch on the shore in an attempt to acquire security and adjustment? You can never really be safe. Someday the branch may break. You may grow weak, or a strong current may take you along.

Instead, and this is the correct way of life, you should swim forcefully with the stream, go in the same direction it is going. You do not have to hold on to anything. You are a part of life; you progress with it. An entirely new, unknown form of security is derived from this attitude. It is dynamic security. It is the right way of life, in accord with the essential laws of human nature, those of constant maturing and growing.

It is a correct way of life, because it is in congruity and unity with the rest of the world and its intrinsic meaning; it provides you with the power and strength to accept yourself in your own right and in full recognition of your eternal values. A correct way of life should and does have as its final result the glorious emergence from the animal state of the godlike creature—man.

11 ■ THE SEARCH FOR IDENTITY

An easy way to test a group of people and its true feelings towards the United States is to mention the word "conformism." There will be little doubt, particularly in a European audience, that this is an expression of an attitude which fits perfectly American life of today.

Yet there is probably no class which is more uniform in its mannerisms and outlook on life than the English aristocracy or no group more set in its ways than average Frenchmen. There are miles and miles of absolutely identical brownstone houses outside of London and modernistic apartment houses in Frankfurt and Vienna that cannot be told apart.

Why is conformity such a truly regretted and decried behavior and individuality apparently the great desired goal?

Some time ago, I was in Western Samoa studying the desire of the people to become independent from New Zealand. They described to me the destiny of Hawaii as a horrible example of what could happen to them. They said: "There are hardly any pure Polynesians left in Hawaii, and all are becoming more and more mixed. We Samoans are 95 per cent Polynesian. We want to preserve our identity and our customs."

At the same time Western Samoa has been under the influence of the London Missionary Society for the last fifty years. There are now only Christians of various denominations on these islands. There is literally no trace left of the original native gods and beliefs. Yet no one there seems to miss these pure Polynesian myths and dogmas. A similar conflict consisted in a desire to preserve the political form of the *matai* system by the Samoans. This system has some resemblance to a feudal village-communism and contains democratic elements only inasmuch as the chief, or *matai*, has to prove his worth to his villagers. They have the power to depose him, and his title is not hereditary. The United Nations insisted for a long time that this semi-feudal system be abandoned before admitting Samoa as an independent state. A final compromise was worked out, making the continuation of the system a subject for a vote in itself. Independence has now been achieved.

In this country, we complain about the fact that we have become a nation of "organization men." At the same time we are worried about the greater efficiency of Russia, her ability to create scientists if she needs them, or to organize all their efforts in such a way as to make a moon shot possible.

We teach competition in our schools and stress at the same time the necessity to co-operate in communities and in our national life. Some time ago a Russian family which had spent some time in this country was asked what impressed them most here. Their answer was that everybody looked out for himself and that this was apparently considered good. In their country, they said, the opposite was true. Before you thought of yourself, you asked yourself what your demand would mean for other people in your group, in your neighborhood, and for your country. After they had been here for a while and had "adjusted themselves" they were interviewed again. At that time they were saving for a car, and they had acquired an apartment of their own. They had learned that one has to look out for *oneself* in this capitalist world and if one does, one can really get ahead.

One of the deepest conflicts of our times is involved in this struggle. In a sense we are being asked to choose all over again between Christian ethics in their original meaning—to love your neighbor—and the law of the jungle, survival.

R. L. Bruckberger in *Image of America* states that the American Revolution is the only one that has succeeded so far because it believes in "the supremacy of the live, real, three-dimensional man, while Europe believes in the subordination of man to abstraction." He considers, further, the most striking difference between the American and the Marxist revolution to be the following:

The Communists also speak of liberty and equality. But for them liberty and equality must await the end of the revolution . . . But how can we be sure that freedom will not be forgotten along the way? How can we be sure that, by the time we reach the goal, we will not have lost our taste and our desire for freedom? . . . the American Declaration, on the contrary affirms that liberty and equality can never wait, that without them life has no human dignity . . . It recognizes that man comes ahead of society. Man creates society; he is not created by society.

We have done a number of studies for young nations, like Samoa, Israel, and Brazil, trying to understand their quest for identity and to act as adviser in the many problems they face in the process of growing up and finding their proper relationship with other nations. In many instances these psychological problems are nothing but a replica of the changing relationship between the members of the family.

The relationship between parents and children is one that involves the problem of command or persuasion. The modern father is confronted with the discovery that he has to permit his adolescent son to talk back if he wants him to become an independent, mature individual; that simply ordering to obey seems not to work anymore after a certain age.

A country like Samoa, for example, feels that it has come of age, that it does not need any more tutelage. The parent nation, New Zealand, in this case stresses the point that Samoa is too young to shift for itself. It will get into trouble because of lack of experience. This is the same line of reasoning taken till recently by England vis-à-vis many of her possessions.

A father refuses his son independence because he does not accept the possibility that he may be able to solve problems for himself. Partly, it is also a reflection of the father's fear that he really is not needed any longer. The answer for the father and for the nation is to realize that the replacement of a relationship of inequality by one of equality carries many rewards. A grown-up son can be a very great help and source of pride.

This search for identity and perfection of individuality works in many fields.

In studies for the liquor industry, we found that the real reason for the large number of brands in existence is not the fact that they are truly different. Probably the only real reason which most people have for drinking, apart from the semirationalization of being social or relaxed, is, to put it bluntly, to get drunk. It would be a shameful thing, however, for a person to go into a store or into a bar and to simply ask for a drink to get drunk. Instead of that, we have developed an elaborate ritual. We want a martini, with just the right amount of vermouth and one or two twists of lemon peel, we are very intent upon buying a specific brand of liquor and not accepting a substitute for it. Our own tests indicate that the majority of people cannot distinguish between one brand of liquor and another. When they are blindfolded and their noses pinched, they cannot even distinguish between gin and scotch. The reason for this insistence on a special brand is partly to cover up the true reason of promiscuity in drinking and to substitute for it the illusion of individuality.

Goethe, the German poet, said a long time ago that nothing is holier to us than our own personality and individuality. The origin of the word "individuality" is one that stresses its importance. Its literal sense is: "indivisible, unique, not replaceable." Traveling through various countries, you are told again and again by Frenchmen, Germans, Englishmen—whatever nationality they may be—"Don't forget, we are different."

Which is true, then? Are we drifting towards more and more conformism or are we witnessing a reawakening of the desire for individuality, the quest for identity? In the last ten years alone, at least fifteen or twenty new nations have come into being. Rationally, probably every one of these nations would have been better off in retaining its relationship with the mother country or at least in joining together with other countries in a new type of federation. The federation principle too, however, has been on the increase. We've witnessed the development of the United Arab Republic; there is a possibility of federation between Ghana and Togo, and there is talk of a North African and Central African Federation. The common market in Europe seems, after centuries of struggle, to be the beginning of the principle of co-operation and a giving up at least partially of this desire for individuality.

In many commercial studies we conducted, we found that this desire for individuality represents a very important appeal. You can sell shampoos better by promising that they are particularly suitable to individual types of hair. Even large, almost monopolistic companies like IBM, General Motors, General Electric have found it necessary to introduce personalities to present their company. General Mills had succeeded in building up the fictitious personality of Betty Crocker. Betty Crocker, for millions of people, is General Mills. She's real enough to receive hundreds of thousands of letters every year—to be asked for advice. The emergence of such programs as Edward R. Murrow's "Person to Person" and "Meet the Press," is an important indication that the desire for individuality certainly has not been swallowed up by conformism. What we are witnessing is another confusion, another false assumption, and therefore the necessity for reorientation and a new kind of thinking in order to find answers, explanations, and consequently patterns for strategy in human engineering.

In many of our analyses, the client points with jealousy or fear to the successes of his competitors as challenges. He orders a study from us when he discovers that a competitor has been moving ahead, when an advertising approach used by someone else has proved to be successful. When a political party finds that their opponent's platform arouses acceptance and sympathy, they often feel that it might be desirable for them to steal this platform and make it their own. In the national and international field, we often attempt to compete with another country by copying its slogans, its techniques, and its goals.

The wrong assumptions which lead to failures in all these fields can be best illustrated on the basis of a simple example. An individual brand is like an individual personality. Each one of these brands or personalities could be represented symbolically by a tumbler filled with a liquid of a particular color. Let's imagine we are dealing with four or five of these competing brands. Brand A may be filled one quarter with a red liquid; Brand B halfway with a green one; Brand C three quarters with a blue one; and Brand D one fifth with a yellow liquid. A misconception of the nature of individuality and its uniqueness, and a misunderstanding of what competition really consists of, often lead to an attempt to take the tumbler that is fullest, therefore apparently most successful—such as possibly Brand C—and to pour it into one's own tumbler.

Carrying this example further, you might be also tempted to use some of the liquid of the other successful brands and mix those with your own. The result is the destruction of the very thing which originally was responsible for the success, no matter how limited, of the individual brand. You end up with a gray, non-distinct liquid which has lost its uniqueness. Several years ago I started using the term "brand image" and "brand personality" for the first time. It has now been widely accepted. What I really meant by it was to remind the advertiser that after all the millions of dollars that he may have expended in advertising and public relations and merchandising, the real measure of his success is the creation of a personality and a uniqueness for his brand and product. If he has failed to establish such a uniqueness, then indeed his advertising program has failed.

The whole American economy is characterized by brand names. In the non-aristocratic, egalitarian culture of the United States, brand names play the role of the "von" before German names, and of the aristocratic titles of other cultures. Even in Poland the cry went up recently for the introduction of brand names. The kind of shirts we wear, the kind of car we drive, and the kind of liquor we drink represent important descriptions of our human personality. Many purchases truly represent a matching between the buyer's personality and the personality of the product and the brand. Most attempts at standardization and grade labeling have failed because the real reason why people buy one brand rather than another is that they feel it suits them, it belongs to them, it matches their own personality. From this viewpoint, a product and the brand can become too successful. There are many examples where a brand name at one point changes into a generic term. This has happened to Crisco, to Frigidaire, to Kleenex, and to a long list of similar products.

In a study we did for one of the largest beer brands, we found that the fact, or the statement, that millions of people consumed this beer began to backfire. It began to rob the beer brand of what we call its "expressive power." Buying it left the consumer with a feeling that he failed to express something special about himself in drinking this beer.

The conflict between individuality and conformism, between older and younger countries, also exists in many professional groups; for example, the conflict between the physician and patient, as we found in a study done for the American Medical Association.

The modern physician is not seen any longer as the medicine man and the all-powerful father. The modern patient wants to be treated as an equal. He wants the medical Bible translated into English. The physician considers himself one of the last remaining true individualists. The vet, the barber, are similar remnants of psychological frontiersmen rapidly disappearing in a society that demands co-operative integration.

The doctor-patient relationship is a symptom of the conflict between individuality and collectivism. In a study conducted for the California Medical Association, we sought to find out how the relationship between doctor and patient could be improved, and why it had deteriorated. We found, in several hundred interviews with doctors and patients, that the doctor considers himself one of the last remaining strongholds of individualists. The patient, on the other hand, does not permit the modern doctor to maintain this role any longer. He wants him to integrate himself into the community and the country.

We found that the doctor's job is a mixture between priesthood and commercialism. He's caught in between, and the patient likewise is not completely clear where the doctor stands. He expects the doctor, on the one hand, to give him love and consideration, to the extent of self-effacement; on the other hand, the patient realizes that the doctor has to make a living. A doctor used to occupy a position of leadership parallel with parish priests, ministers, and teachers. The modern doctor has lost this position. We discovered that most doctors choose their profession for idealistic reasons. While the usually good income expected from it enters considerably into the picture, the idea of helping humanity and doing something worthwhile, non-commercial, and above the doldrums of everyday life, of devoting oneself to helping others, is a very strong incentive. In addition to this, it seems many medical students see the medical career as one of the last possibilities of being independent . . . of fighting against the danger of becoming an organization man.

However, during the course of the medical studies, and particularly during internship, something vital and very important happens. The young doctor discovers the hard realities of life. These realities clash very quickly with his initial highly exaggerated idealism. How important respect for the ego of the doctor, his acceptance as an individualist, matters, is illustrated by the following quote from a doctor of forty-five: "I remember when a young girl of high school age came to me about a month ago and asked for a physical examination. After standing near her for about two minutes, I told her that I couldn't do anything for her today. I told her bluntly that before she comes here, she should pay some respect, and at least take a bath. If she takes a bath before going out with her boy friend, she should at least show me the same respect and come to the office clean. This lecture I gave her must have embarrassed her a great deal, because she didn't come back until a week later. She probably thought I would have forgotten by then. This girl stands out in my mind because she seemed to think that a doctor is just a machine. He doesn't have any feelings, or that all he is concerned with is the fee. These kids get reductions on their examinations, so at least they can come to the office nice and clean. I like patients who come to the office clean, and dressed in clean clothing. Clothing doesn't have to be new, but it should be clean. I hate these workers who, after a hard day's work at the steel mill, come into the office like slobs. The least they could do is go home first and clean up. Coming like that to my office is indicative of being a slob, in my eyes. Those patients don't seem to have any respect for the doctor's dignity, so I treat them with as little respect as possible. They do not deserve anything else."

Listening to a typical patient, on the other hand, we can see how he has begun to attack the exceptional role that the doctor wants to play . . . how he's trying to get the physician to integrate himself into the community and into the rest of the world. He denies him the right to be treated as a priest and an exceptional person. Here is what one patient says, for example: "If I see a doctor doesn't understand me, I simply go to another one. Many patients are afraid to hurt the feelings of a doctor. They think they cannot do that to him. They think that they have to be careful not to disturb him . . . not to ask him too many questions, and not to call him at late hours. In ordinary business, nobody minds being disturbed when he is wanted for some urgent business, and everybody finds it quite natural and ethical to try to get a better deal somewhere else. But in the medical profession, you deal with the ethics and etiquette of the profession." Another patient says: "I think that the patient should have more freedom in his dealings with doctors. As it is now, the patient feels as though he belongs to the doctor—as if he were his property. It is all right for the doctor to be bound by his code of ethics, but the patient should be free to change doctors. It would be better for the patient and for the doctor too, because it would keep him on his toes."

In interview after interview, doctors pointed with pride to the fact that they had chosen this occupation in order to be free. Free usually means free from any kind of interference. There's something of the frontier spirit in them, and the pull of defiance and challenge to dare to attack their bastion. Very few doctors have begun to realize that possibly this rugged individualism is nothing to be really proud of. One such doctor says: "Perhaps in medicine doctors have not had enough teamwork. There's a phrase that doctors are rugged individualists. I sort of feel that they should be ashamed of that, instead of bragging about it. A rugged individualist means that a doctor is self-centered and aggressive and immature to the degree in which he cannot co-operate with other individuals in a society." This feeling of the right to be independent and unconcerned with the difficulties of the community is, however, strongly challenged by the present-day patient. He feels that the doctor has to accept his responsibility of caring for the weak. He has to provide, in a sense, security to others, although he himself had to acquire it the hard way.

The conflict arises from the fact that the strong and independent doctor secretly despises people who want things done for them by others.

We experimented with a group of younger physicians and suggested, for example, that they permit their patients to call them by their first names. To the surprise of the doctors, both parties felt that it established a much greater sense of confidence rather than less. It made it unnecessary for the doctors to waste energy on artificial dignity.

Another idea was to hand the patient a copy of the diagnosis and even to admit when necessary that the doctor was not sure about his findings and needed more research. Another practical measure was to print a plaque which was hung up in the doctor's office. In this plaque the patient was told that the discussion of fees was perfectly proper.

Many of these ideas were put into practice with the help of Rollin Waterson, who was then executive secretary of the Alameda County Medical Association. He was one of the first people to pioneer in the field of replacing the outmoded methods of fee collection (usually through aggressive collection agencies) with more human techniques patterned after social service approaches and handled by medical societies in a friendly fashion, permitting the patient to explain why he had not paid his fees. Often enough the real reason was resentment against the doctor. When this was ironed out and discussed with the doctor, the patient paid. This service became so successful that it is now established in many local county medical societies and usually is self-supporting and even produces a profit.

All of these recommended actions had as their goal the bridging of the gap between the present outdated function of the physician and his potential one in a modern democracy. The gap is still considerable. It is a development which will have to proceed in a number of channels, from a sporadic function of the doctor at present to a continuous one . . . from a primarily biological, etiological one to a social one, and from any isolated function to a shared one, and thus from a non-political to a positive democratic one.

A somewhat different aspect of this conflict between individuality and conformism is represented by the veterinarian. In a study done on this group, we found that about 60 per cent of them told us they went into veterinary medicine only after they found it impossible, for one reason or another, to pursue human medical studies. Many vets, we found, are actually frustrated medical doctors. In contrast to the physician, the vet very often reverses the process of a physician. Because of the intensity of his insecurity, his defensiveness, and his resentment, he seeks a means of self-protection in group membership. Among professional men, he prefers to go along with group action. He requires the most support of his colleagues and his organizations.

One group caught in this conflict are the barbers. They have to adjust to changing economic and historical conditions which have diminished in social importance. The barber is a frustrated professional and wants his expert role promoted in the eyes of the public. He's a small businessman who prides himself in being his own boss and seeks reinforcement of his emotional and economic independence. He is painfully aware that he does not enjoy a high social status and he wishes to be admired and recognized in the community. In his relationship with his customers, he is forced to minister to them physically, but does not receive the psychological and material award of a physician or similar bona fide professionals. Consequently he looks for some means to relieve the menial, subservient aspect of his work. The barber needs to be needed. In a material sense, he needs the loyalty of his customers to safeguard his economic security. In a psychological sense, he wants his customers to regard him as a good professional man whose skill is necessary to them. From Roman times until the twentieth century, the barber's art was called a profession. Formerly, the barber performed the offices of a surgeon. He was a tooth-puller, blood-letter, masseur, and also often a bookseller, matchmaker, expert on marriage, town gossip, and relater of news. In times when psychiatrists and other professional counselors were unknown, he gave advice to his patrons on personal problems. Before the rise of the newspaper, telegraph, radio, and other media of mass communication, he spread the news and served as an opinion leader. The barbershop was the center of discussion ranging from local scandal to international politics. The important role of the barber in human relations has found many literary expressions. We advised a cosmetic company which was our client that by restoring some of this role of the barber they could win his good will.

Another important group with similar problems are the farmers. In several studies done in this field, we've found again and again that the farmer considers his occupation a way of life, a philosophy, and that independence and individuality play a very important role in it. "I'm my own boss," is one of the most frequent expressions used by the farmer to describe his occupation. He often joins co-operative groups, not only because of the price advantages in buying or selling his feed or produce, but also because of the flattery to his ego offered by the co-op. They appeal to him as a strong individual who voluntarily joins an organization of equals. The collectivization of Chinese and Russian farmers has been difficult precisely because of the strong individualism of the man who tills the soil. In a study for a large feed company in this country we found that the agricultural customer was resentful when he was told by this company that it was their wonderful research work and their scientists who had developed new formulas and new feed mixtures. By recognizing the role of the farmer first and crediting him with scientific ingenuity and adventurousness the feed company could increase its success.

PSYCHOLOGICAL PARTNERSHIP

Many of the management problems faced by small and large corporations for which we conducted studies show that they are being forced into acceptance of participation as an incentive to keep their workers happy. Profit-sharing plans, incentive plans, are only psychological symbols of the changing relationship between the economic groups and classes. The modern American consumer, too, wants to be taken behind the scenes, wants to know why a new product is being put on the market. The concept of partnership, of equality, applies also to nations. No nation will permit another one to feel and behave in a superior fashion. We shall have to get accustomed to the idea that the United States is another powerful and big country, but not superior to others.

Sometime ago we were engaged to carry out a research study within the Jewel Tea organization, a large food company (*Sharing a Business,* F. J. Lunding). Our assignment was to investigate the psychological effect which a consciously and specially designed managerial policy can have on the morale and on work happiness of the employees, as well as on their attitudes toward the company.

The thousands of employees of Jewel had been over a period of years exposed to a special philosophy of labor-management relations and, specifically, to two forms of profit-sharing—Jewel Retirement

Estates for the rank and file, and an executive plan which covers the department heads.

In a sense, the given circumstances can be compared to a laboratory, where the experiment conducted is part of real life and has been going on for a number of years. This study was like the first reading of the gauge and represented a check of instruments in order to see what the result of the test had been up to this time. The test tube was a living cell of the social organism—a sizable industrial organization. Furthermore, no artificial circumstances had to be introduced. Life itself and real people in their daily jobs represented the subject.

The goal of this research study, therefore, was to see what changes have been produced by a series of controlled factors, such as profit-sharing plans and managerial philosophy, in the extremely sensitive seismograph represented by the human individual—the employee. How does this different treatment affect him in his job? Does a profit-sharing plan make him feel any happier? Does he feel pampered or neglected, more secure or less secure and, of course, does the psychological effect of all these measures make him into a better worker?

When we undertook our research we were prepared to search for signs of appreciation and gratitude in the employee toward the company and its beneficial profit-sharing and bonus systems. To our surprise, something entirely different and rather unexpected was discovered as one of the outstanding effects which these policies have on the Jewel employee. Rather than seeing the company emerge as an outstanding example of management, we see the individual employee proudly referring to his own qualifications and indispensability. Instead of feeling dependent on protective measures and cradle-to-grave security plans of the company, it appears that the employee is convinced that these various plans have been made possible by his own alertness and contributions to the business.

Such a finding may come as a shock. It may sound like a dangerous and unexpected result for a profit-sharing policy. This feeling, however, cannot last very long when we consider that the true democratic idea involves a competitive-enterprise system in which everyone works in his own interest and has the feeling "I am I" without authority over him; but who, at the same time, works for the benefit of the whole society.

Understanding human nature, we can readily see why the effect of Jewel's philosophy and profit-sharing policies are extremely beneficial to the employees as well as to the company itself. In an authoritarian setup the relationship between management and employees is based primarily on emotionalism. Jewel's democratic system, however, uses modern psychological and education techniques, by which employees are treated in such fashion that they are getting realism rather than emotionalism. Thus, it does not produce resentment, but rather self-elevation for the individual and recognition and respect by his coworkers. In this way the employees get the feeling of maturity, independence, accomplishment, power and self-sufficiency, rather than the feeling of reward and punishment.

We found that the over-all effect of Jewel's setup also creates a strong bond and feeling of belonging, but that in this case it is based on the feeling of independence the employee gets rather than on dependence. The Jewel employee thinks in terms of "we," but the meaning is not "we—I as a part of the company," but rather "we—I and the company in back of me."

This is a psychological solution for the employee's strivings to feel good about himself, and the company represents a means to that solution. The most important thing about the independence that the company offers the employee is that with it he is given security by being given the fulfillment of his inner and outer needs in life. That is to say, by its over-all policies and philosophy Jewel gives the employee the feeling that he is a success in life, in relation to himself as well as to the outside world, and that he is an independent individual standing on his own feet.

In creating this feeling, Jewel provides the employee with work incentive. However, this word has to be properly understood. There are two types of incentive. One type comes from without, the other comes from within. The one coming from without is comparable to the reward and punishment of a child and is therefore immature. Furthermore, it requires constant renewal and stronger and stronger stimuli. Every parent is familiar with the fact that rewards as well as punishments wear off. The incentive which we found to be produced in the Jewel employee is one that comes from within. This inner incentive is self-renewing and of a mature character. It becomes part of the permanent personality of the employee.

This study for Jewel represents a powerful way of resolving on a company level the conflict of the modern era between individuality and organization, between competition and co-operation.

RELATIONSHIP BETWEEN THE SEXES

Similar problems exist in many areas. One of the most interesting changes in this quest for identity has taken place in the relationship between the sexes.

Probably 80 per cent of most movies, novels, and television shows have the relationship between men and women as their main topic. We have been accustomed for so many thousands of years to think primarily of the two sexes in respect to their biological differences. What has been happening, however, over the last two decades or so is a change in roles. The strong male who needs a weak female in order that he may act out his role of protector is disappearing. The weak female, the doll, playing on her weakness to deserve protection and thus in an indirect way becoming the master again, is also disappearing.

The competition between the two sexes is being gradually replaced by co-operation and equality. While this is happening, a major result of it is that we have to get accustomed to thinking in terms of individuals first, and biological and occupational roles second. Rather than worrying about what new type of woman is emerging now, we may have to contemplate the fact that instead of dealing with women, we are dealing with persons. Some of these persons happen to have as a secondary role in addition to their personality and occupation—a biological one of being a sexual partner and mother. An acceptance of this fact could bring about a major revolution in our outlook on everyday life. Women are not just buying a soap for the family—even after they are married they still buy a soap for themselves. Gas stations have to accept the fact that they are catering not only to men but also to women, and not only to women as family buyers, but as individuals with their own cars.

In studying the role of modern gas stations this is exactly what we advised: to introduce the feminine decor, to have exhibits of local art, to have vacuum cleaners available for cars, and to serve altogether as a modern community service center.

Office furniture manufacturers now make desks for women; food for women as individuals is produced. This does not mean, however, further emphasis on difference for the sake of differentiation. Instead, it means that a true, modern, non-corny form of family togetherness can be created only if each individual member of the family is being treated as an independent individual. True co-operation and togetherness depends on individual independence.

This is also true in the relationship between nations. A small country has first to gain its independence before it can become a true member of the United Nations.

Rather than distinguish between the supposedly opposite forms of behavior in competition and co-operation, we may have to introduce such distinctions as those between *true* and *false* competition. True competition would be a kind of technique wherein we agree on a common co-operative goal, such as living peacefully together or securing a happy life. In striving for this goal, however, each individual or country would remain in his own field of ability and try to do his best therein. In a well-balanced family, too, we have agreement on a common co-operative goal for the family as a whole. The individual family members do their best in their respective fields of ability and preference. The husband cares for material security, the wife fulfills her household duties, and both compete with each other for a co-operative goal.

True competition safeguards the individual because it insists that every member of the society do his best in his own field, without encroaching upon the field the other member has chosen. False competition, however, leads to a loss of the individual distinction because each one tries, in an aggressive spirit, to do the same as his neighbor, and to do it better. The end result of this is a leveling out of distinct personalities. The increased search for identity is a healthy sign. It can be another key to progress if the conflict is recognized and actively resolved.

12 ■ MISERY OF CHOICE

One of the basic tasks of modern times is to learn to decide. Democracy represents one of the most difficult forms of life adjustment.

Modern economic life, too, is full of decisions; buying, brand selection, arrangement of one's financial affairs are only a few. Yet few of us have learned to make decisions. Contrary to what we think, changing one's brand, one's candidate, one's jobs, are all miseries of choice rather than pleasures.

We found in our political studies that during elections people are often more motivated by what their vote says about themselves as voters than by the beliefs of the candidate. Few people change their minds after listening to a candidate. They want to see themselves as being consistent in various subsequent elections. This is often considered to be more important than to vote against the candidate who is found to be incompetent. People, in a way, say, "I'm supposed to be a man who has made up his mind. If I were to change my mind during each election, what kind of man would I really prove to be?"

One of the first things we have to learn to recognize is that in many instances, when we make a choice, it is very misleading to study the object of the choice in order to find an answer to what takes place when we decide. Much more frequently, we will find the clue to the mental mechanisms involved by looking more closely at the implementations and consequences of each one of the various choices. It happens very frequently that we do not make a choice so much between objects as between choices.

A psychoanalyst was once asked by a young lady to help her make up her mind among three boy friends. She described the advantages and disadvantages of each one of the possible choices. It did not take long to discover that, in truth, she did not want to make a choice, because in choosing, she would cut herself off from her present state of freedom. Once having married one of the three boys, her life would have taken on a definiteness which she would not like. Therefore, her real problem was one of making any choice as against continuously staying in a state of indecision. Her difficulty had little to do with the object of her choice as such.

Our study of decision behavior has shown that there are actually two major types of decisions possible. One type of decision could be called the "free and intelligent" decision; the other one the "packaged and too routinized" decision.

In a series of radio programs entitled "So You Think You Know People" on N.Y. City Station WNEW, I conducted the following experiment: The audience was asked to vote for one of three candidates. One described in detail all the technical qualifications of the politician, his training, how his mind worked, etc. The second one was described by his previous political record, the decisions he had made. The third one was simply pictured as a human being: his emotionalism, how he loved children, the fact that he smoked a pipe, had a dog, and took long walks. The audience was then asked to vote for the candidate among the three who would make the best public servant. Although there was literally nothing in the description of the third candidate which would tell them what he would do as a congressman or senator, he was the one who won. The decision was made on the basis of emotional factors rather than intelligent ones. It was easier for the public to identify with him than with the others. They could understand him as a real person.

Political history is full of examples where people vote for the person who represents an emotional reality, rather than simply for a record of his qualifications. Even a crook is often preferred as a candidate to a colorless, though intelligent, politician.

We often kid ourselves when making up our minds that we do so on the basis of facts. One of the prime roles in decision-making ought to be "beware of your emotions." In our own analysis of political elections, we have been using such tests as the following to measure the chances of one candidate over another. We ask people for example: "If Stevenson were related to you, or Nixon or

Kennedy, what would he be, a father, a brother, an uncle, etc.?" During the last elections we found that Stevenson was the brother or the uncle but hardly ever the father, while Eisenhower was almost always the father. Another approach measuring more reliable emotional factors which influence our decisions instead of intelligent elements was: "Which one of these candidates would you lend money to? Whom do you consider socially inferior, superior, or on the same level as yourself? Who is more or less or equally intelligent compared to yourself?, etc."

Approaches of this type permit a more accurate insight into real feelings about a candidate than superficial questions such as "For which one will you vote?"

In a study of coffee preference we presented three coffee percolators. One was very modern-looking, the second one rather neutral, and the third one very battered and old. The coffee served out of the old can was almost always considered to be the best-tasting, although all three were filled with exactly the same, previously brewed coffee. The decision was influenced by the appearance of the percolator and not by the actual quality of the coffee.

We make many more such routinized and emotional decisions in our daily lives. There are a number of products which apparently have a great deal of brand loyalty. This is true of razor blades, but interestingly enough also of sanitary napkins. The real reason for this we found to be that people tend to routinize unpleasant things. This permits them to forget about these tasks. They do not have to think about them consciously any longer. This is also true of highly emotional events in life. Marriages, funerals, births, all have been surrounded by a large number of rituals. We don't have to make decisions, everything is organized and structured in a rigid fashion.

During the war I conducted a study for the Columbia Broadcasting System on the problem of war widows. How could this tragic subject be discussed on the air in such a way as to help them as much as possible? We found that many of these women reacted to the tragic event in an unexpected hysterical fashion. A deeper analysis revealed this: Contrary to what they had expected, the first reaction of these young women was an upsurge of energy on receiving the news of the death of their soldier husbands. It was as if they felt they had to face the world now all by themselves and needed all the defense possible. Yet nothing in their previous training or in the things they had read had prepared them for this reaction. They were shocked and afraid that it meant that they really had not loved their men. Often they had married quickly only to cover up this fact from the outside world and, even more important, before themselves they had exaggerated their tragedy and become hysterical. Not having been prepared for their reactions they reached for ready-made, routinized behavior learned from mass media and previous influences.

The answer, and the therapy, was to tell them through subtle forms of dramatization that they were not alone in these reactions and that there was nothing abnormal about their behavior. It did not mean lack of love, it was a biological defense.

One of the large soap companies decided to introduce a new brand. They advertised it as being better in seven different ways than one of the well-known brands such as Ivory soap. The reaction of the housewives was very interesting. Rather than rushing out and buying this new and supposedly better soap, they invented reasons why they really should not buy it. They were reacting to the "misery of choice" posed by the new soap. Rather than logically examining whether the new soap was really better they rejected it to such an extent that it eventually had to be discontinued as a brand. The reason for this failure did not lie in the soap and its qualities. It was an unpleasant task for the woman to make this choice. She solved it by sticking to her old soap.

When we stick to our old job, the reason is often the same. We are afraid of the new decision, we remain loyal, or so we say. In reality we are afraid of making a new move. When we stay in the same old neighborhood or resist making a change in our living habits, we are avoiding the "misery of choice."

We studied the possibility of teaching people how to make decisions in connection with voting. These rules also apply to other situations. Voting is one of the most important forms of decision-making. All young countries have to learn this task. Even citizens of the older countries have never really learned how to make decisions on voting.

Basically the problem of voting is directly related to the degree of communication between the citizen and the government, between the voter and the candidate. There is conclusive proof that people's failure to vote is not due to the fact that they do not believe in voting nor that they are lazy. They do not vote because they feel left out of things. They believe they are isolated from the rest of the community and that their experiences and reactions to the affairs of politics are extremely individual and not shared by others in organized bodies.

The reason why people vote is the presence of a deep feeling. They have a sense of participation in the affairs of their government—their vote counts.

In both cases the answer is not a question of semantic juggling. The bare announcement that "this is your community and, therefore, you should vote" cannot be successful without tangible grass-roots evidence which proves that this is your community.

These are some of the results of a voting study conducted for the city of Portland, Maine, and the American Heritage Foundation.

We found that people do not vote for the following reasons:

1. Lack of communication. The government is too far away psychologically. It is not *my* government.
2. Fear of responsibility. If I vote, I become responsible. If I do not vote, I can keep on complaining.
3. Ignorance about candidates is another factor. We found that even knowing negative factors about candidates brings them humanly closer than not knowing anything at all.
4. Sense of futility.
5. Some people feel that voting is difficult. It means making up your mind; deciding.

Our recommendations based on this analysis included the following measures. Specifically, in Portland, these things worked.

1. Neighborhood Town Hall meetings.
2. Giant footsteps on City Hall steps inviting voters to come in.
3. Not telling voters how few vote but how many have switched to voting this year.
4. *New Yorker* type profiles on candidates rather than stiff stereotype descriptions and pictures.
5. Attack through ridicule the idea that the town was really ruled by a clique and voting was futile.

6. Urging voters to keep a diary: record in it (a little booklet) your present opinions about various candidates, their views about issues, etc. Then follow up during next few months and see how your opinions change or whether these opinions are based on real facts or simply on emotions.
7. A TV show or series of shows intended to dramatize for the voter his own process of opinion formation. Ask for opinions before candidates speak, let them speak, and then check how many people changed opinion and what made them do it; what arguments, what facts, mannerisms, etc. Both candidates and public would learn.
8. Newspapers were invited to print in skeleton form structures of issues, pros and cons and alternatives, and then the voter could register on its views held by the candidates and thus receive a clear-cut picture of where the candidate has failed to express himself, etc.
9. Possibly the most important and most immediate job, however, is to give the voter encouragement. He is capable of voting, of being a good citizen; he always comes through. This, I feel, should be the keynote of any "get out the vote" campaign.

Many of these recommendations also apply to making other decisions. Making decisions in all fields should be part of our school curriculum. How can we expect our young citizens to know how to vote if they have never been taught how to make decisions to begin with? Every school curriculum ought to have a class in decision-making.

In this respect dictatorships have an advantage over democracy. They don't need such classes. Issues, in the psychological sense, are presented in fairy-tale or soap-opera fashion. There are black villains and pure white heroes. No great intelligence is necessary to accept the predigested pattern of political and ethical standards. Every child can know and understand that "all capitalists are basically bad because they exploit the masses." Any time you are called upon to discuss an issue, all you have to do is to fit the opponent or issue into the general structure of the controversy between capitalism and communism. There is the answer, premanufactured. Under fascism, too, evaluations were made on the basis of a clear scheme: "All Germans who are racially pure and believe in the Fuehrer are infallibly right in their actions." It is simple to choose sides.

Without copying fascist methods it is advisable to make it easier for young people to acquire a political education. Why could not our daily papers devote one full page to a clear, simplified, possibly visualized, presentation of the day's news and its influence on major issues? Why does radio or TV not provide such simplifications? All forms of communication should co-operate to bring about an acute awareness of our political life and its meaning. If we reduce the fear in youth that they are incapable of understanding politics and accepting change we cut off an important avenue of escape from the responsibilities of living in and maintaining a democracy.

We, as parents or teachers, might spend some time with our children discussing the day's political events, explaining and clarifying their issues. We might show them that politics is not too difficult to grasp, and that decisions are easy to make. We could teach them how to gather facts, how to compare the pros and cons of an issue. Why could not each City Hall or other centers of community life have a bulletin board sent to schools for discussion? Included would be an explanation of how each representative voted in various debates, what issues were under discussion by the city's governing boards, and other such pertinent facts. Unfinished business would remain posted for public information until action had been taken. The community bulletin board would become the conscience of the town.

The Federal Trade Commission has begun to concern itself with consumer education. It correctly wants to teach the public how to recognize phony advertising claims and not to fall for sensational stories presented in publicity and propaganda. I think it would be a good idea to teach youngsters to recognize their own gullibility, their readiness to be fooled, simply because they want to believe something. I can see students being asked to analyze advertising, to bring in merchandise which they or their parents had bought and which turned out to be faulty and falsely represented. This kind of training would be a better guard than even a self-imposed code of ethics among advertisers or a control by the FTC.

In a study done on political attitudes of young people, we found many disturbing things: A majority of youngsters were not interested in politics and were even proud of the fact. Ruby, who was interviewed in her home in the midst of making a dress for her college wardrobe (she was typical for her age group of seventeen) explained why she was not interested in politics: "Maybe it is because it is all too complicated, all the petty arguments and little details, it goes beyond me. You have to keep up with every little point."

NO ONE IS INTERESTED IN US

Indignation was shown by thirteen-year-old Judy, who expressed herself in the following manner: "I don't feel that there is anything there that I do but hope—outsiders, especially grown-ups, wouldn't be very much interested in your opinions; they think that you are a child and that you don't know much about it, that you don't know what is good for the people or who would be good in office . . . The only thing that I can do is write my congressman and tell him what I think but I don't know if he would take much interest in my letter, my being a child. No, a young citizen cannot have much effect on a congressman. I do think that is one reason why I am not actively interested in politics. It does bother me some, because we are citizens and we think certain things that are worthwhile. I do think that I would be more interested in doing things if I knew that my opinions were worth something."

The moral and religious education of our children starts at a relatively early age. We recognize the importance of giving the child the feeling that he is a part of this world, that what he does is just as important in the eyes of God, the Church, and his fellow men, as if he were a grown-up. When four-year-old Susan hits her brother over the head, we are quick in teaching her the moral implications of this misbehavior. We realize the importance of a a gradual deepening of moral and religious responsibility. Scarcely anyone would suggest that a child not be allowed to enter a church until he is twenty-one, or not be urged to behave in a civilized manner before he has reached maturity.

In sharp contrast, in the political field we let the adolescent feel that no one is interested in his opinions and ideas. We cannot possibly give him the right to vote, but there are many other ways by which we are able to make the young man or woman realize that his opinion is valued. He might be given a much more active role in the determination of all the community affairs which personally concern him. When your family decides where to go for a vacation or how to spend some extra saved-up money, let your children in. Ask them to express their opinion. Decide on the basis of a majority vote. Teach your children not to be afraid of the "misery of choice," to make intelligent rather than routine decisions.

Young people can be shown how to exert their influence on persons of voting age. If you have to answer Joel's questions you may be forced to greater honesty and sharper thinking. The political awareness of young future voters would serve as a very important stimulus for older voters.

The technical forms by which this can be accomplished are not difficult to devise. At election time ask the young people of the community to vote. Although their votes would not count, they would learn to make decisions on important issues and to think objectively rather than to be influenced by personal likes and dislikes.

POLITICS AREN'T GLAMOROUS ENOUGH

With the help of the movies and radio, we have surrounded certain professions with an aura of glamor and excitement. Politics and politicians do not come into this category. To most of the young people we talked to, politics and politicians are drab and dreary. To be interested in politics, to be a good speaker, is nothing of which the American youngster is particularly proud. The social reward certainly cannot compare with the prestige of being a jitterbug or a baseball star or of owning a car. An attractive fifteen-year-old girl, dressed neatly in a light-blue cotton dress which showed up her deep tan, and looking very much like "the American Girl," told us that, "It's not so much that the teen-agers aren't interested when something important happens, but it's that they don't want other kids to think that they are 'brainy' or going 'intellectual.'" In other words, it just isn't fashionable to talk about politics and no one has ever attempted to make it so.

Dictatorial countries, again, have the jump on us, for they understand how to introduce glamor into the political awareness necessary for their own sinister purposes. A student would be considered dumb and backward if he were not fully informed about political issues and could not produce at least half a dozen arguments in defense of his own political convictions. We have to learn to make intellectual prowess and political alertness as desirable and worth striving for as other achievements. Many aspects of our educational system can contribute to such a greater appreciation of "intellectual political" qualities. A vast public-relations job using school, radio, movies, all mass media to bring about such a shift in values is needed.

Young people require ideals for their character formation. It is disquieting to observe how few select politicians as their ideals. Our own study revealed that the majority of respondents did not have too high an opinion of congressmen and senators. Even those who felt that politicians were, by and large, honest found it necessary to introduce a defensive tone into their statement. Listen to some of the statements of condemnation and acceptance. Take, for instance, the testimony of seventeen-and-a-half-year-old Kay: "What do I think about politicians? Most of them are crooks. They're all connected with party machines and all that. The trouble is that people don't vote. If people voted, you wouldn't have all those crooked men."

The preference for a strong leader is the symptom of the basic dilemma of democracy. We want individual freedom, yet we are ready to run away from this freedom, part of our democracy. If physical and other obvious expressions of freedom are being threatened we do not flee, but when psychological freedom is concerned, that is, the privilege of making our own decisions, then we balk. The task ahead seems to be difficult; we are afraid. We try to get around it, we attempt detours. If we are lucky enough to find someone who will help us to escape from this burden of freedom, we readily relinquish it. To have a strong leader who is concerned with the good of the people is convenient, pleasant, and spoils us. When this leader goes and we must resume for ourselves government by the people, we feel insecure, lost, ill-equipped.

It is quite possible that juvenile delinquency has its real cause in this lack of a challenge, a cause for which a youngster can fight. He needs ideals. If he does not have them he constructs them, organizes gangs, defends the flag of the "Crusaders against the Sparrers." What we need is a militant democracy which establishes goals worth fighting for.

Youth is even more entangled in this dilemma. Psychologically, the role of the father and the role of the leader or president resemble each other. The youngster has to decide between growing out of his family's protection, struggling against the pleasant security of the family household, and mastery of the world outside, standing maturely on his own.

In the political sphere the adolescent has to learn to mature similarly. Proper political education would demonstrate to the young man and the young woman that they themselves determine their future and their destiny. The success of this education depends largely on the kind of family the youngster grows up in. Some families have a democratic structure, too many are governed by authoritarian principles. The dictatorial family, where the father makes all the decisions, often functions more smoothly and with less friction than the democratic family. It is more strenuous for the parents to give the youngsters a voice. It takes twice as much time to argue with eight-year-old Tommy that he cannot play in the mud because he would get his clothes dirty than to simply tell him that he will be punished if he doesn't obey.

Too often we think only of physical defense when we are reminded that our freedom must be fought for and defended. It is more important for us to receive training for psychological freedom. We have to learn to beware of the convenience of executing orders and enforcing their compliance. The ability to reason issues out, to think, this kind of education can only start in our homes. Real freedom is freedom from our own enemies, from fears, escapism, and unclear thinking.

13 ■ THE "BURDEN" OF THE GOOD LIFE

Many of our studies over the past few years have uncovered an interesting attitude. Large sections of the population tend to feel worried about the good life. A cobweb of tradition and morality, beginning with the concept of original sin, has painted life as a sequence of worry and toil, if not of misery. Yet this picture does not match the reality of life in the United States where most people have more than enough to eat and a well-shingled roof over their heads. Probably for the first time in the history of the modern world, there seems to be enough for all to live in comfort. Workers, from factory hand to plumber, from farmer to white-collar employees, are proud of their occupations. Yet, there is an over-all question running through the minds of many people, and the answer to it may well make the difference between whether the good life continues or whether it peters out.

The question is "Where are we going? What is the purpose of this good life?" Implied in the question itself is the fear that we do not deserve the good life we have. Somewhere deep in the recesses of our minds, we believe in the superstition of seven good years followed by seven bad. We are frightened by continued prosperity. We consider it almost a sin and many of us feel relieved when the future begins to look rough, as in a depression. Hadn't our critics accused us of paying too much attention to the good life, to the thick rugs and the new leisure, instead of attending to hard work and tough education? That, we are told, is the real reason the Russians are getting ahead of us.

I believe this attitude is erroneous. It is interesting as an expression of our basic feeling of discomfort about the good life. But if our way of life is to continue, we must remove this guilt feeling. We must make the average American accept the fact that a more comfortable life, a life of greater leisure, is one of the major achievements and not one of the major failures of the American way of life. The leisure time must be used for worth-while goals, for goals of growth and personal achievement rather than for lazy contentedness. It is up to the educator, the leader, the advertiser, the government official, to anyone who has access to people, to use his leadership to combat the guilt feeling among the American people, to convince them that it is all right to enjoy life.

There are even broader implications. Our economic world today is based on many products and services that can only be described as non-utilitarian. In many instances, they are superfluous and self-indulgent. If we really wanted to live rationally, we would all live in steel-reinforced concrete bunkers, wear overalls, reject fireplaces, refuse all fashion changes, keep cars for ten or fifteen years, cut out smoking and drinking and overeating, and so on down the line. It does not need much proof to make it clear that our economy, and for that matter the economy of the rest of the world, including that of Russia, would collapse almost overnight on a purely utilitarian basis.

On my recent trip to Moscow and some of the satellite countries, it was very obvious that people there are just as much interested in shiny cars, good food, and sumptuous living, the only difference being that they haven't reached our level yet. They have recently even introduced installment buying with great success. Our modern world will survive or fail not so much because of the right or wrong economic philosophy, but because of the right or wrong moral philosophy. One of the major difficulties the Western world is faced with today is having reached the stage of affluence in many ways without having the accompanying justification for an eventual three-day work week and the life of plenty.

Modern technology and the almost monthly new discoveries of easier ways of living thanks to new gadgets and electronic, atomic, and biological developments, all necessitate abandoning the concept that man is made and born to suffer and to live by the sweat of his brow. The concept of original sin and the humility of man is a dangerous one. It may be a prerequisite for maintaining his dependency on fatherlike figures in the religious or political sense. But if we believe in the final goal of human maturity, it will have to give way to a new insight, the insight that man is only at the beginning of his potentialities, that the more he becomes independently free of superstition and crutches of all kinds, the more he will indeed be fulfilling his final destiny of being in the image of God. The social scientists of the future and possibly scientists in all fields will have to concern themselves more and more with the final goals and destinies of mankind, rather than just with the narrow confines of their particular specialties.

A physician, advising his patient to take a vacation, may have to think first of the guilt feelings that might be the result in a particular individual caught in our contemporary value system which considers leisure immoral. The atomic scientist should possibly worry more or at least as much about the moral consequences of the use of atomic energy for the increased leisure of humans than about the destructive possibilities of atom bombs.

We have reached a new phase, one of affluence and almost overdevelopment. In order to be able to enjoy our daily life without guilt feelings, we have to develop a corresponding morality concept. This morality concept is not one of defending self-indulgence, a soft life, but one of defending the idea that the basic goal of life is human dignity, the ability to achieve self-realization through leisure and control of the technical difficulties of the world which surround us. It is the idea of making possible a new type of creativeness which we once had in very primitive days when the demands of life were at a much lower level and therefore quickly satisfied. This creativeness has now been made possible again since technological advances have permitted us to control very many of the daily physical chores. The introduction of and change-over to this new philosophy is not easy. It seems we have been trained for so many thousands of years to devote the larger part of our energies to survival and struggle against the elements that now when these difficulties have been reduced, particularly in the Western world, we find ourselves at a loss.

Every new so-called convenience product that appears on the scene is first looked upon with suspicion and guilt feelings. Gradually at an ever-increasing speed it is fully accepted. Examples are instant coffee, detergents, washing machines of all kinds. Even when approaching these problems with a complete disregard for ethical problems we must come to the conclusion that in the long run these company-manufactured products that present real advancement and new services and conveniences to the consumer are the ones that succeed and those which simply represent frivolous obsolescence fail.

There is a possible exception in the fashion field, but even there experience has shown that introducing 150 to 200 new patterns every year often results in a clogging of the market, inability on the part of the consumer to make a choice, and a slowing down of sales rather than an increasing of them. As the taste level of the American people rises, new fashions are being introduced. As long as they are, however, real advancements in sophistication, they are permissible and moral technological advancements rather than frivolous obsolescence.

Motivational thinking, even when applied to commercial problems, does not manipulate people, talk them into buying things that they really do not need, by twisting their unconscious. What motivational research truly does, when it is put in its proper framework, that of our present economic system, is to provide a bridge between the consumer and the manufacturer, exerting influence on the manufacturer much more than on the consumer, teaching him that his salvation lies in true technological advancements and in opening new frontiers satisfying the real needs of the consumer.

This might lie in the improvement of existing products, in the invention and development of completely different types of products, or in the opening up of new markets for existing products, such as swimming pools, travel, foreign food, etc.

When Galbraith, in his book *The Affluent Society*, says that "it is all right to put furniture into an empty room, but it is silly to keep on cramming furniture into a room that is already filled with furniture," he makes a mistake. He overlooks the basic psychological fact that human needs are plastic and expansive. Our answer to this is that if the room is filled with furniture one likely event is a desire to enlarge the room and thus make the need for new furniture again operative. At the same time, the same furniture in the existing room becomes out of date either fashion-wise or technologically; and therefore, at one point demands replacement. This is much closer to reality than an abstract, economic analysis of human needs. Human needs change, and almost while they are being satisfied undergo changes by themselves.

This is indeed what is called progress and what life in its psychological superstructure is all about. When we are dealing with a product or technological advancement of any kind, we have to learn to consider and to look upon the individual, the user, the housewife, not as the passive recipient on whom stimuli are being registered. He is an active respondent, and a whole series of reaction patterns are being set in motion each time a contact with a product, with an appliance, a machine is established. Too many of the appliances, products, services are constructed from the viewpoint of physical needs and physical protection rather than from the viewpoint of the psychological needs of the consumer.

In an oven, for instance, the real contact point between a woman and an oven is the bar, the handle by which the door of the oven is opened. If this contact point, as we found in a study for an appliance manufacturer, has sharp edges, a basic barrier against a better establishment of an intimate contact may exist. If, instead, it were round, more pleasant to the touch, this contact would be assured. The way the door of this oven sounds when being closed may be more important than the actual thickness of the steel or aluminum used. This has been recognized in cars for many years. When push buttons are arranged in such a way that the highest degree of heat is at the bottom of the gauge instead of at the top, a conflict exists between the co-ordinate system in the mind of the individual and the engineering co-ordinate system.

Very many of the new developments that appear year after year could have been possible decades ago. They were not introduced because the designer, the manufacturer, did not have enough imagination, not enough acceptance of a "why not" kind of philosophy. To recognize that one way for a woman to take possession of an appliance is to be able to shine it would and should influence the designer to have enough shinable surface on this stove. The ease of cleaning an oven has a technological but also a psychological element.

In many of our studies, we actually have ventured into the field of psychological engineering. In work for the automobile industry, we stated repeatedly that what the modern American wants is to be able to stress his individuality in his car. If this ability to express his individuality is not built into the car, he will reject it. The small car and the compact car are successes because they permit mastery of the car again. The success or failure of American business and industry does not lie only in the ingenuity of the technicians, but possibly much more so in the ingenuity, creativeness, and readiness of the consumer to accept new things. If he is made aware of his desire for improvements, he can be taught to express this desire. The manufacturer then will, for competitive and profit reasons, have to follow suit.

Our role, then, as scientific communicators, as persuaders, is one of liberating these desires, not in an attempt to manipulate but in an attempt to move our economic system forward and with it our pursuit of happiness.

In a study on how to get women to accept colored nylon bed sheets we found that when we asked why they didn't buy them they said they were too expensive. When we showed them the actual price, which was lower than that of cotton sheets, they were surprised. The real reason for their rejection of nylon bed sheets we found to lie in the area of morality. The woman was afraid that using a colored nylon bed sheet would give her husband "ideas." This was reinforced by the fact that the ads showed a young girl in bed sleeping on the nylon sheets. Furthermore, bed sheets are either received as a dowry or bought ten years later to replace the original ones received at the time of marriage. The implication of immorality was found to be such a strong deterrent to the purchase of colored nylon bed sheets that we recommended that instead of the young girl, "grandma" be shown, thus making the buyer feel that such bed sheets were morally all right.

What we are doing is progress engineering. We do not manipulate people. We find out what technological and psychological needs of people have not been satisfied up to now. By offering these satisfactions in the new products, we help competitive selling but we also help technological and economic progress. We are consumers' representatives. We pass on this information to the advertiser and the industrialist, showing him how he can make more money by giving people what they truly want.

This does not mean, however, satisfying their basic instincts, debasing people. If we probe deeply enough, we find that what people truly want is not just more practical products and materialistic values. Very few products have purely utilitarian aspects. They are really bought only because they help us to achieve a number of deeper psychological goals. True commercial success does not rely on giving people superficial satisfaction which might keep them on the level on which they are, but offers them something better than what they have at this moment. "Better" can mean a technological improvement and it can mean a psychological improvement. From what we have said before, however, technological improvements are accepted only if they have a psychological benefit at the same time.

A motion-picture projector manufacturer conducted a survey among schoolteachers (mostly female), who are a prime market for projectors, to find out why they did not use them more frequently, when they professed to value them as important educational tools. The overt reason given was that not enough projectors were available to them. Administrators, however, claimed there weren't more of them because teachers didn't use the ones there were or request more. Eventually the reason for the non-use was ascertained to be that teachers considered them too complicated for unmechanical females to handle comfortably or securely. As a result, engineering efforts were bent on making the manufacturer's projectors comparative paragons of simplicity and ease of operation and increased sales were happily anticipated.

Nothing happened. Why?

Motivational research techniques employed in a "psychological engineering" approach revealed the simple fact that while the redesigned projectors *were* easy to operate, they didn't *look* easy to operate.

Solution: Further redesign aimed at making the projectors *seem* easy to operate as well as *being* easy to operate.

Result: Increased sales in school systems—increased production—expanded economy.

In a study in France we were interested in finding out about tricots and jerseys. We found, contrary to our expectations, that French women were more concerned with clothes as an investment rather than with the fashion aspect of the clothes. The frequency of remarks referring to quality and durability of clothes, and jerseys in particular, proved this. Every purchase of a dress by the French housewife really mobilizes a philosophical concept. The concept of buying to last and to please at the same time are in conflict.

We recommended that stress be put on the beauty and fashion aspect, selling the French woman on what to look for when buying clothes. In contrast to this country, a need for planned obsolescence does exist in France. "I buy to invest and I hold on to it," is still the prevailing philosophy. Standstill is not an answer to the negative aspects of planned obsolescence. This may well be one of the problems of the French economy and the economies of other countries.

To some extent the needs and wants of people have to be continuously stirred up. Unless I want more things, I will not work harder in order to get them. Another example is one I encountered in Western Samoa. The Samoans work only about two or three hours a day. They want, however, increased and improved products, electricity, cars, etc. Sleeping as much as they do and working as little as they do, they cannot get those products.

Even in good restaurants in Australia, South Africa, and India, meat and many other products are not yet up to American standards. When I complained about it, they said, "Yes, we know." The Australians are not willing to pay for better meat. "We could produce better meat, we could corn-feed our steers and would have better steaks, the same steaks that you have in your country, but the Australians do not want to work harder so that they will make more money to pay for the better steaks. Because they will not buy the better steaks, we can't afford to have better steers. It's the chicken-and-egg problem in reverse."

Because of world competition, the easy life and the good life that countries like Samoa or Australia have had up to now cannot be maintained any longer unless they increase their productivity.

America has often been described, at least abroad, as a country where advertising techniques have reached perfection. In recent years, to this accusation has been added a fearful expectation that America is developing the techniques of mass manipulation bringing us close to 1984 and Big Brother.

The reality is quite different. Just take one good look at the reality. If we really had mastered the techniques of mass communication, we would have, for instance, licked the problems of juvenile delinquency and racial prejudice. We would also have licked the problem of our negative image abroad and managed to create a more favorable one. We would have been more successful in our propaganda battle with the Russians.

The truth is that we do not have enough techniques of "persuasion," or at least that we have not learned yet to apply those techniques which are successful. Newspapers and magazines abound with accusations that we fail to improve our educational system.

We blame our soft way of life and we accuse the advertisers of seducing the consumer to spend money. The moment we replace the emotionally charged, consequently misleading words "propaganda" or "persuasion" with such a neutral word as communication, the problem becomes much clearer.

We begin to see then that if we have to communicate—and indeed we have to communicate rather more than less on a national and international level—we must be able to distinguish between correct forms of communication and incorrect forms. After all, we live in a world where communication constitutes one of the most important aspects of interpersonal relations. We have always communicated, either in a hidden or open form. When the lover tries to win his girl friend, when the teacher tries to get a pupil to study his lesson, when a mother urges her children to brush their teeth, they all "persuade," they all communicate, they all educate.

If we strip all ideologies of their political implications, all of them are really trying to develop a formula for the happiness of the individual. By happiness in its true definition we have to understand, however, progress and growth rather than cowlike contentedness. We can assume that Russia, for instance, right now is governed by a partially puritanical philosophy, and yet by its own statements, it is striving for the "affluent society" which Galbraith rejects.

If the fight between the United States and Russia is one of peaceful competition, one could say that it is something very desirable. It will keep us on our toes. It will eventually result in a combination of the ingenuity, efficiency, and work capacity of both countries, each one representing its own interest. The human race as a whole should benefit by it. Armaments and similar expenditures are inhuman, because they do not contribute to the advancement of the human race. They are unproductive, they can only be destroyed and used for destruction and not put into the service of human productivity.

We are not dealing here simply with a problem of morality: that it is more defensible to introduce technological improvements than frivolous innovations. Instead, we are dealing with the necessity of reconciling the technological reality—a reality of affluence, continuous new discoveries, etc.—and the superstructure, the ideology to go with it. We are still utilizing puritanical concepts which probably were fruitful concepts at a time when we were still building the country.

Persuasion or communication is not only not bad, but the more we can learn about communication techniques and the more efficiently and scientifically we can learn to practice them, the better off we are going to be. As far as morality is concerned, this does not lie in the question of using more or less efficient techniques of communication. It lies with the goal, the final end result to be reached by these techniques of persuasion.

A knife has no morality of its own. Making it sharper thus does not make it more or less immoral. Persuasion techniques are like sharpened knives. They are tools. Of course, the wielder of the tool *has* to have moral standards. As long as they are, however, only borrowed from a given culture or political system, they are relative. What is considered moral in one culture can be rejected by another one as viciousness and devilish pursuit. People still are being killed because of differences in moral concepts.

The purpose and the goal for which persuasion techniques are being used have to come from our own philosophy of life as moral human beings. The only way we can make sure that it is a correct one is to make it independent of our own upbringing and the culture or cultures within which we have lived and live. As far as possible, it should also be independent of economic systems. But if we are convinced that the democratic form of life is the closest that we have come so far to satisfying the basic human needs of dignity and psychological self-determination, then the goals which we consider to be moral and right must to a large extent coincide with the psychological and economic goals of democracy and free enterprise. Free enterprise and indeed our whole concept of modern economic life, even that of the Communist world, cannot survive unless we abandon the idea that a comfortable life is automatically an immoral one.

We are ashamed of our thick carpets, good food, and enormous cars. The Russians strive for the very same symbols of affluence but are clever enough to explain them in advance as results of socialistic achievements. What has become imperative for us is to revise our morality. Hedonism, as defended by the old Greeks, has to be brought to the surface again. We have to learn to forget the guilt of original sin.

We had to live by the sweat of our brow because we did not know any better. With atomic energy and electronic computers, we'll have to learn to live with a three-day week and increased leisure. We have to train ourselves to overcome the horror of the vacuum of non-strenuous work. We've been brought up under the Puritan concepts (in Europe even more so than here) that to preserve and to save and to work hard are the mainstays of our morality. We're learning, therefore, to substitute happiness for financial conquests. We are, however, more afraid of what to do with the four empty leisure days than we are afraid of the three workdays.

The misery of choice we have to resolve, if we want our free enterprise system to survive, is to be able to live with the ever increasing technological helper that threatens to make our life easier and better. We have to learn to accept the morality of the good life.

Having enough to eat makes spiritual goals easier to pursue than does being hungry. It is a possibly regrettable aspect of human nature, but nevertheless a true one, that the more threatened we feel in our animal security the more we behave in a primitive and animal fashion. Animals are contented, and usually more so than humans.

We must use the modern techniques of motivational thinking and social science to make people constructively discontented by chasing them out of the false paradise of knowledgeless animal happiness into the real paradise of the life of change and progress. Only in this way can we assure truly human survival. The techniques of persuasion represent the forces which can teach us to resolve the misery of choice between a fearful, cave man, animalistic way of life and the decision in favor of really human, self-assured thinking in a new and changing world.

14 ■ SEARCH FOR A GOAL

Many of the anxieties and discontents of modern man are the result of lack of goals. He is grasping for a clear definition of his personal destiny. Many of today's problems, the individual's as well as those of groups and nations, can be understood and thus eventually resolved if they are seen as aspects and conflicts of growth and a maturing process.

Understanding these conflicts can, I feel, point the way to a better understanding of what motivates people. This insight will help put our strategy on the right side of each dilemma, thus deciding in favor of correct rather than more comfortable decisions.

There are several such conflicts in our era, as I have shown in this book. Each one of them manifests itself in many ways. Political questions of nationalism, the creation of united republics under various banners, really are based on the conflict of individualism and collectivism as forms of security. The samc conflict is involved between the desire to be different and the fear of standing out, and it reveals itself in our daily habits, what we buy, eat, or wear, or the way we vote.

We fight the beginning of the recognition of our irrationality because we want to continue the illusion of our rationality. We consider possessiveness as materialistic and immoral, while we lack at the same time the courage to admit that we have few ideals to replace tangible goods as the goals of our life. We have been taught for so long that to enjoy life is bad that now when we can see a new goal of comfort and security on the horizon we are ready to punish ourselves for the achievement we have worked so hard for.

It is these conflicts that represent the true *Zeitgeist*, the spirit of our era. As contemporaries of this era, we and our actions are largely motivated by its conflicts. As potential victor in these conflicts man can be influenced toward a universal goal of human self-fulfillment. Many of the near goals of human strategy of daily political, educational, and commercial life can be integrated with these far goals of achievement.

This is what this book is about: providing a better structure and understanding for the goals and motivations of man in a conflict era. Certainly the social scientist, whether in the therapeutic field or in the communication field, can only truly find answers to the work he is doing if he knows what he wants to adjust his patient to, or what final goal he pursues by a particular communications approach in the propagandistic advertising or teaching field.

An example of a new kind of thinking was reported in *Look* magazine, March 14, 1950:

President Roosevelt was supposedly worried about whether an atomic weapon would be ready in time to decide the outcome of the war. Dr. Alexander Sachs, his close personal adviser, had estimated the project might cost two billions and told the President that ordinarily it would take twenty-five years to do the job. He explained to F.D.R. that he had searched the history of human thought for an example of how time could be telescoped. He found the example in music, he said. A composer of music has ways of making time three-layered. Remember the old round you used to sing, "Are you sleeping, Brother John?"—three tunes going at once, harmoniously overlapping each other. This, he advised, was what must be done with the atomic project. When you start one part of the project, assume you finish it successfully, you start the next as if you had. That is exactly what was done, probably for the first time with such a huge undertaking.

Our growth takes place on many such layers. Usually we use words like "growth" or "maturity" as if they could stand by themselves. They cannot. To gain a meaning, these words must be qualified and directed toward an object. We must always grow toward, educate for or against something, live for something, adjust or fail to adjust ourselves to a definite set of circumstances.

What then, does one live for, mature for? Life is simply for living. We must live for life itself; the object of life is to be as fully alive as possible. And the more alive we feel ourselves to be, the more meaningful everything about us becomes.

Today, as a rule, we consider our lives meaningful and successful if we have more or less adjusted ourselves to existing circumstances, succeeded in our job, gotten married, raised children, and built an estate. However, the fact that so many among us so often fall prey to feelings of frustration despite apparent success shows that something fundamental is missing in our education and thinking—that the standard of fullness and success is wrong. What we often fail to do is to establish some deeper goals in life, set them forth clearly, and then use them as the measure of our achievements.

But can we establish criteria for these deeper goals? Aren't we here dealing with notions on the one side too personal and on the other hand too vast and imponderable to be captured and dealt with by the minds of ordinary human beings? Basing my conclusions on established biological and psychological facts, I suggest that there are a number of demonstrable criteria for setting goals which can lead any of us to a life of satisfaction and fulfillment.

1. GET SET FOR CHANGE

One of the important questions, therefore, we must ask ourselves is this: To what extent are we prone to do things and think about things in an unvarying, stereotyped manner and to attempt to impose on life a fixity and stability it clearly does not have?

This question is important because any personal or business philosophy or managerial decision which disregards the continuous process of changing is erroneous and must lead sooner or later to psychological maladjustment and to economic difficulties. Given the fact of constant change, the ability to adjust oneself to ever new circumstances and problems becomes all-important. As a psychologist, I admire the wisdom of Mr. J. J. Babb, former chairman of the board of Lever Brothers, who told me about his urge to concern himself with products entirely different from those produced by his own company and to be active on the boards of several concerns. Such activity, he said, refreshes his mind and gives him unexpected insights into the problems of his own firm.

The education our generation received has largely failed to prepare us to face constant change. Is this mistake to be repeated? Are we educating our children to be flexible, to be ready to adjust themselves to ever new sets of circumstances and problems? Or are we intent on fostering in them a sense of "security" by letting them grow up in the midst of the same routine, with the same symbols of stability?

I have already distinguished between two types of security: static and dynamic. The first places its faith in the permanence of the exterior world and exterior circumstances, the second in the permanence of one's capacity to cope with the changing world. Since the first attitude is based on wishful thinking, it is the contrary of real security and can only lead to constant anxiety and tension.

We speak of the time when we will have paid off the mortgage, or become a manager, or acquired a certain income, or married off our children. We envision these events as the great divide when our troubles will be over. But as the Chinese say, there are always mountains behind the mountains; hardly have we solved a major problem when a new one is bound to arise. We must remember, then, that change is the only permanent thing in life, and consider the concept of dynamic security not as a trying injustice, but as a challenging tonic.

2. BE SURE YOUR LIFE IS GROWTH

Life is constantly changing, but man's life must not be permitted to be a random change. Change must become growth leading to maturity. The widening circle of experience must also spiral upward, toward a larger horizon and greater understanding.

First of all, man must avoid the danger of becoming the prisoner of a fixed self-image, of assuming a role and playing it to the bitter end. Such role-playing is understandable. It is a defense mechanism through which a person attempts to achieve identity in a changing world. It, however, kills the possibility of growth.

In our studies for the medical profession we found that some of the thorniest problems in doctor-patient relationships originate in the psychological fact that modern patients often behave like adolescent sons. They feel they are well-informed about medicine, they talk back, show impatience, and put pressure on the physician.

In these situations it behooves the doctor to prove his maturity. As a rule he has an image of himself as an idealist and an authoritative scientist rolled in one, who deserves the greatest deference. He acts immaturely, however, if under the pressure of his self-image he allows himself to take offense at the patient.

The process of growing up applies to business problems as well. All too often businessmen do not take a necessary step because they fear that they will have to assume unfamiliar roles and show a wider grasp of life than circumstances have called for in the past. But no growth is possible without the willingness to enter into new experiences, make bold decisions, and solve conflicts on their merits rather than by fiat.

Whenever confronted with a new situation, one should always vote for growth and maturity, almost to the extent of undertaking to do precisely what one is afraid of doing.

3. CULTIVATE EMPATHY

In novels or in real life most of us have encountered wives who complained that their husbands were "taking them for granted." What is the real meaning of this expression?

At the operative level it means that the husband has lost his sensitivity toward her moods, her emotional fluctuations, the varied stirrings in her soul. Hidden indifference of this kind is not necessarily restricted to married life. It may develop in a person's relationship to his associates, employees, and friends, and to the world. But on whatever level this withdrawal or alienation occurs, its most evident result is an impoverishment of a person's own life. Man's imagination and sensitivities develop to the fullest through human bonds. And the key to this constant, vital stimulation is empathy.

Empathy is spontaneous response to another human being. It is the faculty to understand and to share experiences. When we are overly immersed in our own problems, when we permit ourselves to be obsessed by our own tasks and difficulties, we lose that capacity. Stern single-mindedness, it is true, may permit one to accomplish his task. But the task itself thereby becomes largely meaningless. For in the course of events one has abandoned the richest source of inspiration and satisfaction: feeling vibrantly human toward fellow humans.

Empathy has several levels. From a feeling of tenderness to a feeling of admiration it encompasses a great number of inspiring human relationships. What all these feelings have in common is the phenomenon of release, of giving.

The capacity for release is not only a source of personal enrichment. It is also a great asset in business life. As the sociologist Herbert Mayer stated, the good leader perceives others as individuals with motives, feelings, and goals of their own, whereas the poor leader is more likely to perceive others in relation to his own motives and goals.

4. ASK BIG QUESTIONS

Suppose the son of a corporation president announces one day that he has decided to marry a girl who is not only economically and socially unsuited to him, but manifestly has very low moral and intellectual standards. The chances are his father will ask him how he hopes to find true companionship; how he expects to keep his friends; or whether he realizes that he is casting a shadow over his mother's last years.

These questions, however, would be far off the true mark; they would relate to peripheral areas and not to the essence of the problem. The basic questions in this case would be something like this: "What has gone wrong with the development of my son? What are the root causes of his revolt against values which he seemingly rejects and whose lack will poison his life?"

In other words, in this, as in every other important situation, one must see life in the perspective of fundamental concepts and ask the big questions.

We are, in fact, too often ready to follow the line of least resistance and consider our problems in the terms of ready-made, easy concepts. This is true in business situations as well as in private life.

There are few satisfactions in life comparable to the ones a person gets from using the larger point of view, from asking the big questions. Events and phenomena in life should never become simple illustrations of a routine truth. Life is a big deal and it must be understood in the big manner. Down at this fundamental level everything hangs together, and the real grandeur of the smallest things appears in their relationship to some transcendent, illuminating original cause in the heart of man or nature.

5. REVIVE YOUR SENSIBILITY

Modern man is slowly awakening to the dangers of what is often called "the artificiality of our civilization."

The increasing eagerness of advertising executives, for instance, to buy farms and take up cattle raising or apple growing on the side is an instinctive rebellion against a restricted existence. Fishing and hunting offer similarly desirable direct experiences of nature, of sights, sounds, smells, which have a tremendously refreshing effect, although their value cannot be determined by rational standards.

But simpler exercises too may reawaken your senses and re-establish direct communication with the world. When have you last lifted your head while walking from the railroad station to your home, looked at the houses and noticed the roofs, the windows, the architectural peculiarities in your neighborhood? Have you really been using your eyes? You will be surprised how many new things you can discover in the course of one day.

Are you paying attention to sounds, singling them out, and letting them penetrate your consciousness? Do the voices of your associates have a meaning for you? Are you open to the rustling of leaves, the foghorn on the river, the mysterious noises that always float around any home and contribute so much to its individual atmosphere? How long has it been since you have paid attention to the feel of leather, of wood, the good feel of a good tool, the soul of products? Such training and reviving of one's sensibilities to outside realities will contribute much to the pleasure one takes in life, and to finding one's place in the scheme of things.

From the purely business point of view too, the more open we are to direct experiences, the better we will be able to understand our customers and appreciate what the shape and color of a soap or the colors and lines of a car mean to them. Consumers have surprisingly rich experiences with all sorts of products. A woman may spend half an hour or longer just describing what the color, the feel, the taste of salt mean to her.

Human communication at its deepest and most meaningful level is based not on concepts and logic, but on the rapport created by the sharing and exchanging of intrinsic, firsthand experiences on the largest possible basis.

6. THE NEED FOR A PSYCHOLOGICAL CREED

Until not long ago, religion alone helped man define his place in the scheme of things and advised him about his role and his duties in the world. But, like everything else, religions change and so do their functions and the part they play in guiding man.

Today most religious thinkers acknowledge that together with the answers the various creeds offer to metaphysical puzzles, man also needs sound psychological appraisal of the whys and wherefores of his ambitions, his doubts, his life goals through the dynamism of changing circumstances and values.

The most important message a psychologist can deliver is that life has deep and rich meanings even within our human limitations—even amidst the grinding routine of the factory, the office, the conference room, and the seemingly senseless strains of increasing competition. This meaning is hidden inside every individual. It takes conscious effort to bring it to light and to have it permeate our thoughts and deeds with its fertile radiance. But to know that there can be a superior sense behind our efforts, strivings, sorrows, experimentations, that we can conquer fears, depressions, emptiness, and frustrations by our own strength, this is the most decisive revelation on earth. For it is by acquiring this certitude that a man can become master of his own life.

These basic goals of human endeavor are the same wherever you go. What varies is the specific way in which a people or a culture tries to achieve these results. Nations have not only a physical age but an even more important psychological one. This psychological age is determined, just as in an individual, by the degree of maturity and wisdom with which they found the answer to life's problem of adjustment.

A country or culture may be affluent economically but underage psychologically. A so-called underdeveloped country may be further ahead in its search for true dynamic happiness despite the fact that its citizens walk barefoot. A truly functioning United Nations should concern itself with the therapy of nations. Each of the conflicts on this road to self-realization of a country and its citizens should be properly understood and its solutions studied.

A GOAL FOR AMERICA

One of the major reasons why we have difficulty in our foreign policy and why we seem to be at times losing the propaganda war against Russia is our failure to determine clearly what we want this country to communicate to the world—what this country stands for. It is true that we talk about democracy and similar things. Yet the immediate emotional implication of such statements, the determination of a goal for the individual, particularly the young people of this country, does not exist. The Russian adolescent can have the feeling that he is participating in a militant, aggressive movement, almost a religion, that sets out to conquer the world. We know that this goal is wrong, yet our studies have shown that the American youngster, when asked what he is going to be three or five years from now, usually shrugs his shoulders. He might talk about the kind of job he is going to have, whether he will own a car or not, but he usually fails to have a clear-cut notion of the real goal for his life, the self-realization he intends to achieve.

We must help him. It is too difficult a job to determine one's goals in isolation. Goals in the moral and spiritual field have to come from the country as a whole.

I am suggesting that such a goal can be determined clearly by taking our psychological definition of the goals of life and applying these principles to our country as a whole. Just as the main goal of physical life in its teleological sense is growth, so the goal of mental life is psychological growth: the increased maturity and independence an individual achieves in his normal growth from childhood to adulthood. The real test of the political and economic success of the American way of life is whether it does provide this feeling of growth, self-realization, and achievement.

The new nations that have sprung up over the last ten years

at first glance may represent a regression, if one believes in the eventuality of a brotherhood of nations, in a United Nations, in a world government. At the same time, however, one must understand the psychological necessity that these nationalities have to discover their own uniqueness, separateness, and individuality. Nations usually start out to achieve this by exaggerated nationalism during and immediately after their fight for independence.

Unfortunately, it is Russia who up to now has succeeded in playing the role of the champion of this new nationalism and independence. Our own foreign policy has lacked clarity. We have at the same time defended France vis-à-vis Algeria as we have tried to make friends with Tunisia, Morocco, and other Arab nations. We should have been the nation to play the role of defending idealism and the desire for freedom at all costs. Instead, whether by design or by awkwardness or by mistaken realism, we have been pushed into a role of ambivalence. Many people in many regions of the globe have difficulty in understanding Americans. They do not know exactly where to put them, how to classify them. We found in our studies that Americans themselves suffer from the same kind of dilemma. Do we believe in a conquest of the world under the American flag, or do we really believe in the right of all nationalities to have their independence and freedom? The more mature citizens realize, of course, that the realities of everyday political life cause many difficulties, that solutions are not quite as simple and clear-cut as analysis may indicate. But the basic dilemma of America's foreign policy and goal is another thing. I suggest that a goal parallel with the goal of new experiences and independence for the individual life can be defined for the country as a whole.

The young nations have achieved part of their goal, their political independence. Their next decisive aim must be that of economic independence as the basis of spiritual and psychological independence. In the economic field we have been of help. We have made loans, we have provided machinery, but we are in heavy competition with the Russians, who have successfully done similar things. But another large field is still open to us, the field of helping these young nations to gain their psychological and spiritual independence. This is a bigger job than it may seem at first. Many of these young nations do not know how to behave. They still continue to smash the windows of their own government buildings, as symbols of authority. They still suffer from their past, when any kind of government was foreign. They are often blustering, exaggerating, chauvinistic, because this is a natural form of overcompensation on their part.

What I suggest is to set up an institute for young nations to use all the knowledge supplied by the social sciences to help them to a better adjustment. Permit them to learn through training programs, seminars, group therapy, and studies how best to teach themselves and their citizens their new role. America, with the help of the United Nations, could very well offer to these nations *genuine* help in helping themselves in the most decisive sense possible—psychologically and spiritually. All this would be achieved in line with modern psychological scientific thinking.

In doing this, America would help itself, not only by winning true, lasting friends among other nations, but by establishing and defining its own spiritual goals.

The real lag that we have to worry about is not the one in the field of missiles and the conquest of space, but a lag in a much more vital field. Sputnik and Lunik have only served as a tool in conquering the souls and the imagination of people. What is needed is for America to rededicate itself to the conquest and persuasion of emotions. Modern advertising has become more and more aware of the importance of human emotions. National and international relationships are more than ever based on emotional factors. It is the lack of understanding of the emotions of other nationalities and peoples which has led to present difficulties in selling American ideas abroad.

If an advertiser found out that the "personality" of his product, its image in the eyes of the public, had deteriorated he would take drastic action. "America's image" abroad, among its customers, the people of other nations, has deteriorated to a most appalling degree.

Many of our new assignments abroad have to do with problems

of the common market. A common European market presupposes a common European psychology, which does not exist as yet.

Some of our studies also have to do with European attitudes toward American products. A frightening by-product of these studies was the discovery of the degree to which the major American product, America's image and ideology, has deteriorated.

Here are some suggestions, based on psychological concepts, for remedying the deterioration of our composite personality resulting in the anti-Americanism which is expressed so openly and so vehemently by too many people in many parts of the world:

HELP OTHERS TO UNDERSTAND AMERICA

America is a country of rapid change, of social and economic ups and downs. It is a country of contradictions and extremes which make it difficult to understand. Foreigners cannot understand America. When people have difficulty understanding something, they blame the object. They say, "America is difficult." Difficult objects and ideas are bothersome. The U.S.A. has become a negative challenge. Finding fault with it becomes personally desirable.

The first important step to stop such negative reactions is to provide a proper classification system, a frame of reference, within which America can be understood. In developing a classification and a terminology by which America can be interpreted, we must recognize certain facts. America has become a leading nation, but at the same time it suffers from all the difficulties of a young nation. It has not yet learned its leader role. It can be understood only if it presents itself as an evolving, developing country rather than as a finished product, a country in the process of learning its role as a world leader.

WE HAVE TO SHOW MORE HUMILITY

As Americans we have been brought up to consider ourselves foremost in almost all fields of human endeavor. This belief has subtly changed our outlook on life and in particular our relations with other nations.

Nothing is more resented by others than condescension. It invites active resentment and a desire to retaliate. This has little to do with real facts. The Institute's work in the field of human motivations has brought us to respect the power of emotions.

Magnanimity and admiration for the achievements of other nations are now more than ever a correct emotional approach for improving attitudes toward America.

REAWAKEN THE FRUSTRATED LOVE FOR AMERICA

Most people would like to love America; indeed, at intervals, they do so. The problem is that they feel they are continuously slapped in the face by the many contradictory facets of American policy. People seek the opportunity to love a nation which represents an ideal. France held this position for a time. To many, the Soviet Union has held it from time to time, only to lose it through a series of disillusionments—the purge trials, the Nazi pact, Hungary. For a period, the United States was the symbol of freedom, democracy, and plenty. But today there is a waning love for the United States, and the outright hostility of the rejected lover is more and more prevalent throughout the world. In the seesaw of affection, the United States is losing ground and, in many countries, the Soviet Union is riding its Sputniks to new heights. America must again project the humanitarian qualities which can inspire love.

GREAT DEEDS TO PROVE AMERICA'S CAPACITY FOR GREATNESS

The world is becoming more complex; its problems more impossible for ordinary people to resolve. It is part of a nation's capacity for greatness to offer solutions to the problems of daily life. It would be natural for America to show its leadership by cutting through complexities to simple and understandable solutions. For America to abolish its visa requirements and drastically lower its import duties would be grand gestures immediately understandable to people everywhere. We have attempted to make grand gestures, of course. We have given billions of dollars since the end of World War II. But the effect has been minimized by internal bickering over our foreign-aid program and by the political strings we attached to our aid. We seemed to be giving grudgingly. We need to do something which represents a shift from the inhibitive and protective attitude, which has made people skeptical of America's capacity for greatness, toward a permissive policy in world affairs.

CREATE A SYMBOL FOR AMERICA

Most countries can be described verbally or by symbols. England and France have a long history and a wide range of cultural, even ritualistic symbols by which they are immediately identifiable. Russia has an ideology which can be spelled out paragraph by paragraph. America is too young to have acquired cultural symbols and its composition is too diverse to admit ideological synthesis. The symbol of the Statue of Liberty has been tarnished by many events. There is a very definite experience that can be called "America." For most outsiders, this experience is an impossibility. Even for those who come to America, the experience is difficult without proper guidance. What is needed is a program which will record and disseminate this experience through movies, through pamphlets, through all the channels of communication which can translate experience into understanding.

AMERICA NEEDS PERSONAL HEROES

One of the important emotional symbols which help to create the image of a country is a hero. Our Presidents come and go. They are defeated after virulent campaigns or, even if re-elected, they may be under attack. It is difficult to find heroes among them. Roosevelt was our last hero. England had, and still has, Churchill. India has Nehru. Russia has Khrushchev and its most recent heroes, the Sputnik and the Lunik. America has been represented at trade exhibits and international meetings of all kinds. But it has failed to provide the world with a hero who answers emotional needs. Eisenhower only lately in his trips abroad has attempted to play this role. We have used intellectual symbols—our machines, our architecture, our consumer goods—but we have failed to capture sufficiently the love and sympathy which people are willing to lavish on a hero.

POSITIVE INTERPRETATIONS ARE NEEDED

It is not so much what America does abroad as what happens at home which molds the image of America. Events in Little Rock, for instance, have reinforced all the negative aspects of the American image abroad. Almost all the references in the press, on radio and on TV both here and throughout the world have been negative. Yet Little Rock may actually bring to solution a problem which history has postponed for a hundred years. Little Rock became an inevitability; its solution will become a credit, not a debit. There has, however, been little or no attempt to present to the outside world the positive aspects of the Little Rock story.

STRESS THE INDIVIDUALITY OF AMERICANS

Wherever you go in the world, there is great emphasis placed on the fact of differences among nations. It is a form of pride that these differences exist among nations and among individuals. America, however, is seen as a gray giant with conformity its battle cry. The fact that it is the first truly international country has been submerged. There is no understanding of the differences that exist from region to region, from individual to individual. America is also seen as a nation without culture. Yet there are more museums, concerts, plays, and movies available in New York or Chicago on a typical Sunday afternoon than in any other world capital. There is the stereotype of money economy, a nation built on business and businessmen's values—a money-hungry nation without feeling. A major effort must be made to stress the idea of the rich diversity of American life, not in terms of a rigid government, but rather in terms of a flexible people.

REMOVE THE FEAR OF AMERICA'S VITALITY

The most intangible and probably the most valuable quality in America is its spirit of vitality. Americans, in contrast to Europeans, are willing to try things, to take a chance, to have a go at it. In Europe there is more caution, less experimentation. Yet this American vitality is frightening to Europeans. They see it as a materialistic force, rather than as a liberating force. They see America as a huge machine which grinds up man's individuality. In order to make America's vitality understandable to Europeans, we must dramatize it for its beneficent effect on individual Americans. We must make Europe understand the air of freedom it creates, which is the opposite of the political conformity for which America is so severely criticized. There is a cleavage in the American way of life between the "why not try it" philosophy of the American people and the official policy of the U.S. government. In addition to the many and often contradictory spokesmen for the government's position, we must find spokesmen for the American people and their way of life.

PRIDE IN AMERICA'S ACHIEVEMENTS

Many of the recent stories in the press—many of them picked up in foreign countries—make it appear that we ought to be ashamed of the good life we are leading. This recanting has its origin in a deep-seated guilt feeling, as I pointed out before. This guilt feeling is bad and dangerous. Some of the recanting is directed against a number of specific products, such as electrical gadgets, big cars, luxury and leisure time, merchandise. The real measuring rod of the success of one system over another should be based on the happiness of the citizens, their creativeness, and their constructive discontent. The desire to grow, to improve oneself, and to enjoy life to the fullest is at least equal, if not decidedly superior, to the goal of being ahead in a missile or a satellite program. If it is true that Russia is ahead by four or five years in some of these technical achievements, it is even more true that America is ahead by ten to twenty years as far as the happiness of its citizens is concerned.

Our present life, therefore, should be presented as a challenge to the outside world, not in a boastful way, but as a life attainable by everyone through democratic pursuits. It is wrong, in my opinion, to demand that this life be abandoned in order to bridge the gap of a few months, which Russia may claim to have.

These suggestions are necessarily of a general nature and only indicate the importance of reorienting our thinking. It is possibly one of the fundamental fallacies in American life that, as a country with a fully developed democracy and citizens enjoying its privileges, we still are inclined to talk about the people in Washington as if "they" represented a foreign element.

While I was in South America recently, the owner of a fairly large *estancia* a few hours from Buenos Aires told me proudly that while taxes are fairly high in Argentina, he and many others really do not have to worry much because one can always make arrangements with the tax inspector. Yet, as we drove back to the city, he complained bitterly about the flooded and unpaved roads which forced us several times to make detours.

"The man who is supposed to take care of a stretch of the road," he explained, "plows the sides of the road and uses it for his cattle." As he said this, he waved to a man who was indeed doing exactly what the *estancia* owner had said.

When I tried to establish the relationship between his taxes, the roadman's indifference, and the condition of the state highway, he simply shrugged his shoulders, stating that he hoped the new finance minister might change things eventually.

In Lima, Peru, we were told by a local and successful businessman that the trouble with his country was that the people had it too good. The temperature was even all year round; therefore, they didn't have to work hard.

Both these examples represent important aspects of contemporary conflicts. The time when an absentee owner could insist on high profits without considering the welfare of the rest of the country (isolationism and individualism) are becoming more and more impossible on both a national and international level. The citizen who once felt it was up to him to decide on his destiny is being forced to turn over some of his "freedom" to the community.

The "traffic lights" of regulation and discipline mark the growth of civilization. Buenos Aires still has only very few traffic lights at intersections and every car drives chaotically in its own way. I was told that "traffic lights" of any kind are considered an imposition on freedom. The *estancia* owner also resented taxes as an infringement on his pioneer spirit.

In Iquitos, on the Amazon River, I visited an Indian tribe. They live in blissful fashion, hunting, and planting bananas and yuccas. Who is smarter—we, the hard-working civilized people, or the happy-go-lucky Indians?

Part of the answer was provided by the fact that our guide complained there were fewer and fewer Indians for tourists to see. They were becoming too civilized. In other words, these primitive people who were supposed to be happy are being caught in the inevitable maelstrom of development. They smoke cigarettes, are beginning to wear jeans and shirts.

In most countries I have visited, I find that human desires are pretty much alike. The only difference lies in the level of achievement. Throughout this book, I have tried to stress the fact that growth and progress are the only possible goals of life. Psychological self-realization and fulfillment of all one's potentialities are the real moral issues. In a sense, the more we discover the possibilities of infinite new worlds and new aspects of ourselves, the more we approach, in my opinion, a basic realization of the concept of God—a God within ourselves, rather than the projection of a father-figure in a truly blasphemous, limiting human likeness.

I believe that the clue to man's destiny lies in his relentless training towards independence, not only politically, but also in the psychological sense. We are beset by fears, by inhibitions, by narrow-minded routine thinking. Step by step, year by year, we free ourselves more and more. Jets reduce physical distances; international trade, mass communications, radio, TV, and magazines break down barriers. The world is opening up. The key to this progress is human desire and its strategy. We are on the threshold of the greatest discovery of all times, the vast lands of the human soul and spirit.

Wars are being fought more and more on psychological battlefields. The visits by Khrushchev and Eisenhower, for example, were historic events, because they presented the true fight on a new level. It was as if we had returned on a summit level to the old Greek debates where battles were won by conquering minds, the opening up of new vistas and the planting of flags on the territories of the spirit by the most convincing orator.

We may well have reached on the historical spiral a new level where a return to the truly human values has begun.

Life is strategy, growth. The life force which makes everything move and surge forward is the sum total of all human desires. The fact that the word "desire" itself has become tinged with immorality is one of the diseases which mankind has yet to eradicate.

Rather than forbidding desire, which would be forbidding life itself, it is necessary to set a goal of growth, of dynamic security and constructive discontent; and then to learn and use the techniques implicit in the strategy of desire.

APPENDIX I

TECHNIQUES IN MOTIVATIONAL RESEARCH

Throughout this book I attempted to make it clear that it is not so much the techniques themselves which make the difference in the attempt to understand human motivations. It is the thinking, the concepts, the hypotheses, and the total range of modern scientific thought processes which characterize the interpretative approach in research.

But people still say, "Yes, but what exactly is it that you do?" The detailed discussion of all the steps and techniques, used in interpretative research, can fill, of course, a separate textbook. We still owe it to the reader, however, to give at least some description of the research procedures employed by us.

I. FORMULATION OF HYPOTHESES

In the text of the book I have pointed to the necessity of having hypotheses first in any scientific endeavor. Modern science can only operate with higher level abstracts and thought models, not with a naïve empiricism.

Learning to develop hypotheses is a task not unlike learning to be an artist. It is learning to ask fundamental questions, to see unrelated things as related, to train and develop one's creativeness. The book, as a whole, attempts to spell out, by its examples and by its scientific philosophy, how the discovery of hypotheses can be stimulated and developed.

II. DEPTH INTERVIEWS

A basic description of a depth interview is the following:

Just as a physician would not ask his patient to diagnose his own ills, to tell him why he thinks he has a stomach-ache, so the social scientist, who wants to understand the motivation of his respondent, will pose the kind of question which will permit him to draw the conclusion himself as to what the causative explanation of the phenomenon in question is.

Basically a depth interview is a non-directive interview. The respondent is being urged to talk about a subject rather than to say yes or no to a specific question. The topics he is urged to talk about depend on the subject of the investigation and the problem. There are, however, a number of principles which can be utilized.

1. *The first experience*. Urging a person to talk about the very first car he ever owned, the very first cigarette he smoked, or the first liquor he drank often stimulates the whole range of memories and emotions in connection with a particular commodity and brings the real feelings more out into the open.

2. *Testing the extremes*. We often ask in a depth interview which was the best beer you ever had, which was the worst one. We test the extremes. Again the purpose is to mobilize true feelings, to permit the respondent to talk about real experience rather than to give us considered or biased judgment and opinions.

3. *Being specific*. Contrary to what one may assume of a non-directive interview, it is more concrete than a standardized questionnaire. We avoid asking how often on the average do you watch televsion; when do you usually drink tea; what do you normally do with a cold. In all these and hundreds of other similar approaches the danger exists of asking the respondent to summarize for us his own motivations and to give us the interpretation of what he considers normal, usual, average, etc. What we insist instead is that he report actual events. What did you do last night when you came home? Describe your last cold and all the things that happened while you had the cold. It's up to us, the researchers of human motivations, to determine why you did what you did.

4. *Feelings are facts too*. In our depth interviews we also ask about the feelings of a person. Instead of asking which one of the office machines that you now use have you found most worth while and economical, we ask: Think of your typewriters, your duplicators, your check writers, your postage meters, etc., and tell us all the feelings that come to your mind while you think or look at or remember your experiences with each one of these machines. It is only such an approach which permits us, as diagnosticians, to determine ourselves which one of these machines would really be most missed if it had to be given up; which one has the greatest meaning and really motivated the consumer to buy it, and what might influence him to replace it and to buy a new one.

5. *Test for clues*. In a liquor study we wanted to find out how people really felt about a liquor brand. We asked them to describe to us the last time the boss came for a visit and to tell us what brand of liquor they served and whether or not it was the same one they usually had. Better yet, we knew from the previous part of the interview what the regular brand was.

6. *Permit spontaneity*. Allowing and encouraging a person with some slight guidance to simply pour out his feelings about a particular subject

brings out true motivations in a much more reliable fashion than predetermining the framework within which the answers are to be given. By structuring a questionnaire in a rigid fashion it is really the researcher who determines ahead of time the type of answers that he consider to be most likely. For example, by your asking a respondent to check off on a list which of the following factors were most important in his decision to buy Sanka coffee he is most likely to mark off on the list the advertising claim that it lets him sleep. As our study for this product showed, the real reason for drinking Sanka was that the consumer felt he could now drink even more coffee than before. He might have checked this point had it been included in the list. Since it was not, no answer to the real motivation was received.

Not having included this item at all was due to the researcher's wrong assumption or lack of knowledge that it could be an important motivation.

Permitting spontaneity makes it possible too to observe other clues to human motivations. For example, a person denying several times that he really was bothered by Joe's promotion, and reiterating the phrase: "Don't misunderstand me, I don't mind at all that Joe was promoted, it could not have happened to a nicer guy," admits the opposite. The fact that he phrases his statement this way becomes a clue to his true feelings towards Joe. This is why it is imperative that a depth interview record verbatim every phrase, every gesture, and every intonation of the respondent.

7. *Watch emotionality*. In the car study reported in this appendix we found that people talked at much greater length about the very first car they ever owned than about later cars. This could be literally measured by the space and time occupied in the spontaneous interview. We could legitimately conclude from this that the first car had greater emotional significance than the subsequent ones. Getting up, raising one's voice, getting indignant about a question, all these are possible giveaways in a depth interview.

Many of the aspects of depth interviewing are borrowed from the approaches used in psychiatry, where the problem often is to understand the real reason for a person's behavior. We employ these techniques continuously in our daily lives. When the hostess keeps urging us to stay a little longer, but yawns at the same time, most of us don't need any knowledge of depth interviewing or of psychology to detect a discrepancy between her statement and her actual feelings. We leave.

Even our children have absorbed enough psychological knowledge to know that if the young girl in a TV play repeats several times that she hates Andrew and slaps him, that he will eventually get her. Even the eight-year-old listener will interpret correctly that hatred often is the forerunner of love. Our novelists, artists, and anyone dealing with human beings and their foibles practice depth interviewing—the attempt to go beneath the surface and to discover real motivations.

III. PROJECTIVE TECHNIQUES

In order to uncover new findings and further validate initial hypotheses and depth interviews, we use projective techniques in both initial and final phases of the study. This method of psychological investigation provides verbal or visual stimuli which, through their indirection and concealed intent, encourage the respondent to reveal his unconscious feelings and attitudes without being aware that he is doing so.

Projective techniques have been refined over the last ten years and are widely used in psychological work. They are simply a more rigid form of non-directive interviews where standardized situations are being used into which the respondent can project himself. The classic example is a picture of a little boy looking through a keyhole. You, the respondent, are being asked to tell us what he sees. It is assumed that you play the role of the boy and that what you see reveals some of your own thoughts, fears, and feelings. When applying this to commercial problems such situations are simplified. We may ask you to think of your kitchen ten years from now, or to give us your reactions to a pill which you swallowed daily and which would make tooth-brushing unnecessary. People playing this role, for example, told us that it made them aware for the first time that they really like to brush their teeth, that they did so regularly not so much because it prevents cavity but because it was fun in itself. This feeling was not quite clear to them before. When they were asked directly about tooth-brushing, their first reaction was that it was a nuisance but was necessary.

Here is an example of a projective test which we have used recently.

1. In the last 8 weeks which of the following have you done most frequently?

a ( ) Read.
b ( ) Watched television or went to the movies or sports events or somewhere else to be entertained.
c ( ) Worked on a hobby.
d ( ) Engaged in sports activities.
e ( ) Traveled.
f ( ) Visited with friends.

2. We all generally dislike seeing other people as members of a class —it doesn't appear very democratic. Yet most of us will, from time to time, characterize other people as belonging to the lower class, working class, middle class, or upper class. Considering that we all do this sometimes, which of the following factors would you guess most affect

people's decisions? Number the most important "1," the next most important "2," etc., until you have numbered all those factors you guess other people think are important.

( ) The kind of job he holds.
( ) The type of house he lives in.
( ) His family background.
( ) The amount of money he makes.
( ) The kinds of things he does with his money.
( ) The things he owns—his car, TV set, appliances, etc.
( ) The kind and extent of education he has had.
( ) The nationality and/or religion of his family.
( ) The organizations he belongs to.
( ) The things he does for fun and relaxation—how he uses his leisure time.

3. When a salesman comes to the door:

a ( ) I tell him no immediately.
b ( ) I listen to at least part of what he has to say to see if he might have some item I can use.
c ( ) I let him tell me the whole story because I have no sales resistance.

4. Here are four different views of life quoted from four philosophical writers. Which of them most appeals to you?

a ( ) "The wise man is he who worries of the future. Life being at best uncertain, he wastes not himself nor his money. 'Tis better, he says, to be safe than to be sorry."
b ( ) "Caution, caution is the key. To consider the future as much as we do the present; to enjoy our pleasures, but never to forget that planning ahead is of more importance."
c ( ) "I prefer to enjoy life. Yes, I save a little for a rainy day, but I do not ignore the present to live in the future."
d ( ) "The meaning? It is to be carefree, to live but once and he should live it to get the most from it . . . Live it while you may, now, in the present—the future will live by itself."

5. Below is a list of items. Most people own at least a few of them. Would you please examine the list and *draw a line* through all items that you *do not own.*

( ) automobile	( ) large house
( ) second automobile	( ) small house
( ) hi-fi set	( ) fur coat
( ) camera and/or projector	( ) evening clothes
( ) boat	( ) air conditioner
( ) plane	( ) clothes washer

( ) TV set
( ) personal jewelry
( ) radio
( ) books
( ) automatic dishwasher
( ) garden
( ) food freezer
( ) sports equipment

Now if you were retired, or if your income was cut, or if we were hit by a depression, you might have to do without some of the items you now own. Please examine the list of items not crossed out, and place a "1" next to the item you could most easily do without under those circumstances. Then place a "2" next to the item you could next do without; and so forth until you have numbered all items not crossed out.

IV. PSYCHODRAMA

Often asking people to act out a particular situation, whether a buying act or an interpersonal problem, putting them on a stage, and asking a small audience to participate can bring out fascinating aspects of the problem. The technique used by us is basically an adaptation of Dr. Moreno's Psychodrama, used in hospitals, by the Army and many other organizations. In some of our sessions we found, for example, that in buying a baseball glove, the sound of the fist on the leather played an important role. In shoe-buying situations, fear of having a hole in one's stockings or socks often created tension.

V. OBSERVATIONS

These can be made in our laboratory, in stores, and in hundreds of real situations of everyday life. We can discover that most people close their eyes when drinking beer, that a scratch on a brand-new car can evoke expressions of distress and utter despair, that many women have fights with girls att he checkout counter because they somehow want to project onto her their feeling of guilt at having spent too much.

Practicing such observations of many of the things most of us do can yield valuable knowledge of human motivations. All the training needed for it is to keep one's eyes open and to ask continuously why people are doing what they do. Applying it in research, of course, requires a more thorough and a more systematic control of your observations and often the setting up of special experiments to make sure that your interpretation of what you have observed is correct.

APPENDIX II

Excerpts from a motivational research study on the Plymouth car conducted by Ernest Dichter in 1939–40

THE PSYCHOLOGY
OF
CAR BUYING

A Psychological Study Undertaken to Answer
Two Vital Questions About Car Buying

Prepared by the Research Department
J. Stirling Getchell, Inc.
January, 1940

"Many of the points raised in this study may now seem old hat. But in 1939 when this study was written, they represented a new and fresh approach to the American automobile. Since that time they have come to be generally accepted and practiced by the auto industry."

THE GENESIS OF THIS STUDY

Early in October, 1939, Dr. Ernest Dichter—who has since joined the Research Staff of J. Stirling Getchell, Inc.—called on various executives of the Chrysler Corporation and, upon suggestion of Mr. D. S. Eddins of Plymouth, on executives of this agency.

Dr. Dichter proposed the use of a new psychological research technique to get beyond the limits of current statistical research in an understanding of the factors which influence the sale of cars.

Quite frankly, we were at the onset as skeptical of the practicability and value of the proposed study as, we learned later, executives of the corporation had been when first approached.

Conviction and an acknowledgment of the potentialities of the technique grew out of succeeding conversations.

We investigated the scientific and intellectual integrity of the work with scientists qualified to judge and examined the practical results obtained from previous applications of the technique.

The result was a decision to go ahead with a study which would test, experimentally, how this psychological technique might be employed to aid Plymouth in its advertising and merchandising problems.

Two questions were selected by Plymouth executives as a springboard for the proposed study:

1. Why do most (70%) car buyers buy the same make as their previous car?

2. What influence do women have on the purchase of cars?

Previous statistical studies had suggested, as answers to the first question, only such vague, general terms as "habit," "previous ownership," and "loyalty."

Impressions about the degree to which women influence the purchase of cars were even more elusive.

It was our problem, therefore, to employ this psychological research technique to get practical answers to these questions which might aid us in building more effective advertising and merchandising plans for Plymouth.

HOW CASE HISTORIES ARE USED IN OUR PSYCHOLOGICAL TECHNIQUE

We employ case histories, or detailed conversational interviews, similar to the investigations of criminologists, the diagnoses of physicians or psychoanalyists, although in a much shorter form. The conversation is recorded in shorthand and transcribed for analysis. The slightest detail is sometimes more revealing than a long list of technical generalities.

While more than one hundred interviews were made in the course of this study, varying from thirty minutes to two and one-half hours each, it is not the number of interviews that is most significant, but the depth of analysis in each individual interview.

In order to make our psychological inventory of appeals and motives as complete as possible, interviews were made with people in all walks of life, city and country, all income levels, all different ages, men and women, married and unmarried, immigrants and native-born Americans, car owners and non-car owners.

From each interview, trained psychologists get clues which match up with basic facts about human behavior already confirmed by modern psychology in thousands of experiments. When all of the clues are fitted together they form the behavior structures of car-buying habits. By understanding the character of these behavior structures it is possible to build advertising appeals.

The statistical research technique might be compared to a "still picture," a "snapshot" photograph of the finale of a long story. The psychological research technique gives us a "moving picture," a dynamic biography of the car buyer which goes back into his personal history and also gets beneath the surface.

The detective reconstructs the history of the crime in order to find clues that will help him to understand the motivations of the murderer and to find the criminal. He gets his clues through interviews, but he would be a very poor detective if he believed everything the witnesses told him . . . what they do not tell him is often the clue to the crime. Our psychological technique operates in a manner very similar to that of the detective's.

HOW WE ANALYZED THE PROBLEM

Our first interviews revealed that our two vital questions, repeat buying of the same make and women's influence, cannot be answered in an isolated way. It was necessary to fit them into their proper places in a much larger frame of reference, embracing the structure of all car-buying habits.

Reduced to its simplest terms, our problem is to find out why people buy cars, and once those motives are established, to translate them into appeals which can be used in advertising and merchandising.

If appeals are right, a majority of people will say "Yes" to them.

THE PSYCHOLOGICAL RELATIONSHIP BETWEEN CAR HISTORY AND LIFE HISTORY

Our first significant find was the definite relationship between car history and life history. Our interviews reveal that all dates referring to car ownership stand out in a man's mind. People recall dates concerned with their car purchase in an amazingly exact way.

Since it is true that we retain in our memories only those things which are importunt to us, the importance of car ownership in life is clearly demonstrated. We find that cars are milestones in human life. This fact is expressed in remarks like this: "I never realized that I actually lived my life in terms of cars." Somebody else said at the end of an interview: "Is it possible? Does a man really own so many cars in his life?"

The clearest analysis is contained in this quotation from an interview: "There is something about cars—I've owned cars since I was eighteen years old. I can remember incidents in my life connected with cars. Somehow, the different cars I had represent different periods of my life."

Having established the fact that cars are important in life, we must now discover why they are important, what a car actually represents psychologically.

Our interviews reveal that cars stand for something, they are not just a means of transportation. A car is really a symbol, an expression of human desires. Its appearance, its mechanical functions, and its social functions help to build up that symbolic value.

All our actions are regulated by the psychological mechanism of want and satisfaction. It is logical, therefore, for us to inquire: What desire or want does the car satisfy?

THE "CAR IDEAL" AS A GUIDING FORCE IN CAR PURCHASES

Almost everybody has a car ideal. The car ideal is usually expressed in concrete and vivid language: "I'd give my right eye for one of those real streamlined cars that are set way down low and purr and roar when you step on the gas."

We find that the car ideal is formed very early in life. It is built up through many influences. Every car we see, every ride we take, every advertisement we read adds to the foundation of our car ideal. In looking over the list of cars owned by a man, we find a continuous psychological thread going all the way through his car history. Behind this thread is his car ideal. Sometimes he reaches it, sometimes he keeps on longing all his life, but the ideal is always there as a pulling force.

The following quotation gives us a good inside picture of how this yearning operates: "Sometimes I do wonder if it isn't possible to have one of them bigger cars, and I sit up with pencil and pad, and figger half the night trying to dope out a way it could be financed without it taking too much out of my pocket for too long a time. But I most always come to the final conclusion that it can't be done. I'm pretty good on figgers, but why try to do the impossible. If I got a real good car, I'd get a Chrysler or a LaSalle. There is something about the lines and the clear vision on the LaSalle that I like, LaSalle is a good car. *It fits in a lot of ways with what I have always had in mind that a car should be. It's streamlined and it's fast as hell from what I hear*. It's a car that you don't need to be ashamed of. My Pontiac's nice, but there's a lot of places we might be able to go but we can't because it just isn't a real good-looking car."

Our interviews with college students provide further insight into early manifestations of the car ideal. One nineteen-year-old student says: "Well, I'd like a light-blue convertible with nice comfortable upholstery, and a cigarette lighter. The car has got to have a fancy horn—the old single toot is out of style." Another student of the same age says: "My ideal car would be a blue or gray roadster—nice and streamlined and of good solid construction." A third student says: "Well, I expect to have a Buick—midnight blue with a gray top—a long sedan with a heater and a radio. I'd like one of those automatic clutches—I've driven the new Oldsmobile and like the idea very much."

We also asked unmarried girls what cars they think their future husbands or beaus should have. Their answers are very similar to those of college students.

One typist says: "I'd like a smart-looking automobile—I would look for the body first of all, and of course the comfort inside. I would not get a car unless it was smart looking—a sport model—what I call something smart is the body of Packard. If I could afford it that would be my ideal car. It has a lot of dash to it. Richness—that's exactly what I mean."

Another nineteen-year-old unmarried girl says: "I would like a Ford—an open touring car—convertible, because it is a good-looking car. People say it does not ride very well, but people who really have one say they are satisfied. I think it is a rather outstanding car—not like all the other cars on the street—it looks like 'young people.'"

The importance that a car may have in the selection of a beau is shown in the following statement: "Then came the time when I started to go out and had many friends. I always tried to find young men who had cars. If I met somebody he had to please me very much to go out with me and get more acquainted—but if he had a car I was much more apt to overlook his faults. If I didn't like one too much, and he had a beautiful car, I enjoyed going out with him—that is to say driving out with him—it was almost a passion with me. But even nowadays I feel nowhere so wonderful as in my car. And the quicker I can fly over the roads, the more beautiful it is."

How far these young people will go towards carrying out their car ideal when they reach the age of purchasing a car is difficult to say. They may be forced to compromise, new influences may change their ideal later on, but some of the attributes of the car ideal will persist to maturity.

Throughout our case histories we find that the car ideal is closely linked to convertibles—a significant fact that deserves further analysis.

THE PSYCHOLOGICAL INFLUENCE OF CONVERTIBLES

Although convertibles account for a small part of the car market, their psychological influence is very strong. The desire for perennial youth is symbolized in convertible models. Our interviews indicate that the convertible as the "car ideal" persists into maturity, although it is seldom realized. Many people are first attracted to a company by its convertibles, although practical considerations, such as economies, utility, and wife influence result in a compromise on a closed model of the same make. Although the "car ideal" of a convertible is compromised, its psychological strength is not weakened.

One man justifies his convertible in a cleverly rationalized form: "The reason that I have a convertible is that they have leather seats and with children in the family, they can stand up and can spill stuff on them—get candy all over them. All you have to do is to wipe it off, whereas the regular upholstery looks like the devil when it gets spotted up—which it sometimes does."

Another more emotional man sighs from the depth of his heart: "I hate those sedans! I think that feeling of just driving and driving you lose in a sedan because they are covered. It is too bad my wife does not like it. Maybe I will finally overcome all the objections and get an open car next year."

We got further confirmation of the psychological importance of convertibles during actual observation of car buyers in a Plymouth showroom. A big convertible car in the salesroom window acted as a magnet to stop passers-by on the street. People coming into the showroom invariably walked around the convertible first. They listened to the salesman's questions in a distracted way. Some even dismissed him with the remark that they "wanted to look around first." After they finally turned to the car they actually intended buying and finished inspecting it, they tended to come right back to the convertible.

In many cases, the order was actually signed, or the last conversation about their car purchase was made, while the customer was leaning against the convertible model. Even when people walked out of the showroom, they again stopped on the outside to take a last look at the convertible in the window.

It is our conclusion that convertible models have a far stronger psychological influence in the purchase of cars than has been recognized and capitalized upon by car manufacturers.

THE PSYCHOLOGY OF THE FIRST CAR

"Do you remember when" brings forth many rich and vivid reminiscences about the first car. We find that people love to talk about their cars, but none are so vividly and enthusiastically remembered as the first car. An understanding of the psychology of the first car is vitally important because there we get, for the first time, a full description of what a car means to a man.

To own is one of the most basic human instincts. Ownership signifies, psychologically, an extension of one's own personality. The importance of the first car as the first big object to be owned is indicated in such remarks as this: "Oh, do I remember that first car! Of course, it was a piece of junk—but still, it was my car."

We find that practically all the technical knowledge people have about cars comes from their first car. Almost everybody takes his first car apart: "I know every nut and bolt by name. Every week I took it all apart—I practically rebuilt it." They say they have as much fun taking their first car apart as actually driving.

In analyzing that fact, we find it is not so much taking the car apart, but putting it together again. By putting the car together, the owner gets a feeling of having built the car . . . of having reconstructed it, even of having created it. As one farmer puts it: "You could do anything you wanted to with that Model T. It could stand an awful lot of tinkering —I learned to rebuild it—took it all apart and then had the fun of putting it together again. It was to me a good car."

Because people get their technical knowledge about cars by tinkering with their first car, they often use that technical standard as a yardstick for later cars. This has an obviously important implication in the interpretation of technical details in advertising to people whose knowledge is limited chiefly to technical details in their first car. Buyers seem to understand only those technical details which have not changed very much: "At that time I understood something about cars—now I would not think of touching my car. Whatever is unchanged is still familiar to me—but I would not think of taking the transmission apart, nor the steering wheel."

Acquisition of technical knowledge from the first car, which we will see later is particularly important to farmers, was described to us in a very colorful manner by a farmer: "I learned to drive first. The machine kinda scared me because it made a lot of noise. It was an old Studebaker . . . it was all open and had a high seat and when you'd get her goin', she'd roar and spit like hell. My mother nearly fainted everytime the car started up. You really had fun with a car in them days, because you never knew when it was goin' to break down, and then I got so I could always fix them things pretty good and learned a lot about machines that way . . . We've got an International tractor and sometimes when I'm drivin' that thing, I git the same feelin' I had when I had the original car we first had."

Memories of the first car are rich; later cars never provide as much fun. The period from eighteen to twenty-four years, when most people seem to acquire their first cars, is one of the pleasantest in our lives, consequently people remember their first cars pleasantly: "However, in spite of all defects, no other car has ever been like it . . ."

Here's how another person tells us his experience: "At that time my father would want to run over to town or over to the market for him, and then I would go out raising hell over the place on fun. When I was driving my first car I really thought it was something to have a car that you owned. It was a real nice feeling."

The first car is owned during the time of courtship and romance, and consequently many rich memories are connected with it. When people talk about "the first big thing I bought myself" they actually revel in detail: "I had to go out with a girl one night that I was courtin' and I wanted to make her think that I was some punkins. I hopped into the old car and rode her around to the girl's house and I don't think I ever felt as proud since that day when I drove it up to her house. She thought I was pretty smart. So I took her to the dance and on the way back the damn thing broke down [smiles broadly almost to the point of laughing out loud]—Well, I sweated and spat and tried everything and we was about eight miles from her house and about nine from mine. She got nervous as all hell and madder and madder at me. We wuz there about two hours and she got to walking and said I'd better come along, so I did and left the lizzie standin' there meanin' to come back for it the next morning. It was almost light when I got her back and her father was up waiting and he was plenty burned up and I explained about the car breakin' down. Well, she was hustled off into the house and all her father said was that my father was out looking for me and was as sore as hell and that I'd get some beating when I got home. Well, I never got such a hidin' in all my life . . ."

The first car is a symbol of new independence, of being grown-up, of breaking away from family ties, of expansion and exploration. These tendencies are manifestations of the life period when most first cars are bought—from eighteen to twenty-four.

Adventures with the first car grow out of a deep desire for self-assertion.

Obstacles are welcome at that stage in life; finally life is too stable and safe. "I want to prove that I can be independent" is the underlying thought of all action during that life period. As one respondent sums it up: "The world is so big and just invites me to explore it."

Another respondent gives us a good picture of how the general attitude of the life appears in a specific way in the ownership of the first car. "My first car was a Jordan. I was eighteen years old. It was an open car and I had been working for about two years at that time. I saved up enough money to buy this car and go on a vacation. Oh, it was tremendous! It had been my ambition to own this particular model and type since I was fourteen years old because it was very sporty-looking. I went into a dealer with the cash in my pocket and came out with the car. It was a used car. I spent $425. Then I spent $40 having it painted very flossy—red wheels. I went on my vacation with it . . . I went to Canada.

"There are some very interesting incidents connected with that car. That car to me was adventure. I drove to Canada and I had my musical instrument in the car. I played a banjo. On the way up I had an accident in which I injured a little girl. I fractured her arm. The girl ran into the car. There was a great to-do about it. No one in the village spoke English—it was a French village. The only one that could speak

English was the village doctor. After I got a settlement with the insurance company, I went to Montreal and went on with the rest of my vacation. I found a hotel up in Canada and decided to spend a little time there. I stayed there about two weeks and then got the wanderlust again. Then I decided to go back to work again. I don't know—I just wanted to go, go, and go. That gave me much pleasure. My family did not hear from me once. Then I stopped at a place in the Adirondacks. I did not have any more money left then. I got a job as a caddie at a golf course for which I got room and board. I did much galloping around with the gals on this trip. Took great delight in beating other cars on the hills up the Adirondacks, including a Packard Twelve, the first twin-six they made . . . finally I decided to go home so I came home after an absence of five weeks. All the neighbors stuck their heads out of the windows and said 'He's back again'—because they had the police looking for me for two weeks . . ."

Many people will be able to recognize themselves in the story we have related from one of our case histories. For who has not wanted to run off at sometime during his life . . . disappear just as this young adventurer did? It is not astonishing, therefore, to find that most of the trips undertaken with the first car are very long trips to romantic places . . . usually to Canada or to the South. "My first car was a Hupmobile coupe—I was twenty-five years old and I felt wonderful. I was going to Canada. We had no set plans to go to, but always flipped a coin where to go at each crossroad. We drove over roads which had never had a car on them—that is why the car was useless when we returned, but that was just what we wanted. To go places no one had ever been before . . . and then enjoy all the romance of the South. My tendency when I bought the car was to use it in an exploratory way. To see the country. We used it for a month's vacation, driving through the South. After we were through we wrecked it—we ran it over a cliff."

DRIVING IS A SYMBOL OF LIFE

Tell me how a man drives, and I will tell you what kind of a man he is. An analysis of our case histories indicates that we can do exactly that, because there is a relationship between car history and life history. A car owned in a certain life period reflects the psychological characteristic of that life phase. It is interesting, therefore, to study the characteristics of different life phases; in other words, to discover how youth is psychologically different from maturity.

Studies based on analysis of several hundred biographies and life histories indicate that life can be divided into two large aspects. The satisfaction of desires is the dominant motivating force behind all our actions until the age of thirty-five. After that age the fulfillment of an assignment or a life task becomes more and more predominant.

We can also express this change of dominance in a different way. In the first half the ego is the guiding force. While in the latter half of life it is work per se.

Psychology calls this change of predominance around the age of thirty-five "specification." Our efforts become more and more focused and specified, while before that time, they are largely vague and diffused.

These two large life phases become apparent in a very distinct way in our attitude toward cars. A car first serves largely to satisfy our desires; it is an instrument of pleasure. Later on a desire for efficiency becomes more and more important.

These life phases are also apparent in our driving habits.

SPEED

Speed, and the overcoming of obstacles, is closely tied up with the aims and ambitions of youth. A nineteen-year-old boys says: "I enjoy the sensation of speeding up a hill and coming down again. I like the feeling of the wind rushing past." Another one says: "I like to step on the gas and watch the scenery shoot by. I like to ride in an open car and feel the wind in my hair."

The first experience of driving provides assertion, a factor which youth constantly seeks. The personality of youth is not yet fully developed and grasps eagerly at every opportunity to prove itself.

"My first car was a Reo—second hand. It was over in Woodbury. I was fourteen when I got it. I had it about a year and when I think back it wasn't a bad car for those times. It was a touring car and I tell you I drove that old baby right along. Didn't even have a license. There were only a few constables around then and they did not care much anyway. But the kids around there really thought it was something. Why in them days I could hit sixty like nobody's business on a straightaway. I like to speed. Damn near killed a cow once. Was taking help home, and one of the chains let loose, and I put on the brakes. Well, I missed the cow, but the car went tearing out over the lots."

CONTROL

Control, the wish to make a powerful machine obey your commands, provides another gratification that is important along with speed, which helps to build up the ego during youth. An eighteen-year-old student says: "I like the smooth sensation of power, and the easy glide of the car. I like the sensation of speed. I get a feeling of swift motion. I enjoy a feeling of control over a dangerous machine."

A clerk of thirty-two says: "As a matter of fact I would rather drive a car than fly an airplane. The avoidance of obstacles—the maneuvering —that's what I like. Absolute control."

A woman of thirty says: "I like driving very much. Could drive all day. I like handling a car, steering, avoiding obstacles and missing them."

The following analysis goes a little deeper: "What I like best about a car is the sense of power it gives you—or something like that while driving. I think it is a combination of feelings. At one moment it might almost be like taking some dope—like opium." Although control appears in the same period of life as speed it gets the emphasis during the latter part of the period and really represents a transition to the second phase.

EFFICIENCY

Efficiency becomes predominant during the second phase—it is a characteristic of maturity.

A forty-year-old man describes that change very clearly: "Before I got married I liked to impress my friends with how far I drove and in how many hours, but not now any more—that is kind of kid stuff. I have no feeling of hurrying. You get there twenty minutes later. You just sit there anyway. I enjoy going, and why should I wish to get there quicker?"

Another example of the transition from speed to efficiency is: "When I first started to drive it was really a novelty and I went out of my mind to drive. I was willing to drive anybody any place at any time. While I like to drive so much that it has become mechanical, the feeling of power is gone and I drive for safety and to get where I am going."

Driving becomes a routine, a self-evident necessity: "A car is a part of my life. It is just as important to own a car as washing my teeth . . . a part of living."

A further substantiation: "I live at Manhattan Beach. It takes me about one hour, but I always look forward to driving home. I drive with another chap . . . we have long conversations and time passes so quickly that it almost seems to me I am getting out of the office and am home already. It is like a club to get in the car—I don't notice the landscape or streets we pass through—and I am following for fourteen years the same route morning and evening."

SAFETY

Safety becomes an additional factor after marriage and the building of a family.

"My psychology has changed since I have two children and a wife. Sometimes I have to drive fast, but I put special safety catches on the back door which work from the outside, because I always have the feeling—'God, if that door would open, with the children playing around in the back seats.' I'll probably get those special tires next time to be safer. My psychology has changed in an automobile because of my family."

That concern for safety can also have an agreeable effect! "Since I have been married, I have not had a ticket. Before that—regularly once a week."

COMFORT

Comfort becomes the all important feature of a car with advancing age. Physical ability to drive declines and therefore the desire declines.

The exact age when comfort becomes a predominant factor varies considerably in accordance with the physical and mental activity of the individual. One at the age of sixty says: "I don't enjoy driving—a car gives me a sense of inferiority. I am a very cautious driver and have never had any accidents." One at fifty-five says: "I have the sense of security in a car—she does everything she is asked to do—you don't think when you drive—it is just mechanical. I can hardly stay awake."

Or as a man of fifty-eight puts it: "I don't suppose I can drive as well as I should be able to because my eyes have always been bad, but I might be able to enjoy a ride once in a while if there weren't so many damned fools on the road."

Driving is not only a symbol of life, it is a manifestation of the individual's personality, which we will see as we go a little deeper in our analysis.

CARS HAVE PERSONALITY

Personality is a very complicated psychological structure, made up of many elements. Man has no personality as long you have only heard of him. If you talk to him, drink with him, his personality becomes more and more a living experience for you.

It is the same with a car. The more you live with, or experience your car, the more personality it has.

We probably have our closest contact with a car through hands on the steering wheel. As one person expresses it: "It is like holding the hands of a girl friend. Like looking into the eyes of another person."

Here we get it expressed in another way: "I get the feeling of a car through the steering wheel. I turn it with one finger and sometimes I like to handle the wheel like this—'with flat hands.' I find myself doing it unconsciously. There is no showing off in it."

One statement about the importance of the steering wheel is amplified here: "My present car has a very large wheel, and is very thin. That gives me the feeling of elegance and sleekness. It has a very definite action of its own. Lots of temperament. It flips back like a spring and comes around on her own. I think when I am driving myself the expert manipulation of that wheel, the delicacy of the touch, gives me a certain unconscious satisfaction. It is like a horse—the fine touch—the expertness of the touch."

Here are some excerpts from interviews which indicate clearly how people experience their cars. "My car is more of a companion to me than I figured one could be. If I didn't own a car I'd probably not go out to Long Island so much, and I'd waste my time drinking scotch and soda."

"I never got excited about my other car so much because I was working in a garage and was driving a different make every day, but my Auburn was a humdinger. I wouldn't get over three hours' sleep when I had that. I'd drive sixty or one hundred miles a night and pick up three different women. Just drive up alongside and open the door."

"My father gave me my first car. I was very attached to it. It was a very stable thing—nothing could happen to me. I felt as though the car really fitted me—we belonged together. I felt at home in it, just like in a house."

"Whenever I trade a car in I have the feeling of losing a friend."

"I think in the beginning cars were more personalized than they are now. When I turned my first car in, I just felt as bad about it as if I would have sold my dog."

In a somewhat rough way a farmer describes his experience: "I've had so damn many cars I guess if I once got started, I could sit and tell things about them all day long. It is like a guy that has had four or five wives. He can sit and talk about them all day long."

It must be clear from these vivid descriptions how people actually experience their car's personality.

When we attempt to sell a new car the personality of the new car must compete with the strong personality of the old car. This important fact is frequently ignored both by salesmen and advertising copy writers. It emphasizes the importance of speaking in a kindly way about the old car, avoiding unfavorable criticism of the old car, and hooking up the attributes of the strange new car with the personality of the familiar old car.

We have adequate proof in our case histories that people experience cars as personalities . . . as symbol of their own personalities, as expression of their own power and abilities, even as their own arms and feet. "My car fits me like a hand in a glove." "When I am driving a car the car becomes almost a part of my body."

People point proudly to advertisements in magazines and to billboards displaying their cars, saying: "That's my car," just as though their own names and pictures were displayed.

The following descriptions amplify this point. "When you're driving a Plymouth and you see a big sign with the name 'Plymouth' it gives you a feeling of relationship and identification."

Here is another one: "We bought a Dodge, but it could not be delivered right away. We had to wait several weeks . . . but our car was in the window of the dealer. We made it a regular family excursion and even took our friends along and showed them 'our car' in the window."

Each car has a special personality in the mind of the buyer. That personality is built up both by projections of the buyer's personality and the manufacturer's personality into the car.

THE CAR AS A SYMBOL OF SUCCESS

Psychologically, each motor trip is a life span in miniature.

All of life is composed of minor successes. There is no such thing as a big success. Every motor trip symbolizes an everyday success. The ability to start out, to overcome obstacles and to arrive at a goal successfully and safely is the structure of all life success. This complete structure is present in every motor trip. The street becomes the path of life.

Starting a motor trip is like asking an oracle: "If I get there successfully will I not also be successful in life?"

Every performance of a car is psychologically a dual accomplishment of a car and a driver, as shown particularly in the following quotation: "I enjoy driving very much. It is almost a passion. It gives me a sense of freedom, a sense of objective, flying, actually. I feel just as if I could ride myself without the help of the car—float over the road."

Another respondent reports: "My wife used to say: 'That Plymouth of ours certainly gets us there and brings us back.' "

The psychological role of the car is well described when one person characterizes it as "a silent companion."

It is natural that the close relationship suggested in that word "companion" must lead to an attachment, even the devotion, of the driver for his car.

Cars provide their drivers with "Seven League Boots."

Psychologically, they give people the power to multiply their personalities.

The fairy tale of the Magic Carpet stirs the fantasy of every child.

All stories told in legends satisfy a secret wish . . . an unconscious desire of the primitive child.

But we are never mature enough to lose entirely the taste for those childish wishes.

Even the most conservative man has, in a forgotten corner of his mind, a deep understanding and a sympathetic smile for the tales of wizardry, sorcery, and mysterious powers.

Every man wants to be more than he really is.

We are constantly carrying such a mask of superiority.

The car presents a perfect means of enhancing our feeling of dominance, of superiority, of unusual powers.

After a failure in everyday life, many people get into their cars and drive off, usually at high speed.

They are seeking a re-establishment of their shaken self-confidence.

By driving, they develop their personalities, re-establish their self-confidence in much the same way that a young man builds self-confidence with his first car.

One woman says: "To me driving is a restful thing, even in heavy traffic, even in jams. It takes me away from other things that might be bothering me. In other words, driving is a relief."

Modern man is impatient . . . he cannot wait!

The car provides an antidote for impatience.

Driving provides a means of being somewhere else every second.

It means compensation for our desire of achievement. "I like to drive very fast—there is a certain feeling of power—the ability to direct the thing, and make it go. The feeling of being able to control something. Around here in New York it is not much pleasure—in the Middle West you've got a lot more room and you can drive like hell."

Everyone has a desire for quick success.

When we go to the motion pictures we vicariously share in the quick success of the hero who is a newsboy one minute and an hour later a millionaire.

Similarly, the modern automobile symbolizes such a formula for quick success: "I got there in two hours flat."

We find also that older people and stout drivers especially get a vicarious feeling of mobility that approaches levitation, or floating, in driving a car.

They get their youth and slimness back through the help of the modern motor car . . . the car somehow complements their personality.

Thus, cars become the tools of success, everyday symbols of life achievement. The car as a symbol of success is visualized very early in life. Every social or financial development is translated into a new car. We have innumerable phrases in our case histories to illustrate the importance of the car as an expression of success. "I stood there all excited . . . I could not believe it was mine."

It is a fact that the American automobile industry has made the motor car an integral part of the national character of the country.

Our interviews with immigrants and people with European experience indicate clearly that the opinion prevails in Europe that every real American owns a car.

One lady says: "When I came here about fifteen years ago—to my relatives, I knew perfectly well that one day I was going to have a car—that was my definite resolution in Europe and I was really very much astonished when I came here and found that my relatives did not own a car—I was absolutely convinced that everybody in this country without exception had an automobile."

In our discussion of the psychology of the first car, we saw the close relationship between the first car purchase and first business success.

It is obvious to anyone in the industry that bigger and better cars accompany successive stages in social advancement, as these quotations indicate: "I was the first boy in our gang to be successful enough to have a car. The first thing I did with it was to take a trip to Canada with a couple of friends—also girl friends of course." "It meant a definite advancement for me socially. It always symbolized a definite freedom and independence from my family and my home." "I had that car just about a year and turned it in. Then came the second stage of my development socially." "I got a raise every year—a big raise, I was just beginning to get a good salary." "Then I bought an Imperial Chrysler because I was so satisfied with the first Chrysler. I had that car for one year and traded it in for a Stutz. It had a leather body and was gorgeous-looking. My income was rising all the time, and that certainly had a lot to do with the purchase of the Stutz. I had it for a year and a half and then traded it in against a Cadillac."

But success is a two-edged sword. People want to be envied . . . stared at . . . even conspicuously successful, but there is a very powerful fear in the back of the mind that big expenditures for cars are sinful.

It is obviously important, therefore, that advertising copy should remove the inhibitions to buying by giving moral permission to the "extravagance" of a new car purchase.

A psychological analysis of our case histories reveals that many people actually experience a fear of punishment for the extravagance of their motor-car purchase. People feel that they are not entirely entitled to possess the cars they have . . . that they tempted fate and may expect punishment. "I should not have had that car in the first place—I was overstepping the balance of my income."

A farmer says: "No one else near us had a car. Most everyone had horses—some folks were kinda sore at us gettin' a car—there was talk about us makin' lots of money—we weren't but we were the kind of family that always like to be up on the latest things. When the first radio came out, I remember my father was right there Johnny-on-the-spot to get one."

This quotation indicates the importance of the social group as a distributor of approval or disapproval. This leads us to an important psychological factor in the purchase of cars: social approval.

We have watched the psychological mechanism of "keeping up with the Joneses" too often to dwell upon the subject any longer than is necessary to indicate its vital importance as expressed in these quotations: "You are really only half a man without a nice car." "Every owner feels himself entitled to look down upon the other driver with a shabbier car."

What we deal with in all these reactions is really nothing more than social competition. We are comparing ourselves with other people, our cars with other cars, and we get a superior feeling if we can say to ourselves that we are "better off." Wherever people gather there is a comparison of cars. If we are very frank we must admit we look at other cars primarily in the secret hope that we may be able to make a scornful remark about them.

The same psychological mechanism is at work in our attempt to find out how much money other people make. We do both in the hope that we may say to ourselves: "I am not so badly off, after all." We not only compare our present-day status with our fellow competitors, but we also look back into our own history, as seen in the following excerpts from one of our case histories: "I have very rich relatives, and I also competed a little with them. As a very young man I came to the home of my uncle. He didn't want me to go to college. His idea was to take me into his business. However, I left his home, studied under very difficult circumstances, and then, when I was graduated it was my ambition to prove to my uncle that one can also become rich as a physician, not only as a businessman. One of the first indications of being well off is the ownership of a car. When I got my first shabby Ford, he laughed at me, but it didn't take me long before I got the same make car he had. And I only felt completely happy about it because I knew it would aggravate him."

Nothing is so feared as *loss of social prestige*. The car has been so widely accepted as the most direct translation of success that a sliding off in car standards now means, for many people, the proof of a sliding off in social standards. People keep on buying expensive cars, although they no longer can afford them, just to keep up appearances.

On the other hand, we find that when a certain income level is passed, an interesting reversal takes place. People start to buy cheaper cars. However, the purpose of that tactic is psychologically just the same: "Keeping up with the standard of your class."

You then show off by not showing off. Such people say: "I am so rich, or well established, that I just don't have to care any more." Should they still care, the proof of their absolute wealth would not be 100 per cent.

The importance of social approval can sometimes overshadow technical quality and engineering perfection. A car may be wonderful, but if it is rejected by public opinion, no force in the world will sell that car.

We have an example of this point in the following: "Willys has something very appealing about its streamlining . . . I remember though, a lot of us laughed when it first came out. They were damned good on the road, but who wants a car that people laugh at? No matter how good it is supposed to be. They were good to ride in but they didn't stand up, and they had that damned peculiar look about them. Willys was a little too early—Chrysler was a little too early with that streamline of theirs . . . airflow I think they called it."

We find that one of the most important influences in building standards of social approval and establishing certain makes of cars as symbols of success is motion pictures.

THE PSYCHOLOGICAL INFLUENCE OF ACCIDENTS ON CAR BUYING

Psychoanalysis has demonstrated that everyone to some degree has a subconscious wish to kill or be killed, which in scientific language is called masochism and sadism.

Modern civilization, of course, has repressed these two primitive instincts. To avoid the outbreak of these dangerous instincts, our culture has provided us with a means of making them harmless: sublimation. A motor car is one of the most perfect psychological devices for sublimating our subconscious wish to kill or be killed. The power to destroy others and ourselves is in our hands when we hold the steering wheel of a motor car in motion. It is by conquering the machine itself, that the driver turns a hostile power into an instrument of aggression.

Such expressions as, "Give it to 'em," "Step on it," and recurrent expressions of satisfaction from the "feeling of power" obtained from the car can be interpreted psychologically as a satisfaction of the pleasure of aggression or sadism.

The urge to destruction and the fear of death, as Freud calls them, are deep in the unconscious, and in our interviews we get only the tips, the clues, the circumstantial evidence.

The expression "I just missed that truck by two inches" must be interpreted as an interest in "playing with danger." It is the same interest which we satisfy in attendance of "blood and thunder" movies.

"I could have killed you had I wanted to" is really the thought behind the proud remark after a trip, "Well, I brought you home safely, did I not?" The driver becomes a hero, a savior, a protector. Lives were entrusted to him, and he brought them home safely.

All this he attributes to his skill as a driver, so it is not surprising to find that almost everyone considers himself a good driver.

The wish to kill or be killed is repressed within us early in childhood. But we know from psychological studies that repressed wishes do not entirely disappear. Every accident is a reminder of the dangerous potentialities of the motor car. Every accident, therefore, is a psychological shock which tends to break the chain in repeat buying of the same make. Drivers who have accidents seldom admit that they personally contributed to the cause of the accident. They are much more apt to blame the car, consequently they are much more vulnerable to arguments for a different make of car unless they have developed a strong positive attitude.

THE PSYCHOLOGICAL INFLUENCE OF WOMEN ON CAR BUYING

We have already mentioned the influence of women as related to the several psychological structures of car-buying habits which we have studied.

Less than 5 per cent of the people interviewed said that women have no influence on car purchases.

Woman has a twofold relationship to a car: as a driver and as a passenger. Women spend more total time in family cars than men.

One man whom we interviewed sums up woman's influence as: "I have the money, but she says yes."

Woman's attitude toward car buying is quite different from that of a man. While he looks at the car chiefly as a driver, she looks at the car from both the driver and the rider angle.

"When I got married my wife had an influence on the purchase of the car. She drives a great deal and the Packard was her choice—or rather we both determined the purchase. There was a little upper seat in the back which she decided should be red leather—I determined the make—she the color. She is in the car 100 per cent of the time and driving 50 per cent of it. When I drive with her I do the driving, but she rides in it much more often than I do."

Another man says about his wife: "They have a lot of influence—I would not buy a car without a woman. Seventy-five per cent of my friends would not go to a dealer without their women. He has the money but he needs the yes of his wife. They look at cars in a different way and it also depends on whether or not she drives. If she drives, she immediately sits in the driver's seat. My wife would get in the back and sit down. I want to know all about the technical parts. Women buy a car if they like the color. The same thing seems to be a predominant factor when buying a house. Women have good taste and usually good judgment, but then again some do not. Some friend of mine has a light car—I couldn't stand that. His wife wanted to match her hair—she is a blonde, that is why they have a light car."

The details of a car are a mystery to most men, but they are even more mysterious to women.

The fundamental difference between sexes is that the man will readily admit ignorance of technical detail while a woman will not. Women want to rely on their own judgment. Since they are lacking in technical knowledge, they shift their judgment to details which they really know.

In other words, women use the same buying criteria in judging cars as they use in two fields with which they are most familiar—fashion and housekeeping.

If details she can judge from her experience as a fashion buyer and housewife are of good quality, such as upholstery, color finishes, and so forth, she concludes that the entire car is of good quality.

It should be interesting to detail here a typical incident from our observations of customers in a Plymouth showroom:

A mother and her daughter walked into the showroom and began looking at a car. The mother then had the daughter get into the driver's seat and sit down. After the daughter had adjusted her hat and attained a fairly smart-looking attitude, the mother stepped back and with head cocked to one side surveyed the picture. She made several suggestions, and then went to the other side of the car to get a different view. This time she also made a suggestion or two. After they had fully assured themselves that the car would be a stylish purchase from an onlooker's standpoint, they went into minute detail about the upholstery, rugs, instrument panel, and colors available.

The whole performance brought strangely to mind the typical attitude of a woman buying a dress. She appraises the style first and then examines the quality of the material and details of workmanship, such as seams, and so forth.

Few men are willing to admit that women exert as strong an influence on the purchase of cars as we believe, from an analysis of our case histories exists.

The following gives us a typical example of how a married man rationalizes his wife's influence on the purchase of a car:

"I may give in on one detail and in so doing I get a lot of other things I like. I give her the choice of color. I believe that sometimes you have to give in on little things—you have to give and take—you can't just be the boss all the time, Yes, she seems satisfied with the car we have now."

Here is an example of an unmarried young man, who obviously fears the influence of his future wife: "With the highbrow automobile taste I have, she ought to be satisfied . . ."

A woman is dependent on the technical perfection of the car.

One woman expresses her feeling in the following way: "I often wonder what I would do if I were miles off from everything and the car would just lay down."

The modern car symbolizes for a woman the possibility of being on equal footing with a man . . . "to have a little power of your own."

Her aspiration is to be "just as good a driver as a man."

The driving ability of a woman is an important factor, as indicated in this husband's statement: "If something is wrong mechanically, it is a very bad car, although it may be her fault—but that doesn't make any difference to her."

Superficiality is also evidenced in woman's attitude toward car names: "It sound nices to say, 'I'll send my Packard down to the station.'"

We find that women have much more confidence in car names alone than do men. These two stories are significant evidence of this point: "I had to get a Packard on account of the business, but I had no desire to get a big car. I stood there downstairs with my wife in the Chrysler salon and looked at the cars running around. She saw and said 'that looks good,' but when she saw the name she did not want it any longer. She said, 'I don't like the name.' I had a long discussion with her and asked, 'Why do you want the name? You buy the car.' But she said, 'I just don't like it.' I think that is typical of a woman. Just like Schiaparelli or Saks-Fifth Avenue. This year women seem to be captivated by Bonwit Teller—I don't know why."

"She did not like the Dodge as well as the DeSoto. The name was more ill-sounding to her than DeSoto. I tried to make her believe that the quality had nothing to do with the name, but I do not think I was successful."

Even more significant is the fact that the wife is the economic conscience of the family of the average income bracket. She directly or indirectly controls the family budget.

We have already mentioned the importance of removing by moral permission the inhibition to "sinful extravagances" for new car purchases. The woman is psychologically the representation of the moral conscience, as we can see from the following quotations:

A married woman says: "I think a car is a luxury. I am putting my foot down for a little while, but I am becoming more and more convinced when I see all the cars on the road that it is possibly a necessary part of life. I want a car within our means—I think the best car in the low-priced field is the Plymouth. Maybe also a Buick, but that would be bought on an impulse."

Another woman gives us the following analysis of the breaking down of her resistance: "If you see so many cars on the roads you begin to think everybody seems to own a car. Maybe I really am wrong, but I always feel that we should wait until we can afford it—it is a luxury. We live in Mt. Vernon, and we really need a car to get around in. It is a great inconvenience not having one. It is easy, too, to have a car as they have parking spaces behind the apartment houses."

Here we have the same fact expressed differently: "He thinks very definitely that we should have a car—he thinks it is a great part of your life, especially when you live out of the city. It is also a cheap means of entertainment. You can keep in contact with your friends. Maybe he is right—but I am sort of a little bit on the fence."

From an advertising standpoint, the practical importance of recognizing the woman as the economic and moral conscience of the family is obvious, because only through her can moral permission for new car extravagances be obtained.

According to our study, men tend to step up successive car purchases before marriage. This trend is slowed down, or broken, at marriage. In addition to the obvious economic reasons, the practical conscience of the woman here again exerts a tempering effect. We find that once the husband, through marriage, is placed on a lower car standard, he tends to remain on that lowered standard. It is the wife, after the family budget has been built and standardized, who takes the initiative to step up car purchases.

Once the family budget is stabilized, women take the lead in the satisfaction of needs and become the driving force at an age when the husband is more likely to be easily satisfied.

The practical mind of the wife is also chiefly responsible for changing the man's car ideal of convertibles into a practical compromise on closed models.

The psychological role of the woman, as shown in our survey, is a specific manifestation of the general part she plays in a man's life. When he goes overboard, she pulls him back. When he slows down, she accelerates him.

Women influence the purchase of cars in every life period. Even the first car is bought to impress girls, and their influence continues throughout life, becoming more important after marriage.

Women influence car buying directly or indirectly in about 95 per cent of all car purchases!

We have now answered the second of the two questions asked us specifically by Plymouth executives: What influence do women have on the purchase of cars? We are now ready to give our answer to the first question: Why do most (70 per cent) car buyers buy the same make as their previous car?

If we simply ask buyers why they bought the same make of car again, the majority answer: "Because I was satisfied with the last one."

If the manufacturer interprets such sales as due to previous ownership or habit, there is not much that he can do about it in a practical way unless he understands the structure of the habit.

All of the analysis which we have given you so far has been necessary to understand that structure. We are now ready to consolidate those facts and add some new ones, which will give us the final answer.

First, let us look at the psychological mechanism of decision because decision enters into every car purchase. As John Dewey, the American philosopher, says: "Choice is not the emerging of a preference out of indifference; it is the emerging of a unified preference out of a number of competing inclinations."

Practically applied to our problem, this means that in making a decision to buy a car, all elements, especially the old car, enter the field of consideration.

Consideration is a dramatic rehearsal in the mind before making a purchase. It is an experiment in which many different combinations of elements are tried. The dramatic rehearsal is in terms of actual pictures in the mind.

The fact that 70 per cent of all car buyers repeat the same make is nothing more than a specific form of decision. The figure 70 per cent represents the statistical manifestation of a psychological fact, namely, that the picture of the old car wins!

In the various sections of this study we have analyzed the elements which make up the psychological picture of the car or of its symbolic value.

The fact that a majority of people repeat the same make must mean that the old car represents in a clearer way all the symbolic values of the car.

But repeat buying can, in itself, be done in two different ways:

1. A buyer can purchase the same make of car after looking the market over very carefully, and coming to the conclusion that it is still the best buy.

2. A buyer can purchase the same make without too much looking around, or by looking around with a negative attitude, being unconsciously determined to come back to his old make.

The key to the understanding of our specific problem of repeat buying is in the distinction between the intelligent routine and the stereotype routine.

In the intelligent routine, people buy the same make of car time after time, but each time the decision is made only after careful consideration and comparison of various makes with the old car.

In the stereotype routine, people buy the same make of car time after time without consideration and comparison in making the decision. Such people may give seemingly intelligent, rationalized reasons for their purchases, but their real reasons lie beneath the surface.

In the intelligent routine, such already recognized factors as price, trade-in allowance, dealer service, manufacturer's reputation, and technical features of the new car enter into the dramatic rehearsal in the buyer's mind preceding every purchase.

These are the reasons for purchase which we get when we make statistical surveys.

If they were actually the only ones, it would be sufficient to advertise a car's qualities and get immediate acceptance for it. The best car would conquer the market in a very short time.

The very existence of the phenomenon of repeat buying caused us to suspect that those reasons are surface explanations and are not in themselves sufficient proof of the fact that people repeat the same make of car. Therefore, we felt entitled to focus our study on the possibility of the existence of non-apparent reasons. This approach helped us to recognize many general psychological forces at work. The most important explanation we can find is that there is grave danger that people will stop looking around in an intelligent way for a new car, leave the intelligent routine and turn to the stereotype routine.

So long as the intelligent routine exists, there is an open mind which can be approached by emotional and technical appeals such as we have analyzed. But when the routine becomes stereotyped, which often happens after the consumer buys two or three cars of the same make, it becomes closed to such appeals. It is, therefore, vitally important for us to analyze and understand all of the forces influencing the development of stereotype routine.

In the stereotype routine, we have most of the psychological elements which we discovered beneath the surface and analyzed at some lengths in the earlier sections of this study.

What we formerly could explain only as loyalty, habit, or previous ownership now finds an explanation in the following factors which develop the stereotype routine.

1. Lack of technical knowledge, with resultant uncertainty of judgment. A new make represents to the buyer unknown technical features; the old make at least a feeling of technical understanding.

2. Courage is necessary to accept new technical features. If that courage is not sufficient, it becomes another reason for sticking to the old make.

3. A new decision is full of risks. If the buyer was successful in the selection of one make, he tries to avoid the trouble and chance of an entirely new decision. Selecting the same make is a harmless compromise.

4. Gratification of progress. The feeling of having something better and newer than before is one of the chief gratifications of buying a new car. This is closely tied up with the fact that all life is progress toward a goal, and each car is a milestone symbol of progress. Progress can be more easily measured in the same make. If we know exactly how each feature works in the last model, we can estimate the improvement that has been made in the new model of the same manufacturer better than in a different make.

5. The old car is the strongest picture in the mind of the car buyer.

People do not buy new cars as much as they sell their old cars. They are more likely, for that reason, to buy the same make.

6. Psychological attachment to known things. The old car has become a part of our personality. To give it away is like giving part of our personality away. When asked to switch, we resent abandoning our old car. It is difficult and disagreeable, and we often don't do it. This works as another unconscious reason why people stick to the old make.

7. Fear of the unknown. Experiments have shown that children are afraid of the known face as soon as it is covered with a mask. A car buyer reacts similarly to a new car. He even, unconsciously, invents little tricks to counteract the feeling of strangeness, such as taking familiar objects from the old car and putting them into the new one. A new make is the extreme of strangeness and, therefore, is often avoided.

8. Fear of punishment for unfaithfulness. The wish to be unfaithful to a wife, a job, a friend is very strong. Our education represses such wishes and makes them unconscious. Every appeal made to a buyer to switch to a new make is unconsciously understood as an appeal for unfaithfulness. The stronger the wish exists in our mind, the more violently it will be rejected. The result is often a clinging to the old make.

9. Fear of tempting fate. If we have had no accidents in a certain make of car, we are inclined to be instinctively grateful to that make of car. We fear that by being unfaithful, by switching to a new make, we may be punished through an accident. To buy the same make is a psychological way to placate the gods.

10. Avoidance of strangeness. If you buy a new make of car, you have to see new salesmen, new dealers, new mechanics. People get acquainted with faces and persons. We are apt to develop confidence in a particular dealer, and a strange dealer arouses suspicion. The repeat buying of the same make is a solution of the dilemma.

11. Defense of previous decision. Once we have made a decision in favor of a certain make of car, we feel responsible for that decision. Buying a new make is like admitting we were wrong the previous time. We want to be known as shrewd buyers, and buying the same make will help us keep that reputation.

12. Routine in itself is of such a nature that it insists on its own continuity. It creates uneasiness to break it. To disturb it is like breaking a law. A strong protest is registered in the mind, with the result that the same routine is often restored.

THE PSYCHOLOGICAL INFLUENCE OF YOUTH ON CAR BUYING

Our case histories indicate that the influence of youth on car buying has been greatly underestimated. Three psychological reasons for youth's influence stand out:

1. The car standard of a son or daughter stands for youth. Older people want to be young, so they accept that standard.

2. Generally, children automatically start at a much higher social level than their fathers.

3. Immigrant families, up to the second and third generation, particularly look to their children for advice on car buying.

The car is in itself a symbol of youth, as we have already seen. It is a means of compensating age. Older people feel more youthful while driving a car, and they therefore accept the "taste standards" of their youngsters in the purchase of a car.

While the father in most cases had to work his way up to his social position, his children benefit by his success and therefore have a higher car standard.

More than 60 per cent of all Americans are immigrants of the second and third generations.

We have excluded the many practical recommendations which resulted from this study because they are the property of the client.

Some of them are well known: The greater emphasis on convertibles, the creation of the hard-top convertible as a compromise between the "mistress and the wife."

B. Stirling Getchell, the advertising agency handling the Plymouth account at that time, developed such advertisements as the following:

1. "Do you still remember when . . ." showing an old jalopy and the nostalgia connected with it.

2. "I can drive where I please . . ." dramatizing the freedom experienced in driving.

3. "My car fits me like a glove," appealing to women, and many others. Almost all these advertising themes proved to be highly successful.